NVQ Level **3**

Health &
Social Care

Options Plus

Yvonne Nolan

with Nicki Pritchatt

CML
362 Nol

www.heinemann.co.uk
✓ Free online support
✓ Useful weblinks
✓ 24 hour online ordering

01865 888058

Inspiring generations

Heinemann is an imprint of Pearson Education Limited, a company incorporated in
England and Wales, having its registered office at Edinburgh Gate, Harlow, Essex, CM20 2JE.
Registered company number: 872828

Heinemann is a registered trademark of
Pearson Education Limited

Text © Yvonne Nolan, Nicki Pritchatt 2006

First published 2006

10 09 08
10 9 8 7 6 5 4 3 2

British Library Cataloguing in Publication Data is available
from the British Library on request.

ISBN: 978 0 435464 65 3

Designed by Wooden Ark Studio, Leeds
Typeset by Textech International, India
Illustrated by Hardlines Studio, Oxfordshire

Original illustrations © Pearson Education Limited, 2006

Cover design by Wooden Ark Studio, Leeds
Printed in China by South China Printing Company
Cover photo: © Photolibrary/Botanica

Acknowledgements
Every effort has been made to contact copyright holders of material reproduced in this book.
Any omissions will be rectified in subsequent printings if notice is given to the publishers.

Contents

Acknowledgements

Yvonne Nolan would like to thank Pen Gresford, Jan Doorly and all the team at Heinemann for their unfailing professionalism, enthusiasm and skill.

Expert advice and guidance was provided during the preparation of this book by Jane Bozier, NVQ assessor, and Linda Nazarko, NVQ trainer and assessor for the NHS.

The Waterlow pressure ulcer risk assessment scoring system (page 204) is reprinted with the permission of Judy Waterlow SRN RCNT – more information can be found on her website www.judy-waterlow.co.uk

The authors and publisher would like to thank the following for permission to reproduce photographs:

Alamy Images, pages 4, 112, 118
Alamy Images/Paul Doyle, page 131
Alamy Images/Huw Jones, page 79
Alamy Images/Mediscan, page 250
Alamy Images/Photofusion Picture Library, pages 39, 75, 170
Alamy Images/Janine Wiedel Photolibrary, page 6
Corbis, pages 95, 104, 257 (top), 270 (top)
Corbis/George Shelley, page 154
Digital Vision, page 183 (top right)
Eyewire, page 183 (top left)
Getty Images, page 51
Getty Images/PhotoDisc, pages 8, 14, 121, 141, 188
Getty Images/Thinkstock, page 183 (bottom right)
Harcourt Education/Gareth Boden, page 183 (bottom left)
Harcourt Education/Jules Selmes, pages 157, 159
iStockPhoto/Absolut 100, page 46
KPT Power Photos, page 184
NHS/National Patient Safety Agency, page 229
Photolibrary, pages 42, 92
Rex Features, page 67
Rex Features/GPU, page 147
Science Photo Library/Adam Gault, page 257 (bottom)
Science Photo Library/Andy Levin, page 270 (bottom)
Richard Smith, pages 187, 194, 208, 230, 231, 247, 249
3M Health Care, page 256

Dedication

In memory of John

Introduction

This book is designed to provide further coverage of a range of optional units for Level 3 Health and Social Care. It is simply not possible for a book to cover all the optional and additional units available, but some of the most popular optional units are included here and this will supplement those already covered in the core text *Health & Social Care (Adults)*.

For details of further units, go to the Heinemann website (see below). Each NVQ is presented in the same way:

- **Elements of Competence** divide the unit to make it more manageable
- **About this unit** tells you the subject matter of the unit; it also spells out the scope of the work and the **values** relating to the unit
- **Performance Criteria** tell you what you have to do at work to achieve the standard
- **Knowledge Specification** tells you what you need to know and understand.

You will find that this book follows the structure of the NVQ units closely and gives you the knowledge for each unit. Look out for 'Keys to good practice' as these will help you to satisfy the Performance Criteria.

You will find a grid detailing coverage of the Knowledge Specification points on page 281. For more information about learning materials and resources for S/NVQs in Health and Social Care, visit the Heinemann website at www.heinemann.co.uk/vocational and follow the links.

You will find, I hope, that much of the learning in this book will be useful regardless of the units you are undertaking. The concept of empowerment and putting people in control of the services they need, and the focus on changing attitudes so that people using services are in real partnership with those commissioning and providing them, are both principles that apply to all the work we do in care.

Work in care is changing; links between health and care are leading to far more integrated ways of working, and new roles are emerging which mean that people are able to access health and care services in a far more effective way. These new developments are exciting, and the opportunities for workers to develop skills in both health and care offer a real prospect of offering innovative and effective services to individuals and their families.

I wish success to those who are using this book in order to achieve a qualification. For those using it as a guide for practice, I hope it proves to have lasting value as your career develops and progresses. Continuing to develop your professional skills, expanding your knowledge and improving your practice are among the joys and challenges of working in health and social care. I hope you enjoy the book and put it to good use.

Yvonne Nolan

Support individuals to develop and maintain social networks and relationships

In general, human beings are sociable; we all attempt to develop relationships with other people. Relationships are very varied in their nature, their level of importance and their intensity, but most people would agree that interaction with others is part of what makes us human.

Sometimes people need support in relating to others. This can be for a range of reasons. Illness or social circumstances may mean that a person loses contact with other people; sometimes there are difficulties in making relationships; and some people may have had difficult or painful experiences that have made them wary of becoming involved with others.

This unit deals with the work you will do in supporting individuals to manage the relationships in their lives. Not all relationships are straightforward or easy to deal with, and there can be situations where people need your help and support to cope with awkward, unpleasant or difficult situations. You will need to develop and use a range of skills in order to provide this support. You will also need to understand how relationships and networks develop and know how to ensure that someone is empowered to take decisions about the relationships and networks they want to be involved with, and how to deal with those they don't.

What you need to learn

- What are contacts?
- Social networks
- Different types of relationships
- Reviewing relationships
- Features of relationships
- Effects of relationships
- Maintaining relationships
- When things go wrong
- Support for you
- Getting involved
- New relationships
- Ways to provide support
- Recording contact and relationship information

HSC 331a Support individuals to identify their needs for, and from, contacts, social networks and relationships

Contacts, social networks and relationships are all different aspects of the same thing: interaction with other people. Where they differ is in the level of involvement and commitment that each requires, and the level of benefit they provide. If you are working with people who have recognised that they want to do something about their social connections, then you need to understand the basics of how contacts, networks and relationships work, before you can offer the support and information needed for someone to make changes.

What are contacts?

Contacts can be people whom individuals need to be in touch with for all sorts of reasons. They could be people in local shops, libraries, at GP surgeries, at the bank, or people who supply the services an individual may use. For example, the person organising transport, the administrative staff at the housing association or regular bus or taxi drivers can all be important contacts. Interactions with contacts may not be lengthy, nor are they likely to be very intense or deal with serious emotional issues, but they are an important part of day-to-day life.

Contacts can also provide an introduction into a wider network or to a relationship that will grow and develop.

● *People have many kinds of interactions with their contacts*

Why do contacts matter?

Some people you work with may have lost touch with friends or relatives or have no real social circle. This can happen because of circumstances such as an accident, illness, bereavement or changes in living environments. It can also come about because of social factors, such as the experience of an abusive past, bullying or discrimination resulting in low self-esteem and self-confidence.

Learning or re-learning how to reach out to others and make initial contact is an important part of developing self-esteem, and people grow in confidence as they make contacts and receive positive responses. People who never make contact with anyone never get the chance to become a part of a wider social network and to develop relationships. Humans are social beings who usually live in groups and communities, and very few of us are able to function well in isolation and maintain our emotional health and well-being.

Active knowledge

Make a list of the people you have contact with – including any interaction at all – each day for a week. You will probably be surprised at how many there are.

Now try making a similar list for an individual who is using your support to help develop social links. You will probably find that the list is very much shorter. Try to see where the key differences are and whether that gives you a starting point to work on.

Social networks

Networks are the routes by which things are linked together. Many people are connected to a computer network at work; our public transport system is usually described as a network – a network of railway lines, or a network of roads; most of us communicate through a mobile telephone network, and so on. Social networks are about how *people* link together.

Formal networks

If knowing about networks is useful for big business, it is most certainly useful for care workers in terms of supporting people to extend the ways in which they relate to others.

Some networks are formally established and publicised, for example a 'Diabetes Network', 'Patient Network', 'Mums and Tots Network', 'Musicians Network', 'Women in Business Network', and so on.

The first thing you will notice about most of the networks you hear about or see advertised is that they are based around a common factor which will bring people together.

Did you know?

Big corporations pay consultants large amounts of money to find out who talks to whom, who e-mails whom, who knows what and whom they tell it to. This tells them about the way information flows around the company and how they can best organise the work to take advantage of the networks that already exist. This area of study is called social (or organisational) network analysis.

Valdis Krebs, a researcher into social networks, said in 2005 that there are two basic, powerful drivers which bring people together to form networks:

- 'Birds of a feather flock together'
- 'Those close by form a tie'.

This is the reason why so many networks are based around a shared interest, which could be a hobby, a job role or even a local neighbourhood activity, for example Crimewatch groups. Formal networks are usually organised by an individual, or a committee, and will have a structure, although this may not be very formal. The network will have:

- Using the Internet is an increasingly common way of becoming involved in a network

- a purpose – or common interest
- a membership which is known, and may or may not be recorded
- an agreed means of communication – meetings, or the Internet, for example
- a means of sharing information about itself and attracting new members.

One of the increasingly common ways of being involved in a network is through the Internet. The Internet can provide an excellent way for people to make contact with others across the world and to share views, interests and issues. However, there are always precautions to be taken when people are making contact with others through chatrooms or networking websites. You should advise people to be cautious when using such websites and to follow some basic rules:

- never give your full name, your address or any other contact details to someone you have met on the Internet
- if you decide to arrange to meet someone, make sure it is in a public place and take a friend with you
- never give money or divulge your financial details to anyone you have met through the Internet
- be cautious if you are asked for photos or personal information.

Active knowledge

Choose two information 'hubs', for example the library, the Internet, the local health centre, etc. List some of the networks advertised there. Note how people are able to participate, such as on-line, or by going to a meeting.

Think about how useful any of these networks may be for any of the people you work with. If any of them seems appropriate, pass on the information.

Informal networks

Informal networks can grow and develop wherever people have something in common, whether it is friendship, family, where they live or work. These networks will not be advertised or have a formal structure or established means of communication, and will often not have a set membership.

For example, in some workplaces there is a tradition of going for a drink together after work on a Friday – not usually possible if you work in social care! This would be an informal network, and there is often a core of people who always go, and others who dip in and out. Communication and arrangements are likely to be by word of mouth.

Many families form strong networks with close links between individual members of the family and an overall involvement in the family network.

Most of us have been in a workplace where the informal networks provide just as much support as the formal ones put in place by management. It is often the informal networks that provide support, advice and the sharing of experience and good practice, even if it is only over a coffee in the staff room and not in a formal supervision or assessment session.

An informal network will have:
- a flexible membership
- various means of communication, depending on need
- no definite purpose or goal
- no public advertising of its existence.

Evidence indicator

Think about some informal networks you are involved in. List three benefits you gain from each of them, then list three things you contribute to each. Do the same for formal networks.

You may find this a useful exercise for thinking about the areas to discuss with a service user who is unsure about what sort of involvement he or she may have with a particular network. Make some notes on this.

Remember

Contacts and networks are an essential part of the way we all relate to other people, but they are simply the structures that lead to relationships, the means to an end; it is the relationships with others that are the end itself.

Different types of relationships

Everyone has a wide range of relationships with different people in different aspects of their lives. Relationships range from family to friends and work colleagues. Each of the different types of relationship is important and plays a valuable role in contributing to the overall well-being of each of us as an individual. However, the needs and demands of different types of relationships are varied, as are the effects that relationships can have on an individual's self-image and the confidence with which he or she deals with the world.

Types of relationships	Features of relationship
Family relationships	Relationships with parents, grandparents, siblings and children. Depending on the type of family, they can be close or distant.
Sexual relationships	Relationships that can be long or short term, with a spouse or permanent partner, or can be shorter-term non-permanent relationships. The impact of a sexual relationship is different from family relationships and more intense than the demands of friendship.
Friendships	Friendships can be long term or short term but quite intense. Most people have a few close friends and a much larger circle of friends who are not quite so intimate or close. These may be friends who are part of a wide social circle, but perhaps not close enough to share the intimate details of life. Close friends are often the ones who are an immediate source of support in times of difficulty and the first people with whom good news is shared.
Working relationships	Relationships with employers or with work colleagues. Some may become friendships, but most people relate to work colleagues in a different way from the way they would relate to friends. For example, work colleagues may share very little information about each other's personal life even though they may have very close and regular day-to-day contact. It is perfectly possible to spend a great deal more time with work colleagues than with friends, but not to be as close.

orders that are in force to protect the individual you are working with, and put measures in place to make sure that all staff are alerted to any risks.

Confidentiality

Do not forget to check with the individual that he or she is in agreement that you may share any information about restricted contact. Make sure you explain who will see the notes you are recording, and how they are protected from people who have no right to them. If you feel that you need to tell staff from another agency about any aspect of court orders or other restrictions, remember to check that the person concerned is in agreement with this.

How you can help

If someone is considering changing, extending or even ending some relationships, or the networks he or she is involved with, you can have a useful role in providing support and information. It may also be useful for you to help the person you are working with to analyse the options available by making a pros and cons list.

Often, someone may just need straightforward information about where to contact a particular local network, and you should be able to identify sources of information and assist people, if necessary, in finding out what they need to know.

On other occasions people may have deeper concerns and worries about relationships, particularly if they have previously had difficulties, or never had any close relationships and feel unsure and reluctant to try. In this situation, you will need to spend some time actively listening and encouraging individuals to consider all the options.

CASE STUDY: Developing new contacts

W has recently moved into the area. His wife died last year and he decided to move in order to be nearer his daughter and grandchildren. W and his wife had lived in their home town for over 40 years and this was his first move away from his home area. He is an active and independent man who enjoys gardening, is interested in family history and likes a little flutter on the races. He has had some health problems – he has chronic bronchitis and finds the winter hard to cope with.

1   How would you advise W about ways to develop contacts?
2   What networks would you advise W about?
3   What networks do you think W may have had in his old home?
4   What networks might he have now?
5   What different relationships does W have?

HSC 331b Support individuals to maintain supportive relationships

Features of relationships

Relationships are characterised by certain features. Some may be:

- supportive
- sharing
- equal
- demanding.
- abusive
- violent
- damaging

Some of these features are positive, and some are very negative. It is important to establish the features of a relationship and determine whether on the whole it is positive or negative.

Effects of relationships

Relationships have a significant effect on the development, health and well-being of all individuals. Most people want to be liked and tend to feel happy when they are part of a group, or know that they have friends and are considered to be a friend by others. Very few people are content to be excluded from groups and to live their lives in isolation, never having any close relationships with others. Most people are not loners, and their overall emotional health and well-being depends on the way they see themselves through the responses of others.

Most relationships make people feel good about themselves; they give something and gain something in return from a good relationship. Being liked or loved by someone is excellent for raising self-esteem and confidence.

However, relationships can have equally powerful negative effects. It is not the case that any relationship is better than none. Some relationships are emotionally damaging and even physically dangerous. Sometimes people can be in a relationship where they are belittled, humiliated, bullied or ignored. Relationships with one very dominant partner are not usually beneficial for anyone. Some people become involved in relationships that are violent or abusive, and the effects can be tragic and lifelong.

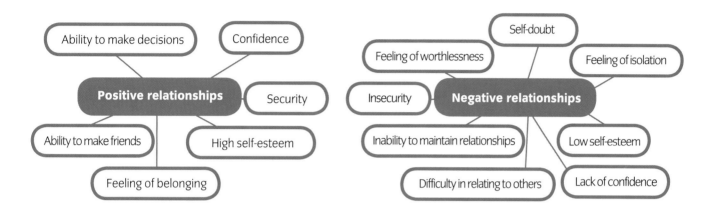

Self-concept and self-image

There is often confusion between self-concept and self-image. Self-concept is how we see ourselves, and self-image is how we value ourselves.

Both self-concept and self-image are influenced by the relationships we have throughout our lives.

Key terms

Self-concept: How we see ourselves.

Self-image: How we value ourselves.

Self-concept

Self-concept is based on our understanding of ourselves and the factors that have influenced our development. It includes our cultural background, our values and beliefs, and our understanding of who we are.

Your self-concept will have many influences: family, friends, environment, race, religion and values. It is fundamental to how you function and relate to the rest of the world. We all have a picture of ourselves, on which we base what we do in our lives. You will probably have said, at some time in your life, 'I'm not the sort of person who…' or 'It's just not me, it's not my sort of thing'. Your self-concept – the way you understand yourself – enables you to make statements like these.

Self-image

Self-image results from the way in which we have been treated by others, and the way this has made us feel about ourselves – our self-esteem. Positive relationships tend to encourage a positive self-image and a feeling of confidence and self-belief. Negative relationships can lead us to see ourselves as being of little value and affect our confidence and self-belief. This is because most of our self-image is formed by the way others react to us. Someone in a relationship where he or she is constantly undermined and belittled is likely to feel of little value as a person and to have little confidence in his or her own abilities. However, someone who is loved and made to feel valuable and worthwhile as a person will have confidence and belief that he or she has something useful to offer society.

● *Positive relationships help us to feel valued and have confidence in ourselves*

Maintaining relationships

Relationships do not generally maintain themselves. Most relationships need a commitment and effort from everyone involved to make them work and to keep them going. There are always some that seem to keep going regardless – most of us have a friend whom we may not see or contact for months or even years, but then meet up and feel as if we had been together the previous week. But these relationships are the exception.

Many of the people you will work with may need extra support in maintaining relationships because there may be barriers that are difficult to overcome without additional help.

Barriers to relationships

There are barriers that can make it difficult to start or maintain relationships. To help and support people in overcoming barriers to relationships you must discuss with them the type of help they want from you, and how much. It is essential that you only provide sufficient support to empower people to take decisions and initiate actions for themselves. Your role is to make it possible for people to do things for themselves – not to do it for them.

Language

If there are language barriers, consider the use of translators, although beware of using family members in this role. This can sometimes lead to difficulties, particularly if sensitive areas are under discussion.

If there are difficulties with verbal communication, then options such as the use of electronic or written means of communication can be explored. It may also be possible for you to support a friend or relative in learning the communication system that works for the service user you are working with.

Access

If someone is experiencing access difficulties, either because of distance or because of the physical limitations of the environment, then you should explore some of the options available to him or her, such as alternative venues, or looking at ways to make a local environment more accessible.

Transport

Transport, or the lack of it, can often be a barrier to relationships. You are likely to be able to help with this if the service user wants you to, either through direct provision such as taxis or a dial-a-ride service, or through information about appropriate means of transport.

Communication

Communication can be a problem for some people who have particular needs, and who are keen to maintain or begin a relationship with someone, especially if the other person also has particular communication needs. You may be able to support someone in overcoming problems by using your own skills and knowledge about methods of communication, or you may need to ask for expert help in areas such as translation, signing or dealing with a sensory impairment.

Environment

The environment can be a major barrier to relationships. For example, living in an environment with a minimal amount of privacy, perhaps in residential accommodation, may make it difficult to develop or maintain a personal relationship. You may need to consider ways in which you can assist someone to have access to quiet and personal time where he or she will have a chance to develop a close personal relationship with someone else.

● *Consider ways in which you can help people have private time together*

Overcoming barriers to maintaining relationships

Apart from face-to-face contact (through visits or meetings), there are various other ways to overcome barriers and maintain relationships by supporting people to keep in touch. Methods of keeping in touch include:

- letters
- telephone calls
- e-mails
- camcorders or videos.

Some service users may need support to use some or all of these, while others may have no problems with using any of these methods once they have been encouraged to consider them.

Barriers to maintaining relationships fall into four broad categories: physical, legal, emotional and communication. Below are just a few examples of the kind of situations you may have to deal with, and some suggestions of ways to respond.

Type of barrier	Example	Ways to overcome barriers
Physical	Wheelchair user wishes to maintain contact with a friend or relative who lives in a high-rise block of flats, which has lifts that are too small to take a wheelchair.	The relative or friend could come to visit the service user instead, or a meeting could be arranged in a location where there is suitable access for both parties.
Physical	A friend or relative living in a high-rise block of flats is house-bound, and the service user is unable to access the flat.	Discuss alternative ways of maintaining a relationship. Relationships do not have to be conducted face to face – if they did, families and friends who moved to different parts of the country or different parts of the world would soon lose touch with each other!

Type of barrier	Example	Ways to overcome barriers
Legal	Contact with a person's children is limited to one day every other month, and must be supervised by a support worker.	Provide support and supervision. Try to make the contact sessions as pleasant as possible for the children and the person you work with. Arrange for some contacts to take place at different venues (provided the court order does not forbid this). Be as unobtrusive as possible.
Emotional	You work with someone who has a long-standing disagreement with a close relative; the two of them have not spoken for years. The relative now wants to heal the split. However, there is a reluctance to forgive and forget.	Provide emotional support, and use active listening skills to support a discussion of the problem. Support the service user by encouraging him or her to look at the positive and negative aspects of the relationship so as to make an informed and considered decision.
Communication	A service user's mother has suffered a stroke, and she now has difficulty speaking. They are both distressed by not being able to communicate.	Help the service user to explore other means of communication such as flash cards, the written word, etc.

Evidence indicator

Look at the types of barriers to relationships that are experienced by the service users you work with.

Choose one person and list all his or her relationships. Next, note down how each one is maintained, and note any barriers that have been overcome. Then note any relationships that have been abandoned or not developed because barriers were not overcome. Think about ways in which you could have dealt with these barriers, and what resources would have been needed. Make notes about these.

When things go wrong

Not all relationships are easy; some are fraught with difficulties, but not all difficult relationships are negative.

Some relationships undoubtedly *are* negative, however, and you will need to work closely to support someone who is involved in a relationship that is clearly having a negative effect on him or her.

The basic principles for offering support in difficult relationships are the same regardless of the reasons for the problems. First, you need to establish the level of help needed from you. As in all your work, you should ensure you are providing help at a level people feel they need, and not at the level you think they need.

Once you have agreed, in discussion with the individual, on the help and support you are able to offer and the limits on what you can do, you need to draw up and agree a plan. This should make clear what actions you will be able to take and what is outside your role and responsibilities.

For example, someone may ask you to make contact with an ex-partner with whom he or she wishes to resume a relationship. You need to explain that this is not an appropriate role for you to undertake, but that you would be happy to assist by providing information on how to locate someone and by providing any necessary support that may be needed in writing letters, making telephone calls, sending e-mails, or any other assistance. However, it is not appropriate for you to become a 'go-between' in a relationship.

● *You may need to give assistance such as sending e-mails on people's behalf*

You may be asked to arrange a meeting with someone with whom contact is prohibited by a court order. You must point out that you are unable to assist anyone to break the law or to deliberately fail to comply with an order of the court.

You may have to deal with pressure from a service user in such situations and it can be difficult not to respond; none of us likes to feel that we have disappointed someone, but you cannot allow yourself to be drawn in and it is essential that you are clear from the start about the limits of your role.

Other situations may not be as clear cut. For example, you may be asked to assist an individual in maintaining a relationship with someone who you are aware has caused problems or difficulties for him or her in the past. For example, someone receiving support with mental health problems may wish to contact a person whose behaviour has been a contributory factor in the deterioration of his or her mental health and well-being in the past. This is a difficult situation and you would need to review this with the care team and the individual, and explain your concerns clearly. Ultimately, the team will have to take a view on the level of assistance and support that can be provided if the individual cannot be dissuaded from pursuing the relationship.

Unless there are court orders in place, decisions about contact, even with people who may have a detrimental effect, ultimately have to be made by the individual. However, you or an agreed team member should discuss the potential effects that such contact may have, and it should be very clear that any decisions are to be made only after full discussion and full consideration of the possible consequences.

Ending relationships

Ending relationships can be very difficult, and in this situation you may need to provide support over a period of time. Relationships end for all kinds of reasons, usually associated with changes in the lives of at least one of the parties involved.

The ending of close personal or sexual partnerships can be an emotionally charged process for all involved. Other types of relationships or involvement in social networks can be ended by, for example, someone moving to a different area or changing his or her living environment, or changing his or her interests or circumstances.

If you need to support a service user through the ending of the relationship, your role can vary depending on whether he or she is the active or passive partner in the process of ending. Where someone is considering making a positive decision to change and move out of a relationship or network, you are likely to be able to help by:

- offering to act as an impartial sounding board
- encouraging a review of action points and the reasons for the change
- supporting any practical arrangements that may be needed
- providing support with any communication issues
- continuing to offer support to complete the changes and move forward afterwards.

On the other hand, when a person is on the receiving end of someone else's decision to end a relationship, your role will be to provide support and encouragement to help him or her through the period of coping with the loss of an important relationship.

Keys to good practice: Supporting individuals to maintain their relationships

✓ Always agree the level of support with the service user.

✓ Do not agree to become directly involved in someone's relationship.

✓ Do not agree to support anyone in flouting or ignoring a court order.

✓ Ensure that the individual has considered the consequences of a potentially damaging relationship.

✓ Remember that you cannot prevent or forbid any legal relationship someone wishes to develop.

Support for you

Never underestimate how hard it can be to be involved in someone else's relationships, particularly if they are difficult or demanding. As a care worker there may be times when you feel distressed or worried by a situation you have become involved in. You may be concerned about the work you have been asked to do or because you feel a relationship is potentially dangerous, either for the person you are working with, or for someone else involved in it. Or it could be that the work has been emotionally traumatic.

In such situations, you should ensure that you get support for yourself. In the first instance, you should go to your line manager. He or she may be able to help, or may refer you for support outside your workplace.

Remember, asking for support is not a reflection on your abilities; in fact it is a positive move showing that you are able to recognise your own need for support and to do something about it, rather than attempting to continue alone, which can result in extreme stress and difficulties in maintaining your own standards of good practice.

CASE STUDY: Dilemmas over relationships

V has multiple sclerosis and uses a wheelchair for mobility. She had a relationship with S, who was not disabled, which lasted for about a year. This finally broke up about nine months ago. V was very dependent on S, who encouraged her dependency and did everything for her. V's independence was seriously affected during her relationship and this undermined her ability to undertake even the most straightforward of tasks for herself.

Since the break-up, which was initiated by S, V (although she was initially very upset) has been able to develop a far greater degree of independence and has been regaining control of her life. She has recently started to receive direct payments and has now established a good team of carers who are able to meet her needs. V has begun working again, which she had stopped doing when she was with S because he thought it was too much for her, and she has developed a new circle of friends.

S had now contacted V again and wishes to re-start the relationship. V was distressed by the break-up, and is keen to get involved with S again. She has told you very excitedly about this. As her key worker, you are concerned at the prospect because of the way S previously made her so dependent. You feel that such behaviour was more about meeting S's own needs than out of any genuine concern for V. You also dislike S and find it difficult to view him in a positive way.

1   How would you respond to V when she told you about this development?
2   Would you share your concerns with V?
3   If so, how would you go about it?
4   Would there be any justification for speaking to S?
5   What factors are likely to influence your approach?
6   List the difficulties you would face in dealing with this situation.

HSC 331c Support individuals to develop new social networks and relationships

Getting involved

You have considered the nature of social networks in the first part of this unit. Armed with that understanding, you will be able to support people in looking at what they need to do in order to make contacts, become involved in social networks and develop relationships.

People with a history of poor social communication and poor relationships may not have had the kind of experiences that enabled them to learn how to manage the way they relate to other people. Sometimes you may find that they have problems with social networks or relationships because they have not had the opportunity to learn which types of behaviour are appropriate, or where the boundaries lie. Sometimes people do not understand that all human contacts are a two-way process and that what you get out of any relationship is in direct proportion to what you put in.

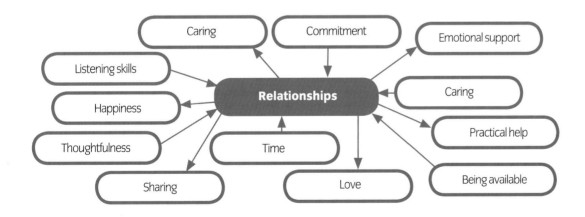

An important part of your role is giving people information so that they can make an informed decision about being involved in any type of social network. Make sure that individuals have the information to find out about:

- the commitments they would have to make to any formal network
- the expectations that other members of the network would have of them
- any access issues about participation in a network
- any legal issues
- areas of risk.

Not all networks are formal, and sometimes people are part of informal networks that they may not even recognise as such. It is often worth sitting down with individuals and asking them to look at who they link with and the networks they are part of. This can often be a useful basis for moving on to look at where the individuals may want to progress and develop new networks and relationships.

New relationships

Your help may be important in developing new relationships or re-starting old ones where people have lost touch. Depending on the circumstances, your help may only be needed to support initial contacts or to provide information, advice and encouragement, or you may need to offer more active help where someone needs your support at an initial contact in order to boost his or her confidence.

If a first meeting is with someone who has made contact on the Internet, you may be asked to be at the meeting as a safety precaution. This would be a very useful and important role.

Your supporting role in new or difficult relationships

As always, you will need to discuss carefully with the individual you are supporting the exact level of support that is needed and appropriate. Depending on the circumstances, your role can vary hugely. Some examples are shown below.

Your role	Key points
You may be asked to be present throughout a potentially difficult meeting with a relative or friend	<ul><li>You are there to support, not to run, the meeting</li><li>You are not there to become involved or take sides</li><li>Agree in advance what you will and will not say and do – and stick to this</li><li>Concentrate on what is happening – be prepared to offer feedback if you are asked</li></ul>

Your role	Key points
Someone may want help in setting up a contact by, for example, finding an appropriate location for a face-to-face meeting with a new contact	<ul><li>Agree the level of help required</li><li>Provide any necessary contact information</li><li>Relay any messages clearly without interpreting or changing them</li><li>Double check any booking or travel arrangements</li></ul>
You may need to provide reassurance before a first-time or potentially difficult meeting, or support and discussion afterwards	<ul><li>Set aside sufficient time for the discussion</li><li>Ensure that the environment is appropriate</li><li>Use your communication skills</li><li>Do not attempt to direct or control</li><li>Support individuals to identify and report abusive relationships</li><li>Be ready to support individuals in coping with any distress</li></ul>
You may need to assist if the contact is to be by telephone or by using an electronic means such as e-mail, chatroom, website or video conference	<ul><li>Act as an intermediary if needed to relay information by telephone or electronically</li><li>Relay any messages clearly without interpreting or changing them</li><li>Provide access to specially adapted electronic or telephone communication, if necessary</li></ul>

It is always important to clarify exactly what help you are expected to provide. You must ensure that the expectations are realistic and you are not being asked to do anything which exceeds your job role, or which may break any conditions that have been laid down in respect of any particular contact.

How circumstances can affect new networks and relationships

A person's physical or emotional condition or current mental health can affect any of his or her relationships, or the potential for relationships. For example, if you are working with individuals with a degenerative condition and they are attempting to re-establish contact with people they have not met for a long time, it may be important to discuss whether they wish to prepare a contact for any changes in their condition.

The same may apply if you are working with individuals with a history of mental health problems. The people they wish to contact may not be familiar with their condition, or may be unaware of the effect their mental health problems have had on their behaviour.

Alternatively, individuals may be looking to set up new relationships with people who have only previously met them during a difficult period for their mental health, and they may be anxious about re-establishing contact. It will be important that you can provide the support and links for an exchange of information to allow contact to be re-established.

Active knowledge

Think of an occasion when you have been apprehensive about meeting someone new, or someone you have not seen for a long time, or where a meeting was likely to be difficult. This could involve being introduced to members of a new partner's family, or a school reunion or a college get-together. It could be a meeting with a relative or a family member with whom you disagreed on the last occasion you met, or with a senior manager whose last contact with you involved a disagreement or disciplinary matter.

Think of one or two such examples and make notes about how you felt, and also whether the meeting justified the nervousness that you felt in advance.

Ways to provide support

If you have been asked to be present during a meeting, you need to be clear about the role you are being asked to play. If your role is simply to provide support for someone who may feel more confident and relaxed because you are there, then you may not need to take an active role in the meeting itself.

However, if you are there as an advocate, you should be very clear in explaining the limitations of that role and how you can handle it. As a general rule, if you are undertaking advocacy it should be because of something an individual is physically or emotionally unable to do for himself or herself – not simply because either you or the individual think that you would do a much better job!

The role of an advocate is to put forward the views of the person he or she represents. However, be careful that you are not drawn into a position where you are being used to back up or support someone's point of view.

Support before or after a meeting

If you are not attending a contact meeting to support an individual, because you have not been asked or it is not appropriate, you may nevertheless need to provide support before or after initial contact. The support you give can range from straightforward reassurance and information to relieve anxiety and apprehension, to using basic listening and supportive skills to resolve some of the questions, issues and concerns that result from a meeting. If you find yourself having to offer extensive or in-depth support, you should talk to your line manager as you may need advice or guidance before you undertake this. Otherwise, make sure you do the following.

- Follow basic procedures of good communication. Make sure you create an appropriate environment where everyone can be relaxed and comfortable.

● *Your task includes creating an environment where everyone can be relaxed and communicate easily*

- Remember that you are doing the listening, not the talking.
- Listen actively to what you are being told, and prompt speakers by nodding and using encouraging words.
- You may need to mirror and feed back what you have heard to show that you have understood.
- Use paraphrasing if appropriate to show that you are listening.
- Try to avoid giving direct advice, but encourage the examination of options.

CASE STUDY: Preparing for a difficult meeting

D is 24 years old. He lives with his parents and has used a wheelchair since a serious road accident three years ago. D suffered serious head and facial injuries in the accident but has, apart from mood swings, recovered well from his brain injuries. However, he has been left with a changed appearance following his facial injuries.

D has been communicating by e-mail with a woman he met through an Internet chatroom. The communication has been going on for a couple of months and D has now made plans to meet the young woman. His parents have expressed their concerns, but D flies into a rage when he is challenged. D's support worker has spoken to him at length about the intended meeting and has discovered that D has not prepared the young woman in any way for meeting him; she is unaware that D uses a wheelchair and is also unaware of the effect that the accident has had on his appearance.

D's support worker knows that he will need to attempt to bring about some change in D's intended course of action in order to avoid a potentially difficult situation.

1 How would you tackle the issue of this meeting?
2 What action can the support worker take if D continues to be adamant?
3 What advice should be given to D's parents?
4 What steps should the worker take:
   a before the meeting
   b after the meeting?
5 What are the potential difficulties for D that could follow?

Recording contact and relationship information

It is important that information on a service user's contacts and key relationships is kept up to date in his or her records. The rest of the members of the care team will need to know if any information has changed, such as contact details for people who are important, or the arrangements for meetings and contacts with others, or if the legal position has altered. It is also essential that new and developing relationships are noted and any potential difficulties identified.

Changes should be recorded clearly and immediately. It is no good you knowing that someone's mother, whom he sees every week, has changed her address if you are off work sick and no one else knows about the change, which may mean that visiting arrangements break down.

You must also ensure that all information of a personal nature is kept securely, and complies with the Data Protection Act 1998.

Evidence indicator

You have been asked to design a new form for recording information about people's contacts, networks and relationships. Think carefully about what needs to be in it in order to make sure that everyone in the care team will have all the important information.

When you have designed the form, try it out for a real or imaginary individual – or even for yourself!

When the form is completed, ask a colleague to look at it and tell you whether it seems to record everything necessary about an individual's relationships with other people. If there are items missing, add them in.

Checklist for recording decisions
- Copies of any court orders should be obtained from the relevant agencies, and details of the consequences of failure to comply should be recorded.

- Plans for supervised contact visits should be noted carefully, so that the service user will not be disappointed if someone has to take over from you and the plans change.
- Agreements reached about assistance to overcome physical barriers to relationships should be noted, and will need team discussion if they involve resources.
- Make a note of discussions about the emotional factors around relationships and any previous difficulties. It is important that others in the team know about the issues.

Remember always to transfer information from your head into the notes!

Active knowledge

Choose a set of records for someone you work with. Check how many entries provide information about relationships. Think how much you know about the person's relationships that is not recorded in the notes. Work out how much you could discover about this person's relationships by reading the notes alone. Asking the following questions will help:
- Who are the people who are important in this person's life?
- Who are the people with difficult relationships?
- What are the plans for approaching the difficulties?
- Are there any court orders or other restrictions?
- What are the consequences of failure to comply?

Test yourself

1 Identify two ways to support someone to participate in social networks.
2 What are the key aspects of practice to remember when supporting someone in a difficult relationship?
3 Why might you need to be involved in supporting someone in a relationship? Give at least two reasons.
4 Why is it important to record relationship information?
5 What sort of information should be recorded?

HSC 331 UNIT TEST

1 What are the different types of relationships?
2 What are the main features of relationships?
3 How are families structured in different ways?
4 What are the factors that affect how we see ourselves?
5 What are the factors that affect how we value ourselves?
6 How do relationships affect self-image?
7 How can relationships be affected by legislation?

Support the social, emotional and identity needs of individuals

All of us have needs. They range from the basic human needs we all share to highly personal and individual needs that we have because of our unique backgrounds, genetics and life experiences.

Whatever your job role, you must be aware of how important it is for well-being that people understand their own needs and recognise how to meet them. You will need to look at the nature of well-being and recognise that this is about far more than physical condition. Ensuring well-being means looking at all the factors that contribute to it: health, self-esteem, a clear identity and self-concept, positive relationships, mental stimulation and challenge, as well as factors such as economic circumstances and a decent living environment.

Everyone benefits from being able to understand who they are, to look at their own life journey and recognise how their development has been influenced.

Needs change with time as people grow and develop, and they also change as people's circumstances change. You will need to understand how these changes happen and how you can make sure that you respond in a supportive way.

What you need to learn
- Human needs
- Theories of human behaviour
- Feeling good/feeling bad
- Planning to meet different needs and wants
- Self-concept
- Self-esteem
- Planning for individuals
- Life stages
- Change
- What about you?

Human needs

Although everyone is different and an individual, we all share some basic needs as human beings. The basic, shared human needs can be broadly split into the following categories:

- physical
- intellectual
- emotional
- social.

This way of putting needs into categories has given rise to the acronym PIES.

This is one of simplest ways to think about needs and to remember what they are, as the illustration below shows.

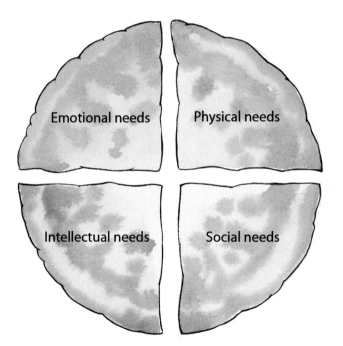

Emotional needs

Physical needs

Intellectual needs

Social needs

- *Human needs can be divided into categories*

Physical needs

These are things like food and drink, warmth and shelter, sleep and exercise.

Physical needs are usually very basic, and it is impossible to survive without fulfilling them. Of course, needs will vary with the age of the individual and the stage of life he or she is at. But generally, human beings have a greater range of physical needs at the start of their lives and in old age. These tend to be the times when physical needs are greater than just food, warmth and shelter. At the beginning of life, a baby needs care and help with moving, feeding and cleaning of body waste. In the later stages of life, or because of a disability or accident, people may also need help to meet some, or all, of these needs.

Intellectual needs

This is not about being clever! Intellectual needs are about mental stimulation and having varied interests. Everyone needs to keep his or her brain active – this is not to suggest that everyone should try to be Einstein, but simply that all humans need to have something that holds their interest or makes them think.

Like physical needs, intellectual needs change to fit the life stage: a baby will be stimulated by colours and simple shapes or by new sounds. But an older child or adolescent requires considerably more to prevent boredom! An adult will benefit from having interests and opportunities that offer a challenge and a change. Later adulthood is a vital time to ensure that intellectual needs are met, as maintaining interests and having access to mental stimulation become increasingly important if physical abilities decline.

Emotional needs

The keys to emotional fulfilment are being clear about who you are, and liking who you are. If people are confused about their own identity or are unhappy with themselves, then it will always be difficult for them to reach out to others and develop good relationships. Most people like to be liked; most people like to love and be loved. At the various stages of our lives, the needs will be different, but basically everyone needs to feel secure, nurtured and loved. A new-born child needs to feel safe and secure, or he or she will become distressed. As children grow, they benefit from receiving love and caring, as well as having boundaries, limits and routines which provide security. As adolescents progress into adulthood, emotional fulfilment is likely to come from developing a close emotional bond with another person.

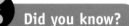
Did you know?

Children who are deprived of love and affection become silent and withdrawn. They fail to thrive and are slow to develop.

Social needs

Social needs are about relationships with other people. No one lives in a vacuum, and most human beings like to relate to other human beings. As a species, we have never lived a solitary existence. Humans have always sought to meet their social needs by living in groups alongside others. All cultures have a history of people grouping together in villages and towns or simply in tribes or families.

Evidence indicator

Think about the different needs you have: make a list to include at least five needs under each of the PIES headings. Ask a friend or colleague to do the same, then compare and find how many are different and how many are the same. Make notes on your findings.

Theories of human behaviour

Behaviourism

There are many psychological theories that attempt to explain human behaviour. Some are based on the view that humans develop behaviour directly through learning about the consequences of what they do – we do some things because we have learned that we get a response we like, and don't do others because we get a negative response. If you put your finger in a flame you will get burned and it will hurt – so you won't do it again! This is generally called **behaviourism** and incorporates the theories put forward by people such as B.F. Skinner and Ivan Pavlov.

Cognitivism

An alternative approach suggests that the human mind develops like a computer and processes information. Children receive information, organise it and adapt their behaviour according to the information they receive about the world around them. This happens in stages with children responding differently at each stage in the process. This theory is known as **cognitivism** and was primarily developed by Jean Piaget, with later adaptations by people such as Albert Bandura.

Psychoanalysis

Sigmund Freud put forward the view that all human behaviour is driven by our subconscious and unconscious urges and he considered, like Piaget, that we all pass through stages of development. In Freud's view, personalities consist of basic human biological urges, a series of processes enabling people to function and meet the demands of their unconscious urges, and a part which controls behaviour so that people fit in with the norms of society. This is a **psychoanalytic** approach, and suggests that as individuals we do not ultimately control our behaviour, as it is largely determined by our subconscious and unconscious minds.

Interactionism

Interactionists put forward a view that there are some basic personality traits, as follows.
- **Emotionally stable:** People who tend to be calm, secure and content rather than anxious, insecure and self-pitying.
- **Extrovert:** People who tend to be sociable, fun-loving and affectionate instead of sober, shy and reserved.
- **Open to experience:** People who tend to be imaginative, responsive and independent rather than practical, routine and conforming.

- **Agreeable:** People who tend to be sympathetic, trusting and helpful rather than suspicious, ruthless and uncooperative.
- **Conscientious:** People who tend to be organised, careful and disciplined rather than careless, disorganised and impulsive.

The theory argues that these basic personality traits interact with circumstances and environments to cause people to behave in particular ways, so that although someone may have a particular personality trait, the situation may cause a different reaction. For example, someone whose personality normally displays strongly agreeable traits such as being friendly and approachable may nevertheless become quite ruthless and aggressive if put into a situation where he or she is defending a loved one.

Humanism

A **humanist** approach to understanding behaviour argues that the way individuals feel about themselves is more likely to affect how they behave than the environment. Carl Rogers' theory claims that human beings are capable of growth and positive change in behaviour if they are supported and if they have a positive view of themselves. Humanists believe that all human beings are capable of improving their lives and that everyone has the ability to develop and reach their full potential. Abraham Maslow took a humanist view of behaviour, and developed an interesting approach to understanding human needs and their effect on the way we behave.

Maslow's hierarchy of needs

Maslow believed that human beings all have needs at different levels – thus it is known as Maslow's hierarchy of needs. This is usually shown as a triangle or pyramid with needs at different levels (see the next page). Maslow's theory is that people need to have the lower-level needs met, or they will never be able to move on to the higher levels.

As you look at the levels in his hierarchy, you can see that there is a progression from basic physical needs to more complex needs relating to relationships, self-esteem and fulfilment. Maslow's argument, put simply, is that people cannot enter into positive and happy relationships if they are starving, neither can they go on to extend themselves and achieve their full potential if they are not content with who they are.

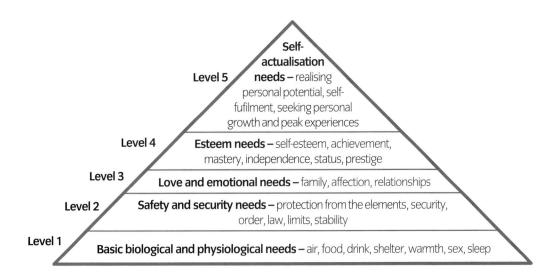

Level 5 — **Self-actualisation needs** – realising personal potential, self-fufilment, seeking personal growth and peak experiences

Level 4 — **Esteem needs** – self-esteem, achievement, mastery, independence, status, prestige

Level 3 — **Love and emotional needs** – family, affection, relationships

Level 2 — **Safety and security needs** – protection from the elements, security, order, law, limits, stability

Level 1 — **Basic biological and physiological needs** – air, food, drink, shelter, warmth, sex, sleep

Basic physical needs

People will do whatever is necessary to meet their basic physical needs. These needs rank as the most important when people are placed under threat. Most people are fortunate enough to be able to take the basic physical needs for granted, but all human beings, if they are deprived of them, will go to great lengths to satisfy those needs. For example, if a person is starving it becomes his or her overriding priority to find food. All of the other higher-level needs fade into insignificance when compared to needs such as food, warmth and shelter.

Safety and security needs

These are the needs that people will try to satisfy once they have met their basic needs. When they have sufficient food, some heat and a shelter, they will look to feel safe and secure. Safety and security means different things to different people, but safety from physical danger is what most people will look for. Freedom from fear is important to everyone, and individuals will try to achieve that and will see it as a higher priority than establishing relationships. Stability and security also include the need to live in a stable and unchaotic society. Humans also need to be free from anxiety as well as from fear, and will take steps to try to regulate the environment in which they live to achieve this.

Love and emotional needs

Human beings need to reach out and form relationships with other human beings. They need to love and to be loved in return, to express affection and caring for others, and to feel cared for and nurtured in return. This is about more than having a close relationship that we would define as love. It is also about contacts with others – friends, colleagues, neighbours – and the opportunity to co-operate and work alongside others. Most individuals dislike feeling like outsiders or not being accepted by a group, and a failure to make relationships with others is likely to make people feel very badly about themselves. The need to form relationships with other human beings, however, only becomes important after basic needs and safety and security needs have been met.

Esteem needs

Self-esteem is about the way people feel about themselves. It is important that people feel they have a valuable contribution to make, whether it is to society as a whole or within a smaller area such as their local community, workplace or their own family.

Feeling good about yourself also has a great deal to do with your own experiences throughout your life and the kind of confidence that you were able to develop as you grew up. All human beings need to feel that they have a valuable place and a valuable contribution to make within society, so achievement and knowing that what you do is valued is also a key factor.

Self-actualisation needs

This is about every human being's need to reach his or her maximum potential. This might be through setting out to achieve new goals or meeting new challenges, or through developing existing talents. Abraham Maslow suggests that if our other needs have not been met (from the most basic needs up to self-esteem needs), then this need will never be met, because people will continue to try to achieve the needs lower down the hierarchy, and will never attempt self-fulfilment and never reach their full potential.

Remember

Maslow may be right in his hierarchy of needs. Think about the number of times that you have seen people who are confused, depressed, dirty and malnourished who, within a few days of having their basic needs of warmth and food met, have started to make relationships and to try to meet some of their higher needs.

Did you know?

Maslow developed his theory by studying healthy, creative, productive people's lives; figures such as Abraham Lincoln, Thomas Jefferson, and Eleanor Roosevelt. He noticed that all high-achieving people share characteristics such as openness, self-acceptance, and love for others.

CASE STUDY: Meeting higher needs

Miss J had lived alone in a very large, cold house since her mother died about 15 years ago. She was always viewed as a bit odd by the local neighbours. She appeared quite grubby and unkempt and never spoke to or smiled at anyone. She was very thin, and seemed to be just skin and bone. The milkman and paper girl, who were the only people who ever went to the house, said that it looked very messy and dirty inside and there was never any evidence of heating, even in the depths of winter.

She was admitted to hospital one day after the milkman looked through the window and saw her on the floor when she didn't answer his knock. She had fallen and fractured her femur.

At first, Miss J didn't speak to anyone apart from asking to be left alone. She agreed to a bed bath and having her hair washed, and ate the meals which were brought to her. The nurses and health care assistants noticed that after about a week, she began to respond to their conversation and seemed to look forward to having a shower and eating her meals. Gradually, she began to talk to other patients on the ward and it became clear that she was a well-informed and intelligent woman with a keen sense of humour.

When she was ready for discharge, she decided to go on to convalescence and to sell her house and buy a flat in a retirement community, where she would meet other people and yet retain her independence.

1 Which of Miss J's needs were met by coming into hospital?
2 What effect did that have on her behaviour?
3 What level of needs is Miss J going to meet next?
4 What may have happened if she had not had the fall?

Needs recognised by the law

The Care Standards Act 2000 was the basis for the development of national standards for the provision of services for older people and vulnerable adults. All of the standards require an assessment of needs, including social and emotional ones, regardless of whether they relate to residential or domiciliary services, or services to older people or vulnerable adults.

The national standards form the basis for inspections undertaken by the Commission for Social Care Inspection. This makes sure that people's needs are considered by everyone providing a social care service. The National Health Service has a series of National Service Frameworks that provide the benchmarks for the standard of service required. Similarly, it is a requirement that people providing health care must consider the full range of people's needs.

Active knowledge

Look at the tree diagram above. It shows people at a great many stages and in a great many different situations. Study them all carefully.

1 Where do you think you fit? Are you the person at the top of the tree smiling, or the person near the top of the tree but not very happy? Are you falling, or being pushed? Are you hanging on by a thread, or having great fun? Are you climbing up, or sliding down?
2 Which figures look the happiest?
3 Which figure would you most like to be?
4 Which figure would you least like to be? Why?

Remember

The people you provide care for all see themselves at different stages on the tree, and have probably seen themselves at different stages at various points in their lives. Nobody stays at the same point on the tree forever. As circumstances change, so do people's views of themselves.

Feeling good/feeling bad

People can find it difficult to work out exactly what it is that is causing problems with their lives. The chances are that some of their needs are not being met. Working out where the issues are is not always easy, and sometimes people need support to do this. If you are asked to help someone you will need to encourage them to think about a few key areas.

- First, which parts of their lives are working well and which parts are not? This is not always a simple question. Sometimes people are going through such a difficult time that they may not be sure exactly what is working in their lives and what is causing a problem. Starting with the basics is always a good idea, so try discussing the points in the following table.

Relationships	Work	Environment	Health	Values, beliefs and culture
Partner, parents, siblings, friends, colleagues	Lack of work, job role, work colleagues, looking for work, not able to work	Housing, area, access, transport, shops, libraries, community facilities, closeness to family	Mental and physical health, understanding of condition, treatment – is it working, is health restricting activities?	Are things happening that are hard to deal with, are people not behaving as expected, are local, national or world events shaking a faith?

- Next, when individuals have been supported to look at which parts of their lives are difficult, it may be easier for them to see which of their needs are not being met. For example, if relationships have gone wrong, or in the case of a bereavement, people's emotional needs will not be met and this could be an area they can identify. Alternatively, the fact that they have no job and do not go out much may mean that they are feeling low because their social and intellectual needs are not being met. They may have little chance to interact with other people and very little that offers an intellectual challenge.
- The third stage is to look for ways to meet the needs that have been identified. This could involve supporting someone to look for a job, or helping to find ways to meet new people. You may be able to give information about where people can find support if they have been bereaved – or you may just be able to offer a shoulder to cry on!

What people say

Most people are not going to describe their unmet needs in professional terms – you are very unlikely to hear 'I think my problem is that my social and emotional needs are not being met'. What you will hear is 'I'm so lonely, I feel as though no one cares'. It is your job to recognise what that means, and to work alongside individuals to find the way to meet their needs.

Planning to meet different needs and wants

There are many practical ways in which people's needs can be met through the way in which you provide the services they need. Being recognised and valued as an individual is hugely important for people's self-esteem. When an individual either requests, or is referred for a service, the assessment and planning cycle begins. Throughout the consultation and planning that follows, the individual and his or her needs should be at the centre of the process. You will need to make sure that individuals have every opportunity to state exactly how they wish their needs to be met. Some individuals will be able to give this information personally; others will need an advocate who will support them in expressing their views.

Recognise the power you have

You need to be very clear in your understanding of the responsibility you carry in relation to the individuals you support. Working to provide care for someone gives you a great deal of power. It also means that you are able to influence people because they will have faith in what you say and do.

Unfortunately, trust is sometimes abused and care workers can be among those who exploit vulnerable people, by recognising their weak points and using them either to make money or satisfy their own sexual or emotional needs.

Of course, the vast majority of care workers use their power and influence positively and responsibly, and they encourage and support individuals to recognise their own needs and find ways to meet them.

Test yourself

1 List the different types of needs all humans have.
2 Note down two examples of each different type of need.
3 Explain the theory of Maslow's hierarchy of needs.
4 Describe a humanist view of human behaviour.
5 Describe a Freudian view of human behaviour.

HSC 332b Support individuals to develop and maintain self-esteem and a positive self-image

The concept of self is usually described in terms of self-concept – the person we think we are; and self-esteem or self-image – the value we attach to that self-concept.

Self-concept

Self-concept is about how people see themselves. This is one of the fundamental questions that philosophers and psychologists have sought to explore. How would you answer this question about yourself? Would you describe who you are in terms of what you do, such as being a care worker? Perhaps you would describe yourself in terms of your relationships with others, such as being a spouse, or a parent, or a child. Have you ever described yourself as 'So-and-so's mum or dad', or 'So-and-so's son or daughter'? You might think of yourself in terms of your hopes, dreams or ambitions. What is perhaps more likely is that all of these ways of thinking about yourself play some part.

Active knowledge

Think about the number of different ways you could describe yourself.
List them all, then look at:

- how many describe your relationship to other people – e.g. someone's parent, sibling, friend
- how many relate to what you do – e.g. care worker, volunteer at the youth club, gardener
- how many relate to what you believe in – e.g. honesty, loyalty, being a Christian or a Muslim
- how many relate to what you look like – e.g. short brown hair, blue eyes…

You may be surprised when you see the different influences on how you view yourself.

● *Everyone has a self-concept, making an individual sense of identity*

Self-concept is about what makes people who they are. Everyone has a concept of himself or herself – it can be a positive image overall or a negative one, but a great many factors contribute to an individual sense of identity. These will include:

- gender
- race
- language/accent
- values and beliefs
- religion
- sexual orientation.

All of these are aspects of our lives that contribute to our idea of who we are. As a care worker it is essential that you consider how the individuals you work with will have developed their own self-concept and identity, and it is important that you recognise and promote this.

The values, beliefs, tastes and preferences which individuals have are what makes them who they are, and must be supported, nurtured and encouraged, and not ignored and disregarded because they are inconvenient or don't fit in with the care system.

Self-esteem

Self-esteem is about how people value themselves – their self-worth or self-image. People have different levels of self-confidence, and it is very common to hear that somebody is not very confident or does not have a very high opinion of himself or herself. It is important that people feel they have a valuable contribution to make.

Feeling good about yourself also has a great deal to do with your own experiences throughout life and the kind of confidence that you were able to develop as you grew up. All human beings need to feel that they have a valuable place and a valuable contribution to make within society.

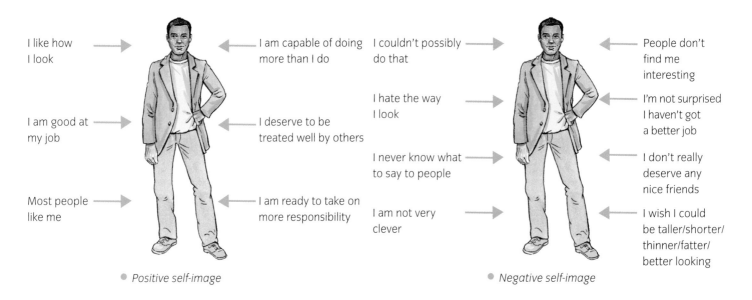

Positive self-image

Negative self-image

The reasons why people have different levels of self-esteem are complex. The way people feel about themselves is often laid down during childhood. A child who is encouraged and regularly told how good he or she is and given a lot of positive feelings is the sort of person who is likely to feel that he or she has something to offer and can make a useful contribution to any situation. But a child who is constantly shouted at, blamed or belittled is likely to grow into an adult who lacks belief in himself or herself, or finds it difficult to go into new situations and to accept new challenges.

Not all the reasons for levels of self-confidence and self-image come from childhood. There are many experiences in adult life that can affect self-confidence and how people feel about themselves, for example:

- being made redundant
- getting divorced
- the death of someone close
- the loss of independence, possibly having to go into residential care or into hospital
- the shock of being burgled
- having a bad fall, which results in a feeling of helplessness and a lack of self-worth
- being the subject of discriminatory or stereotyping behaviour
- being the victim of violent or aggressive behaviour.

All of these experiences can have devastating effects. Very often, people will become withdrawn and depressed as a result, and a great deal of support and concentrated effort is needed to help them through these very difficult situations. People can be very vulnerable at these low points in their lives, and it is important that you make sure that you have followed the procedures in your organisation for assessing and managing the risk of self-harm where you are aware that someone is going through a period of low self-esteem. When you identify signs of extremely low self-esteem in an individual, you should seek advice and support to help resolve the problem.

Active knowledge

Check your organisation's policies and procedures to identify the key criteria that will trigger a risk assessment for someone who has been showing signs of low self-esteem and feelings of worthlessness.

However, self-esteem is also very closely tied into the culture we live in, and the values that culture has. For example, among a group of young car thieves, the person most admired might be the one who has stolen the most cars, and the self-esteem of that person is likely to be high because of this admiration and approval, even though these values would not be shared by other people in the community! So never forget the strong influence that values and culture have on self-esteem and self-concept.

Clearly it is vital to balance the rights of individuals to meet their own needs against their responsibilities to others – in the example above, obviously the car thief cannot be allowed to continue to steal cars in order to maintain his or her self-esteem! However, there are other, less clear-cut situations where it can be difficult to balance the needs and rights of individuals with the responsibilities they have to themselves and others. For example, a young woman who believes that she will feel more confident if she is as thin as all the models and pop stars she admires may decide to eat only 200 calories each day in order to achieve the weight loss she wants. This is obviously going to result in her becoming ill, and is a situation where a balance needs to be established.

Ways to support self-esteem

Feeling valued as an individual is vital to increasing self-esteem and making people feel good about themselves. After all, it is very hard to feel good about yourself if you don't believe that anyone else thinks much of you. If you are able to feel that people respect and value you, you are more likely to value yourself.

In your role as a care worker, you will come across situations where a little thought or a small change in practice could give greater opportunities for people to feel that they are valued and respected as individuals. For example, you may need to find out how someone likes to be addressed. Is the use of 'Mr' or 'Mrs' considered more respectful and appropriate, or is a first name preferred? This, particularly for some older people, can be one of the ways of indicating the respect that is felt to be important by users of care services.

You will need to give thought to the values and beliefs which service users may have, for example:

- religious or cultural beliefs about eating certain foods
- values concerning forms of dress
- beliefs or preferences about who should be able to provide personal care.

What do you need to do?

You need to make sure that people have been asked about religious or cultural preferences and those preferences are recorded so that all care workers and others providing care are able to access them.

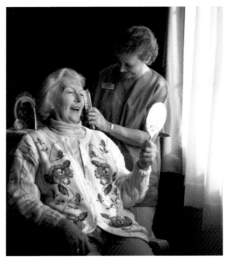

There may already be arrangements in your workplace to ask for and record this information. If so, you must ensure that you are familiar with the process and that

- *It is important to find out how people like to be addressed*

you know where to find the information for everyone you work with. If your workplace does not have arrangements in place to find out about people's choices and preferences, you should discuss with your line manager ways in which you can help to find this out.

How do you need to do it?

The prospect of having to ask people questions about their background, values and beliefs can be quite daunting. But it is quite rare for people to be offended by your showing an interest in them! Simple, open questions, asked politely, are always the best way: 'Excuse me Mr Khan, the information I have here notes that you are vegetarian. Can you tell me about any particular foods you wish to eat?'

You can obtain some information by observation – looking at someone can tell you a lot about their preferences in dress, for example. Particular forms of clothing worn for religious or cultural reasons are usually obvious (a turban or a sari, for instance, are easy to spot), but other forms of dress may also give you some clues about the person wearing them. Think about how dress can tell you about the amount of money people are used to spending on clothes, or what kind of background they come from. Clothes also tell you a lot about someone's age and the type of lifestyle they are likely to be used to. Beware, however – any information you think you gain from this type of observation must be confirmed by checking your facts. Otherwise it is easy to be caught out – some people from wealthy backgrounds wear cheap clothes, and some people in their seventies wear the latest fashions and have face lifts!

Equally, be careful that you do not resort to thinking in stereotypes, rather than working with people as individuals. Avoid making assumptions about people based on any of the factors that make them similar to others, such as:

- age
- gender
- race
- culture
- skin colour
- job
- wealth
- where they live.

All of these factors are important in giving you information about what may have influenced the development of each individual, but they will never, on their own, tell you anything else about an individual. If people make stereotypical assumptions about individuals it can result in very low self-esteem and a negative self-image. For example, if everyone assumes that just because you are 85, you are too old to be interested in current affairs, or the latest sports news, you may decide that perhaps you are too old to bother after all; or if employers keep refusing to give you a job because you live in an inner city, are 16, male and black, you may well decide that its not worth bothering to try any more.

Evidence indicator

Look at the form or other means of recording information which is used in your workplace to set down the cultural or religious preferences of individuals. Fill it in for yourself as if you were a service user. Now note down all the factors that make you who you are. Think about:

- gender
- age
- background
- economic and social circumstances
- nationality
- culture
- religion
- sexual orientation
- food preferences
- entertainment preferences
- relaxation preferences
- reading material preferences.

Look at the form you have completed – would it tell care workers enough about you so that they could ensure that all your needs were met and you did not lose aspects of your life that were important to you? If not, think about which other questions would need to be asked, and note them down. Make sure that, if appropriate, you ask those questions.

Planning for individuals

The process of providing care should be carefully planned and designed to ensure that the service is exactly right for the individual it is meant to be helping. This is of key significance, not just because it is a right to which everyone is entitled, but also because health and well-being respond to emotional factors as much as physical ones. Individuals will benefit if the service they receive is centred around their own needs and the ways in which they wish those needs to be met. Feeling valued and recognised as a person is likely to improve the self-esteem and self-confidence of the people you work with and thus contribute to an overall improvement in health and well-being.

Making it all positive

You can support people to maintain a positive self-image and to maintain and improve their self-esteem by encouraging and supporting them to achieve their goals, and by offering recognition of their achievements when they do. Working with people to look at what they want to achieve is vital in promoting well-being; you should help individuals to think about what they want to do, but encourage them to be realistic and to set goals that are achievable. We all know that nothing boosts our self-esteem more than achieving a goal we have set, or overcoming a challenge.

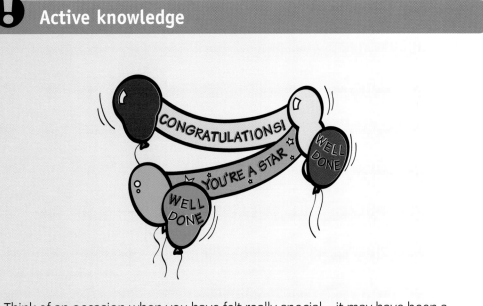
Setting goals

Beware of situations where either you or the individual are setting out to achieve the impossible. It's a bit like trying to stop smoking and lose weight at the same time – you are setting yourself up for failure! Try to encourage people to move away from unachievable goals, or try to get them to break the goals into smaller ones that are more realistic. Someone recovering from a spinal injury may say 'I will be back at work in three months'. This is not a goal that should be dismissed, but it is certainly one that needs to be modified. With support and encouragement, such a goal can be broken down into achievable stages, such as: 'I will walk down the corridor with support in six weeks'.

When you are working with individuals where there are goals of this nature that have to be broken down into smaller parts, you must always:

- check with the relevant professional that the goals are appropriate for the individual's physical condition (physiotherapist, doctor, speech therapist, etc.)
- plan and agree with the individual and his or her carers and family what the goals are and how they will be achieved
- assist if necessary to monitor progress and achievement
- readjust and modify goals in the light of progress
- celebrate achievements.

Active knowledge

Take a real or imaginary individual and look at a simple achievement. Think of the ways you can encourage the individual and recognise the achievement.

Then take a different (real or imaginary) person and look at a more complex, longer-term goal. Think of how you can assist to break this down into achievable stages. Make notes or a chart to show how you have worked or could work alongside someone to help him or her achieve such a goal.

The importance of personal appearance

The way people look can often help to raise or lower their self-esteem. Apart from the reasons of physical health that make it important for people to remain clean and well groomed, appearance is an important factor in how people feel about themselves. Offer support and encouragement if necessary to someone to select clothes, have hair washed, cut or styled, and have nails cleaned and manicured.

Remember

Maintaining self-esteem and a positive self-image is about a range of factors:

- background and upbringing
- values and beliefs
- being treated with respect and valued as an individual
- achieving targets and goals
- overcoming challenges
- feeling good about how you look.

You can make a real difference by recognising where the needs are and working to meet them.

Test yourself

This poem was said to have been found, after her death, in the locker of Kate, a long-term patient on a geriatric ward in the early 1970s.

What do you see, nurses, what do you see?
What are you thinking when you look at me?
A crabbit old woman, not very wise,
Uncertain of habit with faraway eyes,
Who dribbles her food and makes no reply

When you say in a loud voice 'I do wish you'd try',
Who seems not to notice the things that you do
And forever is losing a stick or a shoe,
Who, unresistingly or not, lets you do as you will
With bathing and feeding – the long day to fill.
Is that what you're thinking? Is that what you see?
Then open your eyes nurses – you're looking at me.
I'll tell you who I am as I sit here so still
As I move at your bidding, as I eat at your will.
I'm a small child of ten with a father and mother
Brothers and sisters who love one another.
A young girl of sixteen with wings on her feet
Dreaming that soon a lover she'll meet.
A bride soon, at twenty my heart gives a leap
Remembering the vows that I promised to keep.
At twenty-five now I have young of my own,
Who need me to build a secure happy home.
A young woman of thirty, my young now grow fast
Bound to each other with ties that should last.
At forty my young ones now grown will soon be gone
But my memories stay beside me to see I don't mourn.
At fifty, once more babies play round my knee
Again we know children, my loved one and me.
Dark days are upon me, my husband is dead;
I look at the future, I shudder with dread.
For my young are all busy rearing young of their own
And I think of the years and the love I have known.
I'm an old woman now, and nature is cruel
The body it crumbles, grace and vigour depart
There is now a stone where I once had a heart.
But inside this old carcass a young girl still dwells
And now and again my battered heart swells –
I remember the joys, I remember the pain
And I'm loving and living life over again.
I think of the years – all too few – gone too fast
And accept the stark fact that nothing can last.
So open your eyes, nurses, open and see
Not a crabbit old woman… look closer, see ME.

1   What does this poem tell us about Kate's self-concept?
2   What do you think could/should have been done for Kate?
3   What does this poem tell us about Kate's self-esteem?
4   What do you think could/should have been done about this?
5   Which of Kate's needs were not being met?
6   Who should have been meeting those needs?

HSC 332c Support individuals to address changing social, emotional and developmental needs

It is inevitable that everything changes, as people's circumstances and health change with time. As people change, so do their needs. For example, a baby has its emotional needs met by having lots of cuddles and being held close to the smell, touch and feel of its mother. For an adult, emotional needs are met in a different way.

Everyone is different, but all humans broadly develop at a similar pace. People move through life stages and their needs will inevitably change with each stage.

Life stages

The chart below gives a broad picture of life stages and their associated needs.

	Intellectual/ cognitive	Social/emotional	Language	Physical
Infant, birth–1 year	Learns about new things by feeling with hands and mouth objects encountered in immediate environment	Attaches to parent(s), begins to recognise faces and smile; at about 6 months begins to recognise parent(s) and expresses fear of strangers, plays simple interactive games like peekaboo	Vocalises, squeals, and imitates sounds, says 'dada' and 'mama'	Lifts head first then chest, rolls over, pulls to sit, crawls and stands alone. Reaches for objects and rakes up small items, grasps rattle
Toddler, 1–2 years	Extends knowledge by learning words for objects in environment	Learns that self and parent(s) are different or separate from each other, imitates and performs tasks, indicates needs or wants without crying	Says some words other than 'dada' and 'mama', follows simple instructions	Walks well, kicks, stoops and jumps in place, throws balls. Unbuttons clothes, builds tower of 4 cubes, scribbles, uses spoon, picks up very small objects

	Intellectual/ cognitive	Social/emotional	Language	Physical
Pre-school, 2–5 years	Understands concepts such as tired, hungry and other bodily states, recognises colours, becomes aware of numbers and letters	Begins to separate easily from parent(s), dresses with assistance, washes and dries hands, plays interactive games such as tag	Names pictures, follows directions, can make simple sentences of two or three words, vocabulary increases	Runs well, hops, pedals tricycle, balances on one foot. Buttons clothes, builds tower of 8 cubes, copies simple figures or letters, for example 0, begins to use scissors
School age, 5–12 years	Develops understanding of numeracy and literacy concepts, learns relationship between objects and feelings, acquires knowledge and understanding	Acts independently, but is emotionally close to parent(s), dresses without assistance, joins same-sex play groups and clubs	Defines words, knows and describes what things are made of, vocabulary increases	Skips, balances on one foot for 10 seconds, overestimates physical abilities. Draws person with 6 parts, copies detailed figures and objects
Adolescent, 12–18 years	Understands abstract concepts such as illness and death, develops understanding of complex concepts	Experiences rapidly changing moods and behaviour, interested in peer group almost exclusively, distances from parent(s) emotionally, concerned with body image, experiences falling in and out of love	Uses increased vocabulary, understands more abstract concepts such as grief	May appear awkward and clumsy while learning to deal with rapid increases in size due to growth spurts
Young adult, 18–40 years	Continues to develop the ability to make good decisions and to understand the complexity of human relationships – sometimes called wisdom	Becomes independent from parent(s), develops own lifestyle, selects a career, copes with career, social and economic changes and social expectations, chooses a partner, learns to live co-operatively with partner, becomes a parent	Continues to develop vocabulary and knowledge of different styles of language use	Fully developed

	Intellectual/ cognitive	Social/emotional	Language	Physical
Middle age, 40–65 years	Continues to develop a deeper understanding of life – sometimes called wisdom	Builds social and economic status, is fulfilled by work or family, copes with physical changes of ageing, children grow and leave nest, deals with ageing parents, copes with the death of parents	Vocabulary may continue to develop	Begins to experience physical signs of ageing
Older adult, 65+ years	Ability may be influenced by health factors; some individuals will continue to develop 'wisdom'	Adjusts to retirement, adjusts to loss of friends and relatives, copes with loss of spouse, adjusts to new role in family, copes with dying	Ability may be influenced by health factors; some individuals may continue to develop language skills	Experiences more significant physical changes associated with ageing

A knowledge of life stages will not tell you about an individual, but will help in identifying the ways in which people's needs are likely to change.

Change

Changes can be exciting and challenging, but they can also be frightening, upsetting and unsettling; much depends on individual personalities, the nature of the changes and how well prepared people are. Changes in circumstances can mean a change in people's needs; someone who moves into a residential care facility a long way from a former home may find that he or she has little social contact, having moved away from friends, neighbours and acquaintances. So whereas previously an individual may have had no need for support with meeting social needs, new circumstances may mean that you will need to work with the individual to make links to new networks and social contacts.

How people cope with change

Most people who receive care will experience a change at some point. Whether it is something as comparatively small as a new home carer or something as great as the closure of a residential home and a move to a new location, it is still likely to be worrying for the individual concerned.

There are two types of change that affect most people's lives. One is caused by predictable events and one by unpredictable events. Predictable events are things such as:

- starting school
- leaving school
- getting married
- moving house.

Unpredictable events are things such as:

- a sudden death
- redundancy
- accident
- winning the lottery.

People tend to cope in different ways with the two different types of event. Generally, it is easier to cope with a predictable event because people have had time to plan, organise and get used to the idea that it is going to happen. Unpredictable events can be much more difficult to cope with. Even positive changes such as winning the lottery can be quite traumatic, although it is probably a way in which most of us would be willing to be traumatised!

● *Even positive changes such as winning the lottery can be difficult to cope with*

Active knowledge

Think of major events or changes that have happened in your life. Make two lists with three or four items on each: one of the unpredictable events, and one of the predictable events. Write down what you can remember of your feelings about each of these events. Some of your memories may be vague if they happened some time ago, but try to remember the important feelings and write down as many as you can.

When you carry out the activity above, you will probably find that many of your feelings, even about the planned and predictable changes in your life, were connected with anxiety and worry about how things would turn out. A new job can be something that you welcome, look forward to and are excited about, but that can still be mixed with feelings of worry and anxiety, and questions such as: Will it be alright? Will they be nice people? Will I be able to do the job?

Imagine how much stronger those feelings must be when people are moving from one care setting to another. Even a planned move can bring with it a great many concerns and worries.

Unpredictable or unplanned events can obviously be even more difficult for people to cope with. Having to move into residential care, perhaps as the result of the death of a partner, the illness of a carer at home, because of a fall or because of illness, can make it very difficult for people to adjust to the new setting. This is hardly surprising – they have had no chance to think, to adjust, to plan or to ask questions and receive any answers. Their needs will be changing, and in a time of uncertainty, people will react to not having some of their needs met – remember Maslow's hierarchy.

Did you know?

The expression 'ringing the changes' is not about change at all! It comes from bell-ringing, and is the art of ringing a set of tuned bells in a mathematical sequence, called 'change ringing'.

Supporting people through transition and change

The best way for people to cope with change is generally to have the maximum amount of information available. One of the key roles you will have in supporting people who are going through a change is ensuring that their questions are answered and that they have information on which to base decisions and make plans. Many studies have been carried out into how people cope with major changes caused by loss – the death of a close relative or the loss of a limb, or major physical changes following an accident or an illness. Although a transfer from one type of care setting to another may not seem as drastic as any of these changes, it can certainly have similar effects for some people, and one of the underlying reasons is that people's needs may not be met in the way they were previously.

One of the most common findings in all the research is that there are a number of stages in people's reactions to major and traumatic change. In general they follow a pattern of:

- *Stage 1: Shock and disbelief*
- *Stage 2: Denial* – people may pretend that the change is not happening or that it is not as large a change as it appears to be
- *Stage 3: Frustration* – the change is still not accepted and there is a great deal of frustration and anger about the fact that nothing can be done to change the situation
- *Stage 4: Depression and apathy* – this is the stage at which people say 'What is the point? How can I carry on?'
- *Stage 5: Experimental stage* – people begin to accept that the change has happened, and start to experiment with the new situation

- *Stage 6: Decision* – people start to decide how they are going to move forward from this point in their lives; they accept the change and begin to come to terms with it
- *Stage 7: Integration* – change is now fully integrated into a person's life, he or she has completely come to terms with it and it is now a part of the way he or she lives.

All of this takes time, and the length of time varies depending on the nature of the change. The accepted time to work through these stages in serious cases, for example after a bereavement, is about two years. Clearly other situations may take less or more time.

Adjusting to a change to a new care setting is unlikely to take as long as adjusting to a bereavement, but nonetheless acceptance may not be immediate. So do not be surprised if a new resident, admitted as an emergency, does not seem very friendly or want to take part in the activities of the care setting.

The best way to support people through the coping stages is to ensure that they are constantly reassured and constantly given information, so that they can reach their own conclusions about the new situation. Always offer information and always make sure that you take the time to answer questions. Information is one of the major needs during times of change and transition.

You can help to ensure that information is correct by reporting issues and decisions to the appropriate people within your own and other organisations, and recording them accurately. Of course, you will need to respect confidentiality when you do this, and follow organisational and legal requirements.

● *Offer all the information you can and take the time to answer questions*

✔ Keys to good practice: Helping people to cope with change

✓ Always give people as much information as possible about changes.

✓ Make sure that the information you give is within your role and responsibility.

✓ Recognise that people go through stages in coping with change.

✓ Take time with people to help them adjust.

✓ Offer reassurance and support.

✓ Report on and record actions, processes and outcomes according to organisational and legal requirements, including confidentiality.

CASE STUDY: Coping with planned change

T has been a resident in a small children's home for the past two years. She is 13 years old and attends the local school. Her mother died following an overdose, and during most of T's life had an intermittent drink and drugs problem. T maintains occasional contact with her grandmother, who is not able to care for her. Her father has had no contact with her throughout her life.

T has generally adjusted well to life in care. She has made good relationships with the other young people and the staff, and apart from the occasional outburst and tantrum, has never presented any major difficulties with behaviour.

A decision has been taken by the Social Services department that, in line with its policy of extending community provision for young people, T's children's home is to close along with three others. The young people are to be relocated, either in one of the remaining children's homes in the city or in foster care.

Individual reviews have been held with all of the young people from the home and plans have been made. T has decided that she wants to go to a foster home, and the care team are happy to agree to this. T was asked if she had any preferences about the kind of family she wants to live with. She decided that she would like other children to be in the family, but that she did not mind if there were one or two parents. T wanted to live in town rather than in the country, did not mind if she had to change school and wanted a family who have a dog.

A suitable foster home was found for her, and she was told about it and shown photographs. T decided that she would like to meet the family. Introductory visits were made, after which both T and the family decided that they wanted to go ahead. Finally, the date has arrived for T to move on a permanent basis.

1   What do you think T's feelings will be?
2   Which of T's needs will be met by this change?
3   How will her needs change?
4   What sort of behaviour could you expect from T?
5   What help do you think T may need in the immediate future?

In the case study of T it is clear that she was given a lot of information. She was able to meet her new foster carers and visit them, the reasons for the home closing were explained to her, and she had time to plan. However, this is not always the way things happen, as the following case study shows.

CASE STUDY: Coping with sudden change

Mr P has terminal cancer. He is 65 years old. He was cared for by his wife, with the support of Macmillan nurses. He remained at home for most of his treatment and both he and his wife were adamant that they did not want to consider any form of hospital or hospice care. Mr P is now at a stage where he is taking a fairly substantial number of painkillers and his mobility has decreased. Although he gets out of bed each day, he only moves into the lounge, where he sits by the window overlooking the garden. On mild days he is able to walk out onto the patio, but this is the furthest he can manage.

On the way back from the local shops one day, his wife was involved in a serious car accident. She was admitted to hospital and is likely to be there for several weeks. Mr P was taken to the local hospice by his Macmillan nurse. He had never been to the hospice before, but he has been told about his wife's condition and knows that he may have to remain there for some time.

1 What is Mr P likely to be feeling?
2 Which is his needs are not being met?
3 How have his needs changed?

The two case studies show two very different situations – in one there was plenty of opportunity to plan and gather information, and in the other there was an emergency situation where virtually no information was available. The two individuals concerned are likely to have responded very differently to their experiences and your role in each situation would be different, but both circumstances are about changing needs and the importance of services being able to recognise and meet needs as they change.

What about you?

Some of the situations we have looked at can be difficult and distressing to deal with. It can be hard to support someone who is feeling very low, and if someone you are supporting harms himself or herself, it is easy to feel that you are to blame.

Make sure that you have regular access to supervision from your manager; this will be an essential part of helping you to work more effectively and to plan and review the work you are doing. You do not need to struggle alone with any problems or worries – you should always make good use of professional supervision.

Evidence indicator

Work individually on this exercise, although you may want to discuss the results with a small group of colleagues.

Choose an individual with whom you work. Check whether he or she is willing to participate and to give you some information about important events in his or her life history. Note down these important events. Some examples are obvious and will apply to everyone:

- year of birth
- starting school
- leaving school
- starting work.

Other items will be different for different people:

- birth of any siblings
- achievement of qualifications
- meeting a partner
- marriage
- progress in job
- birth of any children
- death of people close to them
- major illnesses
- other important events
- retirement from work.

Be sure to ask about your subject's feelings, hopes and fears connected with each of these important events. Use the information you have gathered to prepare a timeline which shows all the important dates in his or her life in order.

Make notes at each entry on the timeline, identifying:

- what the person's needs were at each point
- how the needs were met.

When you have finished, look at how the person's needs have changed during his or her life. Identify the points at which the needs changed, and what the different needs were.

Make sure you observe all the confidentiality safeguards by not including names – only initials – and by gaining the permission of the individual to do the exercise.

Test yourself

1 Why might a knowledge of human life stages be helpful in assessing individuals' needs?
2 Why is a sudden change often more difficult to cope with than a planned change? Give some examples.
3 Name some of the stages that people may go through in the process of coping with change.
4 What are the most important points to remember when you are supporting someone who is coping with change?

HSC 332 UNIT TEST

1 What are the basic human needs?
2 What can cause needs to change?
3 What factors influence self-esteem?
4 Note down three ways of supporting someone to improve his or her self-esteem.
5 Why can self-esteem be linked to culture and values?
6 What factors contribute to someone's self-concept?

Contribute to the protection of individuals from harm and abuse

This unit is for those who are likely to make a significant contribution to protecting people and minimising the risk of them being subjected to harm, abuse or danger.

In this unit you will look at some of the most difficult issues that you will face as a care professional. You need to know how our society handles abuse, the causes that give rise to harmful, dangerous or abusive situations, and what to do about them. It is a tragic fact that almost all disclosures of abuse are true – and you will have to learn to *think the unthinkable*.

If you can learn always to think about the risks, always to be alert to potentially abusive situations and always to *listen* and *believe* when you are told of harm and abuse, then you will provide the best possible protection for individuals you work with. In recent years, there has been a high level of public interest in and reporting of abuse of children. The protection of vulnerable adults has not had such a high profile, although a structure of policies and strategies is now in place to support and protect vulnerable adults.

What you need to learn

- Danger, harm and abuse
- Structures for protection of vulnerable adults
- Abusive situations
- Warning signs of harm or abuse
- Neglect
- Patterns and nature of abuse
- Risk factors for abuse
- Empowerment and protection
- How to reduce individual risks
- Consent
- Abuse by professional carers
- Protection of Vulnerable Adults scheme
- How to respond to concerns
- What happens next
- How to deal with abusive behaviour

HSC 335a Recognise and report on factors that may cause danger, harm and abuse

Many different factors will place people at risk, and it will not always be possible for you to protect everyone from everything; neither is this desirable. There are many situations in which you will have to balance the rights of individuals to place themselves in potential danger in order to take control over their own lives. This does not mean that every disabled person you work with will want to take up wheelchair rock climbing, but the element of risk can equally apply to a vulnerable adult with deteriorating memory function who wants to go out alone on a shopping trip. There is undoubtedly a significant risk in such a situation, but this needs to be balanced against the importance of empowerment, dignity and control.

Danger, harm and abuse

There are vital differences between danger, harm and abuse. In the National Occupational Standards, danger and harm are defined in relation to abusive situations:

- danger is about the possibility or risk of abuse
- harm is about the results and consequences of abuse.

Whether your job role means that you are responsible only for your own work, or whether you also have some responsibility for the work of colleagues, you will need to give thought to your role in protection. There are likely to be differences depending on your working environment; for example, the dangers and risks presented in an individual's home will be different from those in a residential or health care setting.

Clearly, the concepts of danger, harm and abuse are inter-linked; someone who is abused may be in danger and will be suffering harm – but not everyone who is exposed to danger is being abused, and people can be harmed through accident or carelessness rather than deliberate abuse.

Active knowledge

Think of three possible ways in which an individual could be exposed to danger:
- at home
- in residential care
- in hospital.

List three ways in which the individual could suffer harm in these situations.

The Law Commission, in its consultation document 'Who Decides?' published in 1997, suggested that 'harm' should be taken to include not only ill treatment (including sexual abuse and forms of ill treatment that are not physical), but also 'the impairment of, or an avoidable deterioration in, physical or mental health; and the impairment of physical, intellectual, emotional, social or behavioural development'. This gives a far broader definition of harm than previously considered and means that acts that cause reactions such as distress, fear, loss of confidence and anxiety are also identified as abusive.

● *Danger: Yes, but balance against empowerment and choice*
  Harm: Possibly, but balance against empowerment and choice
  Abuse: No, unless forced to do it!

● *Danger: Yes*
  Harm: Yes
  Abuse: Yes

Structures for protection of vulnerable adults

All local authorities have to have a policy for protecting vulnerable adults. There is a set of guidelines published by the government about adults, called 'No Secrets'. These guidelines state that older people have specific rights, which include being treated with respect, and being able to live in their home and community without fear of physical or emotional violence or harassment.

The guidance gives local authorities the lead responsibility in co-ordinating the procedures. Each local authority area must have a multi-agency management committee for the protection of vulnerable adults, which will develop policies, protocols and practices. The guidance covers:

* identification of those at risk
* setting up an inter-agency framework
* developing inter-agency policy – procedures for responding in individual cases
* recruitment, training, and other staff and management issues.

A government White Paper published in 2001, 'Valuing People: A New Strategy for Learning Disability in the 21st Century', sets out the ways in which services for people with a learning disability will be improved. 'Valuing People' sets out four main principles for service provision for people with a learning disability:

* civil rights
* independence
* choice
* inclusion.

The White Paper also makes it clear that people with a learning disability are entitled to the full protection of the law.

Recent policy approaches to protecting children and vulnerable adults have concentrated on improving and monitoring the quality of the service provided to them. The principle behind this is that if the overall quality of practice in care is constantly improved, then well-trained staff working to high standards are less likely to abuse service users, and are more likely to identify and deal effectively with any abuse they find. This type of strategy is also concerned with the qualities of people who become professional carers, and a national scheme was introduced in July 2004 – the Protection of Vulnerable Adults Scheme (POVA) – which enables criminal record checks to be made on people in the care workforce. People who are found to be unfit to work with vulnerable adults are placed on a list to which potential employers must refer before allowing anyone to start work.

Abusive situations

Abuse may happen just once, or it can be ongoing; either situation should be viewed as serious. If abuse has happened once, the risks of it happening again are far higher. It may be physical or psychological abuse, or deliberate neglect.

A failure to provide appropriate care can also be abuse. A vulnerable person might be persuaded to enter into a financial arrangement to which he or she has not given or cannot give informed consent, and this is abusive in the same way as persuading someone to enter into a sexual act for which informed consent either has not been, or cannot be, given.

Remember

Abuse of vulnerable individuals can take many forms. An individual may be subjected to more than one type of abuse.

A wide range of people may abuse vulnerable adults, including family members, friends, professional staff, care workers, volunteers or other service users.

Abuse may take place within an individual's own home, in nursing, residential or day care facilities or hospitals. Incidents of abuse can affect one person or a group of people at the same time.

Some instances of abuse will constitute a criminal offence – for example assault, rape, theft or fraud – which can be prosecuted, but not all abuse falls into this category.

Warning signs of harm or abuse

There are warning signs that indicate you should consider harm or abuse as a possible cause, and these are discussed in the following pages. Each of them can be the result of something other than abuse, but they do act as pointers that should make you look at the possibility of abuse.

Different types of abuse have different remedies in law, and some have no legal remedies, but are dealt with through policies, procedures and guidelines. The remedies for different types of abuse are also set out below.

Physical abuse

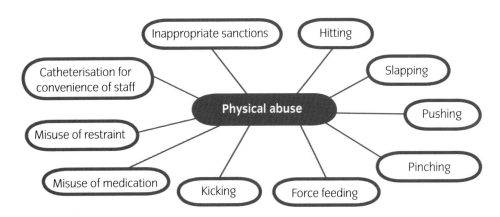

Potential indicators of physical abuse are listed below. Remember that none of these factors are evidence of abuse on their own – they are a warning sign only.

- Multiple bruising or finger marks (especially in well-protected areas such as eye sockets, inner arms or thighs)
- Fractures, especially twisting fractures, and dislocations, especially when accompanied with bruising or finger marks
- Scratches or cuts
- Pressure ulcers and sores or rashes from wet bedding/clothing
- Black eyes or bruised ears
- Welt marks – especially on the back or buttocks
- Scalds/cigarette burns
- A history of unexplained minor falls or injuries or a history of accidental overdoses/poisonings
- Injuries not consistent with the explanations given for them
- Clinical interventions without any clear benefit to the individual
- Deterioration of health without obvious cause
- Loss of weight
- Inappropriate, inadequate or soiled clothing
- Reluctance by a vulnerable adult to be alone with a particular person
- Withdrawal or mood changes
- Resistance by carers to allowing people to visit the individual

Relevant legislation, regulations and guidelines

The following remedies may be appropriate for cases of physical abuse.

- Criminal prosecution by the police under the Criminal Justice Act 1998 for assault, or under the Offences Against the Person Act 1861 for more serious offences of actual bodily harm or grievous bodily harm.
- Civil action by the victim for assault, battery or false imprisonment.
- Under the Care Standards Act 2000, cancellation of registration for residential and nursing homes. However, it is the driving up of quality as a result of this Act which offers the best protection against abuse.
- Injunctions and non-molestation orders under the Family Law Act 1996.
- Action under the Mental Health Act 1983, particularly S37 (the powers of a local authority, relative or court to undertake guardianship of a vulnerable

adult), S115 (powers of entry and inspection for Approved Social Workers), S135 (powers to remove people to a 'place of safety'), S127 (preventing ill treatment of patients with mental health problems) and S117 (providing aftercare for people with mental health problems).

- Under the Police and Criminal Evidence Act 1984, S17, police have emergency powers to enter premises if they believe there is danger to 'life and limb'.
- The Mental Capacity Act 2005 make it a criminal offence to ill treat or neglect a person who lacks capacity.
- The National Health Service and Community Care Act 1990, S47, provides for assessment for services and support.
- The Criminal Injuries Compensation scheme can provide payments for survivors of abuse which was the result of a criminal act.

Sexual abuse

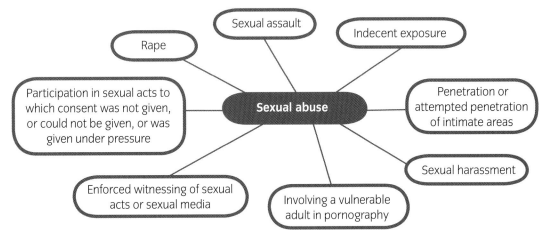

Potential indicators of sexual abuse are listed below. Remember that none of these factors are evidence of abuse on their own – they are a warning sign only.

Physical signs
• Bruises, scratches, burns or bite marks on the body
• Scratches, abrasions or persistent infections in the anal/genital regions
• Pregnancy
• Recurrent genital or urinary infections
• Blood or marks on underwear
• Abdominal pain with no diagnosable cause

Behavioural signs
• Provocative sexual behaviour, promiscuity
• Prostitution

- Sexual abuse of others
- Self-injury, self-destructive behaviour including alcohol and drug abuse, repeated suicide attempts
- Behaviour which invites exploitation and further physical/sexual abuse
- Disappearing from home environment
- Aggression, anxiety, tearfulness
- Reluctance by a vulnerable adult to be alone with a particular person
- Frequent masturbation
- Refusal to undress for activities such as swimming/bathing

Relevant legislation, regulations and guidelines

The following remedies may be appropriate for cases of sexual abuse.
- Criminal prosecution for rape, indecent assault, etc. under the Sexual Offences Act 2003. This Act has greatly increased the protection of people with mental health problems or a learning disability.
- The Care Standards Act 2000, as described on page 63.
- Injunctions and non-molestation orders under the Family Law Act 1996.
- The Mental Health Act 1983, as described on pages 63–64.
- Declaratory Relief from the High Court (common law) providing for supervised contact only.
- The Mental Capacity Act 2005 makes it a criminal offence to ill treat or neglect a person who lacks capacity.

Psychological abuse

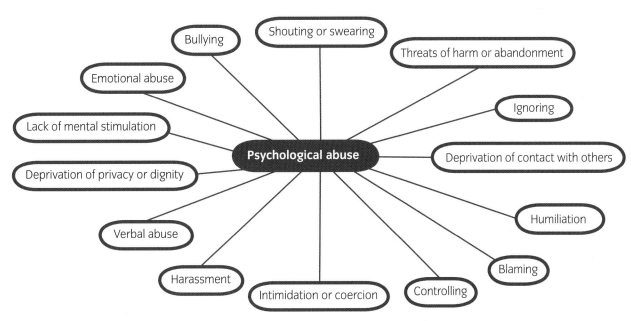

Potential indicators of psychological abuse are listed below. Remember that none of these factors are evidence of abuse on their own – they are a warning sign only.

- Reports from neighbours of shouting, screaming, swearing
- Reluctance by the vulnerable adult to be alone with a particular person
- Fear of raised voices, distress if the vulnerable person feels he or she may be 'in trouble'
- A culture of teasing or taunting which is causing distress and humiliation
- Carer seeming to ignore the vulnerable person's presence and needs
- Carer referring to the cared-for person in a derogatory way
- No valuing of basic human rights, e.g. choice, privacy and dignity
- Vulnerable person being treated like a child – infantilisation

Relevant legislation, regulations and guidelines

The following remedies may be appropriate for cases of psychological abuse.
- Protection from Harassment Act 1997 – this provides protection from harassment and from fear of violence.
- The Care Standards Act 2000, as described on page 63.
- The Mental Capacity Act 2005 makes it is criminal offence to ill treat or neglect a person who lacks capacity.

Financial or material abuse

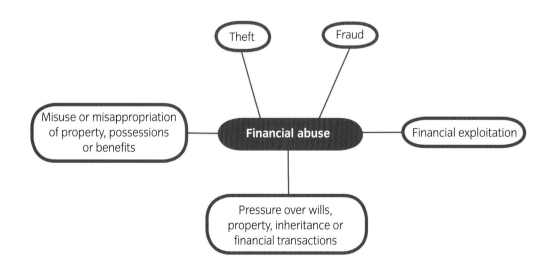

Potential indicators of financial abuse are listed below. Remember that none of these factors are evidence of abuse on their own – they are a warning indicator only.

- Individuals not being allowed to manage their own financial affairs

- No information being given to a vulnerable person where consent is required

- Family unwilling to pay from a service user's funds for services, although the service user has sufficient capital or income

- Service user not made aware of financial matters

- Enduring power of attorney set up without consulting a doctor where the vulnerable adult is already confused

- Other people moving into a service user's property

- Family regularly asking for money from a personal allowance

- Vulnerable person having very few or no personal possessions

- Unusual and unexplained changes in spending patterns

- Unexplained shortage of money despite a seemingly adequate income

- Unexplained disappearance of personal possessions or property

- Sudden changing of a will

Relevant legislation, regulations and guidelines

The following remedies may be appropriate for cases of financial abuse.

- Criminal prosecution under the Theft Act 1968.
- The National Assistance Act 1984, S47, deals with the protection of property.
- The Mental Health Act 1983, S127, relates to people who are hospital patients.
- The Mental Health Act 1983, as described on pages 63–64.
- Under the Mental Capacity Act 2005 it is criminal offence to ill treat or neglect a person who lacks capacity.
- The Court of Protection/Public Trust Office deals with the financial affairs of people who are judged incapable of managing their own property and affairs for the present, but this will change following the implementation of the Mental Capacity Act.

Discriminatory abuse

This includes racist and sexist abuse, abuse based on a person's disability, and other forms of harassment related to a person's age, gender, sexual orientation or religion. It is also the case that discrimination can underpin other forms of abuse – particularly physical or psychological.

Potential indicators of discriminatory abuse are listed below. Remember that none of these factors are evidence of abuse on their own – they are a warning sign only.

- Exclusion from activities based on inadequate justifications
- Restricted or unequal access to health care and medical treatment
- Individuals are not supported in challenging discrimination
- Unnecessary barriers restrict participation
- Individuals experience loss of self-esteem, fear, withdrawal, apathy
- Many of the emotional indicators are similar to other forms of abuse

Key terms

Discrimination: In care work, discrmination means treating some categories of people less well than others. People are often discriminated against because of their race, beliefs, gender, religion, sexuality or age.

Relevant legislation, regulations and guidelines

The following laws and guidelines may be helpful in cases of discriminatory abuse.
- Race Relations Act 1976.
- Race Relations Amendment Act 2000.
- Sex Discrimination Act 1975.
- Disability Discrimination Act 1995.
- Special Educational Needs and Disability Act 2001.
- 'Valuing People' White Paper 2001.
- National Service Framework for Older People, March 2001.
- Human Rights Act 1998.

Active knowledge

How many types of abuse does your workplace have guidelines to deal with? Look at the policy and procedures for dealing with abuse. See how many types of abuse are listed and what the procedures are. Ask your supervisor if you cannot find any information.

Neglect

Neglect and failure to care can occur where carers are ignoring medical or physical care needs; fail to provide access to appropriate health, social care or educational services; or withhold the necessities of life, such as medication, adequate nutrition and heating.

Remember

Neglect occurs when a person's needs are not being met.

Potential indicators of neglect

- Medical condition deteriorating unexpectedly or not improving as expected
- Hypothermia, or the individual is cold or dressed inadequately
- The vulnerable person is hungry
- The living environment is dirty and unhygienic
- Risks and hazards in the living environment are not dealt with
- The individual has sores and skin rashes
- There is unexplained loss of weight
- Clothes or body are dirty and smelly
- The vulnerable adult is reluctant to be alone with a particular person
- There are delays in seeking medical attention

Legislation, regulations and guidelines on neglect

There has previously been very little legal redress for neglect, unless the neglect has resulted in a situation which would be actionable as a form of abuse (for example, if someone was so badly neglected he or she suffered physical harm). Now, under the Mental Capacity Act 2005, it is a criminal offence to ill treat or neglect a person who lacks capacity. Not all vulnerable people are covered, but it is a step forward for some.

Where neglect is suspected, an assessment for services can be undertaken under the NHS and Community Care Act 1990.

Self-neglect

Self-neglect is different from neglect or abuse by others, but it is still a situation that can put individuals at risk of harm and, potentially, place them in serious danger.

People may neglect their own care for a range of reasons. The commonest are:
- increasing infirmity due to old age
- physical illness or disability
- memory and concentration problems
- sensory loss or difficulty
- mental illness and mental health problems
- learning difficulties/disabilities
- problems with alcohol and drug misuse
- a different set of priorities and perspectives.

Clear indicators of self-neglect include:
- poor personal hygiene
- dirty and unkempt appearance
- lack of food, or no interest in eating
- cold and/or dirty living environment
- failure to seek medical advice or help
- refusal to accept support or assistance with daily living or personal care.

However, what may appear to be self-neglect may in fact be an informed lifestyle choice, and it is important that you do not attempt to impose your standards and values on individuals who have made a decision to live in a particular way. Decisions in these situations are very difficult, and a balance must be achieved between safeguarding and protecting people who are vulnerable and respecting people's right to choose to live as they wish.

Obviously, where someone has a deteriorating mental or physical condition, then you can and should act in order to protect them. A deliberate choice to follow a particular way of living is an entirely different matter.

Patterns and nature of abuse

Abuse can happen because someone deliberately sets out to abuse a person who is vulnerable, but it can also occur where someone fails to provide adequate care for a vulnerable person, or does not know how to look after the person adequately, or is simply unable to cope with the pressures of being a carer.

The nature of abuse can vary and patterns of abuse take place in different ways. These are described below.

Serial abuse

The perpetrator may seek out and 'groom' vulnerable adults for abuse. Sexual abuse and some forms of financial abuse usually fall into this pattern. These are often, but not always, criminal offences committed by people who deliberately prey on vulnerable people. Examples can range from the confidence trickster who poses as an official in order to gain entry to an older person's home, to the abuser who 'befriends' someone with mental health problems through an Internet chatroom and later subjects him or her to abuse or assault.

Serial abuse can also involve criminals who attempt to commit fraud or threaten vulnerable people in relation to wills, property or other financial assets.

Situational abuse

Abuse can occur in a particular situation as a result of pressures building up and/or because of difficult or challenging behaviour. Physical abuse is the most common type of situational abuse, although there can be verbal or emotional abuse and sometimes neglect, where a carer no longer seeks out necessary medical treatment or other support.

Long-term abuse

In the context of an ongoing family relationship, there can be long-term abuse, for example domestic violence, or the regular humiliation of a family member with a physical or a learning disability, or an older relative having money and belongings gradually taken from him or her over a period of time.

Neglect of an individual's needs because others are unable or unwilling to take responsibility for care is also likely to take place over a long period of time.

Institutional abuse

This arises in organised settings from poor standards of care, inadequate staffing, lack of response to an individual's complex needs, or from staff with inadequate knowledge, skills, understanding and expertise. It can also involve unacceptable treatment programmes including over-medication, unnecessary use of restraint, or withholding food, drink or medication.

Remember

Abusers can be:

- individuals
- groups
- organisations.

Risk factors for abuse

People can be abused for many reasons, but there are certain situations where experience has shown that the risk of abuse increases. It is important in highlighting these contributing factors to be clear that the factors alone do not mean that abuse is taking place. It is perfectly possible for several risk factors to be in place and no abuse to be occurring – equally, there may be no obvious risk factors in a case but, nonetheless, abuse is happening.

Some of the factors known to contribute to the risk of harm and abuse of adults by unpaid carers are:

- poor communication between a person and his or her carer; this could be because of a medical condition, or a social/relationship issue
- challenging behaviour by the person needing care
- a carer who is young or immature
- a carer who feels unable to carry on
- strong feelings of frustration on the part of the carer
- a relationship with a troubled history
- a carer who has an alcohol or drug dependency
- a carer who believes that the individual is being deliberately difficult or ungrateful
- a carer who took on the caring role unwillingly
- a carer who has had to make major lifestyle changes
- a carer who has more than one caring responsibility – such as for young children as well as an older relative
- a carer who has suffered violence at the hands of the person needing care
- a carer who has disturbed sleep
- social isolation
- financial or housing pressures
- delays in providing support or insufficient resources to fund adequate support
- an older person needing care who is isolated and lacks family support or contact – particularly a risk in relation to financial abuse.

Some of the factors known to contribute to the risk of harm and abuse by professional carers include:

- poor quality staff training
- lack of knowledge and understanding by staff

- inadequate staffing numbers
- lack of investment in continuing professional development
- little or no staff support or supervision
- low staff morale
- lack of opportunity for care workers to form relationships with individuals
- an organisational culture that fails to treat people with dignity and respect as individuals
- a culture of bullying of staff members by management.

Active knowledge

Research a case of abuse of a vulnerable adult. Ask your supervisor or line manager about any situations he or she can tell you about from experience. Otherwise, look at a case study, or a report investigating an incident that took place in another workplace. See how many risk factors you can identify in the situation. But before you start thinking that people should have seen the potential risk, remember that hindsight is always 20:20 vision!

Evidence indicator

You can complete this activity by yourself, or in a group. Produce an information pack that can be referred to by other members of staff if they have to deal with a situation involving abuse. You should assume that all staff will have access to a computer, so you can produce an on-line pack if you prefer. Your pack should include:

- a list of all the different forms of abuse and neglect, with a brief explanation of each form you identify

- a list of the types of behaviour changes that may indicate abuse has taken place, showing what type of abuse may be indicated by different behaviour changes.

Include the abuse and protection policies and procedures of the organisation you work for. Write explanatory notes about how these fit in with legal requirements.

Research national and local sources of support for people who have been abused, and include information about the services offered, contact points, addresses, websites and details of the kind of support that can be provided and who the service is aimed at.

Responding to concerns

Information about abuse you suspect, or situations you are working with that are 'high risk', must be recorded after being reported to your line manager. Colleagues may report concerns to you, and it then becomes your responsibility to act and to pass on information and concerns.

Where there is a disclosure of abuse, or you have clear evidence of abuse, your duties are straightforward – there will be clear guidelines in your workplace. But often you may only have information that needs to be included in a service user's plan of care or personal records, particularly if you have noticed a change, or any 'early warning' signs that indicate the care team needs to be especially observant. Your workplace may have a special report form for recording 'causes for concern'. If not, you should write a report, making sure you include the following:

- what happened to make you concerned and who you are concerned about
- whether this links to anything you have noticed previously
- what needs to happen next.

Discuss your report and your concerns with your supervisor and colleagues.

You must report anything unusual that you notice, even if you think it is too small to be important. It is the small details that make the whole picture. Sometimes, your observations may add to other small things noticed by members of the team, and a picture may begin to emerge. Teamwork and good communication are vitally important.

CASE STUDY: Seeing the whole picture

One domiciliary support worker had a nickname – he was known as 'Cecil', short for Cecil B. de Mille, the film director. Cecil was known for regularly phoning the day centres, care managers and GP surgeries of the families he visited every time there was any event, incident or change. Cecil always started his conversation with 'I'm just keeping you in the picture', hence the nickname!

Cecil provided support to the G family, where a mother cared for her 23-year-old brain-injured son. It was thanks to being 'kept in the picture' by Cecil that the care manager was made aware of the arrival of the mother's new boyfriend. When his details were checked, it was discovered that he had a record of fraud and financial abuse, and had previously been prosecuted for stealing money from an elderly relative.

When this information was put together with the fact that the day centre staff had noticed the mother becoming very edgy and seeming to be worried about money, alarm bells began to ring and support was offered. The mother was given information about how to manage her finances. She was helped to keep a tighter control over her money – and the boyfriend disappeared fairly soon afterwards.

1 What was Cecil doing that was important?
2 What might have happened if the information had not been passed on?
3 Why was Cecil in a good position to keep everyone informed?
4 What were the alternative ways this could have been handled?

In serious cases, your written evidence may be needed by a social worker, doctor or case conference, or even in court proceedings against an alleged abuser. So you must make sure all reports are written accurately and factually. If you have witnessed, or intervened in, an act of abuse that may constitute a criminal offence, you must *not* remove any possible evidence until the police have examined the scene.

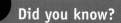

Did you know?

If you were to take one piece from a jigsaw puzzle, it would be very difficult to guess from it what the complete picture was – if not impossible. You could easily guess wrongly! You would need quite a few pieces before you could begin to draw a conclusion. The same applies to identifying the true picture in cases of abuse.

Test yourself

1 Identify three potential signs of sexual abuse.
2 What is the difference between danger and harm?
3 Name three risk factors for abuse by professional carers.
4 Name three risk factors for abuse by unpaid carers.
5 What is the focus of current policy in protecting vulnerable adults?

HSC 335b Contribute to minimising the effects of dangerous, harmful and abusive behaviour and practices

Empowerment and protection

Current thinking in relation to policy for vulnerable adults is to focus less on the individual as someone with a 'problem' that needs to be resolved, and more on empowering vulnerable people in their role as citizens. If people are contributors to decision making and are a recognised and valued part of a community, then abuse is less likely to occur, or if it does, people feel more able to report it and to take steps to stop it. Even the term 'vulnerable adults' tends to make people sound as if they have no power and are a target for bullies, but it is intended to indicate people with a particular need to be protected from harm and risk.

Key terms

Empowerment: Making sure that people have choice, that their self-esteem and confidence are promoted, and that they are encouraged to take action for themselves where possible.

● *The emphasis today is on empowering people in their role as citizens*

This type of policy change will take time to come into effect. Not so long ago ideas about rights, dignity, choice and anti-discriminatory practice were almost unheard of in the care sector, but now all of these form a vital part of good practice and everyone understands how essential they are. The same thing will happen to the concept of empowerment as a means of protection, and it will become the basis for efforts to reduce the incidence of abuse and protect vulnerable people.

There is a direct comparison with the field of child abuse, where for over 20 years the focus was on risk analysis, individual intervention and the removal of children into 'care'. Sadly, this often replaced one type of abuse with another. The 'Quality Protects' initiative in the late 1990s began a change in attitude, and professionals began to recognise that improving the quality of children's services was an effective means of safeguarding against abuse. It was the introduction of the 'Sure Start' and 'Connexions' programmes that really made clear the fact that children and young people are an integral part of society and a 'whole system' is needed rather than separate parts working together. The 2005 Green Paper 'Independence, Well-being and Choice' (quickly followed by the White Paper 'Our Health, Our Care, Our Say') sets out this thinking and is likely to follow the same rapid route to legislation as 'Every Child Matters', the Green Paper that quickly became the Children Act 2004.

Did you know?

Stephen Ladyman, a government minister with responsibility for communities, said in 2004: 'Local communities and the public in general need to be sensitised to issues of abuse and become as angry about adult abuse as they are angry about child abuse.'

Information is power

Giving people information and making sure that they are aware of their rights is very important. It is surprising how often a vulnerable adult who has been in an abusive situation did not even realise that he or she was being abused, or that anything could be done about it.

Ways to empower vulnerable adults

For people to feel that they are able to take control and deal with difficulties, they need to have the means to do so. Many of the changes that need to be made will be outside your area of responsibility, and need to be undertaken by other agencies. However, your own practice can make a huge contribution and you can make suggestions for improvements. The following are some examples.

- Awareness of abuse of vulnerable adults must be promoted in all information sources. These should be available in a wide rage of formats – print, audio, braille, appropriate languages, in picture format, and large print.
- Information should be made available about what abusive behaviour is, how to recognise it and how and where to report it.
- Information should be available in leaflets sent out by agencies, and in posters in libraries, leisure centres, schools, hospitals, churches, community centres, cinemas, pubs as well as in places providing services for vulnerable adults.
- Reporting procedures for abuse must be easily accessible – one easily remembered free telephone number, or a 'one stop shop' in a central place.

- Publicity should be given to these through local newspapers, TV programmes and radio programmes.
- Survivors of abuse should be involved in policy-making forums to look at ways of improving responses.
- Vulnerable service users should be involved in decisions about how services are planned and commissioned.

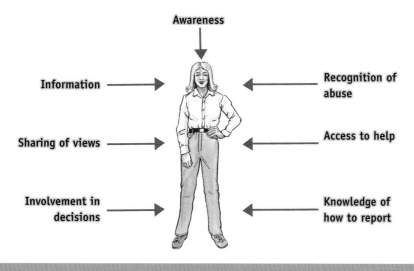

CASE STUDY: Taking responsibility in the community

K works in a post office in a small Midlands market town. She has known Mrs J for many years – she always used to stop for a chat when she collected her pension. K also sees her at the local church every week. Mrs J has always been active in the local community and very friendly and sociable.

Mrs J's son and daughter-in-law have recently moved into her house. They have arrived from another part of the country and are not working. Mrs J had never spoken much about her son P, and K was quite surprised when she mentioned he was moving in. Mrs J said that he had 'had a bit of trouble' where he was living, but didn't seem keen to talk about it. After P moved in, Mrs J did not come to church or to the post office for a few weeks. Eventually P came in to the post office. When K asked how Mrs J was, P said that she was very confused and could not look after herself any more. K was surprised and sad as Mrs J had always been so well and such an active person.

A few weeks later, K was walking past Mrs J's house when she saw P and his wife carrying boxes out of the front door. Mrs J was watching through the window and crying, obviously unhappy about what they were doing. K was very concerned and asked what was going on. P shouted at her that he was having to cope with looking after his mother, who was too confused to communicate and unable to go out, that he was doing his best and that K should mind her own business. K left because she was quite frightened by his aggressive attitude, but she still felt that something should be done.

1   Should K report her concerns, and to whom?
2   What barriers could K face in reporting her concerns?
3   How could the barriers be reduced?
4   How would you find out what Mrs J wants?
5   Is abuse everyone's business?

How to reduce individual risks

The kinds of attitude changes needed before whole communities take responsibility for the well-being of their vulnerable members are going to take time. In the meantime, vulnerable people still need to be safeguarded and protected, and whatever your role, regardless of your work setting, you will be able to have an impact in reducing the risks of harm and abuse for vulnerable adults.

No one can guarantee to prevent abuse from happening – human beings have always abused each other in one form or another. However, using the information you have about possible abusive situations, you are able to work towards preventing abuse by being alert to where and how it can happen.

Working with carers

Try to ensure that people in stressful situations are offered as much support as possible. A carer is less likely to resort to abuse if he or she feels supported, acknowledged and appreciated. Showing that you care and understand about a person's difficulties can often help to defuse potential explosions.

If you work directly with carers, you might express this by comments such as, 'It must be so hard caring for your mother. The demands she makes are so difficult. I think you're doing a wonderful job.' Such comments can often help a carer to feel that he or she does have someone who understands and has some interest in supporting him or her.

So many times the focus is on the individual in need of care and the carer is ignored. If your role involves the management and support of colleagues who are working directly in the community, you can ensure that they have an awareness of the need to focus on carers too and to meet their needs.

How carers are supported in law

The first national strategy for carers – 'Caring about Carers' – was introduced in 1999. Since April 2001, carers have had further rights under a new law, the Carers and Disabled Children Act 2000. This entitles carers to an assessment of their needs if they wish. This can be done when the person they care for is being assessed, or separately from any assessment for the person needing care. Carers can, with guidance from a social worker or care manager, assess themselves.

The Carers (Equal Opportunities) Act 2004 came into force in England on 1 April 2005. The Act gives carers new rights to information and ensures that work, life-long learning and leisure are considered when a carer is assessed.

Working alongside carers is an essential part of protecting vulnerable adults. Even if there are no immediate concerns, working with carers to make sure that they are accessing their rights and have the support they are entitled to reduces the risk that an abusive incident can develop out of anger and frustration.

Did you know?

The 2001 census identified that there are six million carers in the UK. This is 12 per cent of the adult population. The increasing numbers of older people, along with the policy of empowering people to remain active in the community for longer, means that the number of carers is forecast to rise by over 50 per cent to almost nine and a half million by 2037.

Supporting carers in the community

Some situations require much more than words of support, and giving practical assistance to a carer or family may help to reduce the risk of abuse. The extra support provided by a professional carer can do this in two ways: first, it can provide the additional help which allows the carer to feel that he or she is not in a hopeless, never-ending situation; and second, it can provide a regular opportunity to check an individual where abuse is suspected or considered to be a major risk.

When resources are provided within the community rather than at home, this also offers a chance to observe someone who is thought to be at risk. Day centres and training centres also provide an opportunity for people to talk to staff and to feel that they are in a supportive environment where they can talk about any fears and worries and they will be believed and helped.

● Because there are increasing numbers of older people in our society, the number of carers is forecast to rise

Situation	Solution
Carer needs to be able to take breaks when necessary	Either regular or flexible breaks can be arranged. Some areas operate voucher schemes so carers can organise breaks when it suits them; other have regular planned breaks.
Carer needs aids, equipment and adaptations	The physical environment can be adapted to make caring easier. Hoists, ramps, accessible bathrooms, and electronic equipment can all make the caring task less burdensome.
Carer needs support to work or undertake training	Carers can be provided with support for the cared-for person while they are at work, and they can be helped to undertake training courses in order to return to work.
Carers need some time to pursue interests for themselves	Carers can be provided with support while they are involved in leisure activities. Advice and information about opportunities as well as practical support are available.

Protecting carers from abuse

Never forget that sometimes, the carer can be the person who is vulnerable to abuse. For example, an older parent caring for a son or daughter who has mental health problems or who exhibits challenging behaviour may be very much at risk. It is important to look at the whole picture when looking at a risk assessment, and to offer support and protection to any vulnerable adult who is at risk.

CASE STUDY: Carers at risk

Mrs C is 75 years old. She is quite fit, although increasingly her arthritis is slowing her down and making her less steady on her feet. She has been a widow for 15 years and lives with her only son, R, who is 51. When R was 29, he was involved in a motorcycle accident which caused brain damage, from which he has never fully recovered. His speech is slow and he sometimes has problems in communication. His co-ordination and fine motor skills have been affected, so he has problems with buttons, shoelaces and writing. R also suffers from major mood swings and can be aggressive. Mrs C is R's only carer. He has not worked since the accident, but he goes to a day centre three days each week. Mrs C takes the opportunity to go to a day centre herself on those three days because she enjoys the company, the outings and activities.

Recently, Mrs C has had an increasing number of injuries. In the past two months she has had a grazed forehead, a black eye, a split lip and last week she arrived at the day centre with a bruised and sprained wrist. She finally admitted to the centre staff that R had inflicted the injuries during his periods of bad temper. She said that these were becoming more frequent as he became more frustrated with her slowness.

Despite being very distressed, Mrs C would not agree to being separated from R. She was adamant that he didn't mean to hurt her. She would not consider making a complaint to the police. Finally, Mrs C agreed to increase both her and R's attendance at their day centres, and to have some assistance with daily living.

1   What do you think Mrs C should have done?
2   What action can be taken?
3   What action should be taken?
4   Why do you think Mrs C will not take any action against R?
5   Whose responsibility is this situation?

The kind of situation described in the case study above may cause a great deal of concern and anxiety for care workers, but there are limits on the legal powers to intervene and there is no justification for removing people's rights to make their own decisions.

Consent

A key point in the protection of vulnerable adults is the issue of consent. Vulnerable adults have a fundamental human right to decide how and with whom they live. A person who is able to make decisions is entitled to refuse protection and to limit what you are able to do. In general, any action you take in relation to protecting a vulnerable adult must be with his or her consent.

The issue of gaining consent before taking any action applies not only to reporting abuse; it also applies to providing evidence for any prosecution and to having any medical examination to record and confirm injuries or other forensic evidence. If you are faced with a situation where it is clear that abuse has taken place and the vulnerable person is refusing to make a complaint, or to undergo a medical examination, then your only way forward is to try to give as much clear information as possible and then to refer the situation to your line manager for consideration as to whether further action is possible.

The steps you can take are limited; there is no legislation giving vulnerable adults an unconditional right of protection as there is for children. But some things you can do in a case where an individual refuses help are detailed in the table below.

Reason for refusal	Information to give
Fear of reprisals from the abuser	Reassure that it will be possible to make certain there is no need to have contact with the abuser, and the individual can be protected.
Belief that it is his or her own fault	Emphasise that abuse is *never* the fault of the abused person. Give information and reassurance about rights, and the fact that abuse is against the law. Confirm that abusers are bullies and criminals.

Reason for refusal	Information to give
Fear that services will be withdrawn	Reassure that a complaint against a professional is taken very seriously, and that services are provided as a right. No one will remove services because of a complaint. The service provider is on the side of the survivor, not the abuser – even if the abuser is an employee.
Fear of medical examination	Ask medical staff to explain the procedure and to reassure. Explain why it is important to provide evidence, and show the types of evidence that can be found from examination.
Fear of police investigation/court appearance	Explain the support available for police interviews and for court appearances.

Medical treatment

A refusal to undergo medical *treatment* following injuries is an entirely different situation from refusing to undergo a medical *examination*. If you are faced with someone who has been injured and is refusing treatment, then you must refer the matter to a doctor immediately so that a decision can be made on the best way forward depending on the nature and severity of the injuries. This is not a decision for you to make without medical support.

Capacity

If a person lacks the mental capacity to make a decision about reporting abuse, or there is an overriding public interest (for example, other vulnerable adults are at risk), then other courses of action will have to be considered.

The question of capacity to make decisions is highly complex and must be considered carefully. It is very easy to make the assumption that because someone has dementia, or has a learning disability or a long-term mental health problem, he or she lacks the capacity to make decisions about important issues. But if you think about it, the capacity to make a decision can often depend on how much help we have. For example, if a government minister has to choose between two different highly advanced fighter aircraft to commission for the RAF, he or she will ask for help from experts across the aviation industry, from experienced civil servants from the relevant departments, and from the pilots and senior officers who are going to use the aircraft. The minister will make the final decision – but he or she lacks the *capacity* to make the decision alone, and so uses plenty of advice and support.

Similarly, most of us would need help to make a choice between two different types of central heating system; we would ask for advice from experts before

● *We all find that some decisions are beyond our capacity*

deciding. So remember – capacity to make a decision is relative to what has to be decided, and depends on the circumstances.

The legal position

With this is mind, an Act of Parliament was passed in April 2005. The Mental Capacity Act sets out a framework for supporting people to make decisions, and lays out the ways in which people can be supported. The Act is underpinned by five key principles:

- a presumption of capacity – every adult has the right to make his or her own decisions and must be assumed to have the capacity to do so unless it is proved otherwise
- the right for individuals to be supported to make their own decisions – people must be given all appropriate help before anyone concludes that they cannot make their own decisions
- individuals must retain the right to make what might be seen as eccentric or unwise decisions
- the principle of best interests – anything done for or on behalf of people without capacity must be in their best interests
- least restrictive intervention – anything done for or on behalf of people without capacity should be the least restrictive of their basic rights and freedoms.

The new Act sets out clearly how to establish whether someone is incapable of taking a decision. The 'incapacity test' is used only in relation to a particular decision; no one can be deemed 'incapable' in general simply because of a medical condition or diagnosis.

The Act introduces a new criminal offence of ill treatment or neglect of a person who lacks capacity. A person found guilty of such an offence may be liable to imprisonment for a term of up to five years.

Active knowledge

Active knowledge

Think about decisions you have had to make recently, large and small. List those where you have needed help or advice in order to make them.

Abuse by professional carers

Responding to an abusive situation in your own, or another, workplace can be very difficult. There may be many reasons why you feel that you should not intervene; you might think it will mean problems with colleagues; that you will make yourself unpopular; that it could jeopardise your promotion prospects; that no one will trust you again; that you might be wrong.

You may therefore feel that you should leave matters to sort themselves out. You shouldn't, and they won't.

'Blowing the whistle' about an abusive situation among colleagues is never easy, but you have an absolute duty to do so; there are no ifs or buts.

The government has recognised this, and following several well-publicised cases, passed the Public Interest Disclosure Act 1998. This protects whistleblowers and ensures that you cannot be victimised by your employer for reporting abuse, or any other illegal acts. The Act protects people making disclosures about any of the following:

- a criminal offence
- the breach of a legal obligation
- a miscarriage of justice
- a danger to the health or safety of any individual
- damage to the environment
- deliberate covering up of information tending to show any of the above matters.

The basis for obtaining protection under the Act is that the worker is giving information that he or she 'reasonably believes tends to show that one or more of the above matters is either happening now, took place in the past, or is likely to happen in the future'.

It is important to realise that you must have *reasonable belief* that the information tends to show one or more of the offences or breaches listed above. You may not in fact be right – it might be discovered upon investigation that you were wrong – but as long as you can show that you believed it to be so, and that it was a reasonable belief in the circumstances at the time of disclosure, then you are protected by the law.

If you believe that your line manager will not take action about possible abuse, either because of misplaced loyalty or an unwillingness to confront or challenge difficult situations, then you must make a referral to a more senior manager. You must keep moving through the management chain until you reach the person you consider able and willing to take action. If there is no one within your own organisation, then you must make a referral to an outside agency.

Contact your local authority and make the referral to the Social Services department.

If you believe that the abuse you are aware of is potentially a criminal offence, such as physical or sexual assault, theft or fraud, then you should refer the matter to the police. At the same time, you should refer it to the Commission for Social Care Inspection, which is responsible for standards in all care settings.

How are cases investigated?

Each local authority must have a multi-agency management committee for the protection of vulnerable adults. This committee is responsible for setting out procedures and policies, identifying and protecting those at risk, and ensuring each agency has an appropriate response to abuse. It is likely that the procedure for your workplace in relation to abuse by a professional carer will involve:

- immediate suspension of the person accused
- investigation by the police if appropriate
- investigation led by an independent agency
- disciplinary procedures following the outcome of any police or protection investigation.

CASE STUDY: Abuse by professional staff

Mr B is 89 years old. He has lived alone in his three-bedroom house since his wife died several years ago. He has impaired sight and hearing, and his mobility is limited after a recent fall in which he hurt his back. For the past month he has had twice-weekly visits from a physiotherapist from the local primary care trust. Mr B has domiciliary care support daily from a private provider contracted by Social Services.

S has been Mr B's carer for the past year. She has noticed over the past few weeks that Mr B has been losing weight and that his meals, which are delivered daily, are largely uneaten. In response to S's enquiries, Mr B will only say that he is feeling a bit down and hasn't felt very hungry recently.

One day, S arrived at the door and heard someone shouting 'Get on with it – you're not trying at all, you're so lazy!' As S walked into the hall, the physiotherapist looked shocked to see her and said that she was just leaving. After the physiotherapist left, S tackled Mr B and asked if everything was going well with the physio's visits. He replied that there was a long waiting list for physiotherapy and he was very lucky to have anyone.

1 What can S do?
2 What barriers may she face in trying to deal with this issue?
3 Is this abusive behaviour?
4 How would you try to empower Mr B?

When the organisation abuses

You may want to blow the whistle about the way an organisation is run, or the quality of a service. You could find yourself working in a setting where standards are not being met and vulnerable people are being abused because of the policies and procedures of the organisation rather than through the behaviour of any particular individual. There may be a policy of over-medication, or vulnerable people may not be given sufficient food, people could be left in wet or soiled clothing or bedding, or the organisation may have a policy of restricting rights or freedoms.

In this situation, you should contact the local authority Protection of Vulnerable Adults Committee or the local office of the Care Standards Commission (CSCI).

Public Concern at Work is a national organisation that provides legal advice to individuals concerned about malpractice at work; its service is free and strictly confidential.

Challenging the potential for abuse

All abusive behaviour is unacceptable. However, you may come across other types of behaviour which you may not be able to define as abusive, but which are certainly close to it, or could lead to an abusive situation if not dealt with.

Generally you can define behaviour as unacceptable if:
- it is outside what you would normally see in that situation
- it does not take into account the needs or views of others
- people are afraid or intimidated
- people are undermined or made to feel guilty
- the behaviour is likely to cause distress or unhappiness to others.

Examples of unacceptable behaviour include:
- threatening violence
- subjecting someone to unwelcome sexual harassment
- verbal abuse, racist or sexist innuendo
- spreading malicious gossip about someone
- attempting to isolate someone
- playing loud music in a quiet area, or late at night.

Unacceptable behaviour from colleagues

You may come across unacceptable behaviour in your colleagues or other professionals in your workplace. You may see or hear a colleague behaving in a way that is not abusive as such, but may be oppressive and unacceptable. This can take various forms, such as:
- speaking about service users in a derogatory way
- speaking to service users in a rude or dismissive way
- humiliating service users
- undermining people's self-esteem and confidence

- bullying or intimidation
- patronising and talking down to people
- removing people's right to exercise choice
- failing to recognise and treat people as individuals
- not respecting people's culture, values and beliefs.

In short, the types of behaviour that are unacceptable from workers in care settings are those that simply fail to meet the standards required of good quality practitioners. Any care worker who fails to remember that all people he or she cares for are individuals and that all people have a right to be valued and accepted, is likely to fall into the trap of behaving in an unacceptable way.

All behaviour that is oppressive to others needs to be challenged, whether it is behaviour by colleagues, visitors, carers or service users. You can probably think of many other situations in your own workplace which have caused unhappiness. You may have had to deal with difficult situations, or have seen others deal with them, or perhaps you have wished that you had done something to challenge unacceptable behaviour.

Active knowledge

Ask three colleagues in your workplace to state one behaviour that they would find unacceptable in (a) a service user and (b) a colleague. Compare the six answers and see if they have anything in common. Discuss with your supervisor the type of behaviour that is challenged in your workplace, and that which is allowed.

How to challenge unacceptable behaviour

The steps to follow when dealing with difficult situations are described below.

Step 1 Consider all the people involved in the situation

If you have some knowledge of an individual's background, culture and beliefs, it may be easier to see why he or she is behaving in a particular way. This does not make it acceptable, just easier to understand. For example, an individual who has been in a position of wealth or power may be used to giving people instructions and expecting to have immediate attention, and may be quite rude if it does not happen. This type of behaviour is obviously not to be tolerated, but approaching the situation with some understanding allows people to maintain their dignity while adapting their behaviour.

Step 2 Be aware of everyone's needs

In a care setting, it can be that the person whose oppressive behaviour you are challenging is also one of your service users. In this case, it is important to ensure that you challenge the behaviour without becoming aggressive or intimidating yourself, and that you do not undermine the individual.

Step 3 Decide on the best approach

How you decide to deal with an incident of unacceptable behaviour will depend on:

- whether the behaviour is violent or non-violent – if the behaviour is violent, what the potential dangers of the situation are, who may be in danger, and what needs to be done to help those in danger
- who is involved, how well you know them and know how to deal with them
- whether you need help, and who is available to help you
- whether the cause is obvious and the solution is easy to find.

Clearly, you will need to weigh up the situation quickly, in order to deal with it promptly. You will, no doubt, feel under pressure, as this is a stressful situation to be in, whether you are experienced or not. Try to remain calm and think clearly.

Step 4 Deal with non-violent behaviour

If the behaviour you have to deal with is not physical aggression or violence, then you will need to ensure that you challenge it in a situation which provides privacy and dignity. You should challenge without becoming aggressive, remain calm and quietly state what you consider to be unacceptable about the behaviour. Do not try to approach it from various angles, or drop hints. Be clear about the problem and what you want to happen.

For example: 'Bill, you have been playing your radio very loudly until quite late each night. Other people are finding it difficult to get to sleep. I would like you to stop playing it so loudly if you want to have it on late.' You may well have to negotiate with Bill about times, and the provision of headphones, but do not be drawn into an argument and do not be sidetracked into irrelevant discussions. Keep to the point:

Bill   Who's been complaining? No one's complained to me. Who is it?

You   Bill, this is about your radio being too loud. The issue is not about who complained, but about the fact that it is upsetting other people and I want you to stop doing it.

By the end of this discussion, Bill should be very clear about what is being required of him and be in no doubt that his behaviour will have to change.

Step 5 Attempt to calm a potentially violent situation

It is always better to avoid a violent situation than to respond to one, so you need to be aware of the signals which may indicate that violence could erupt. Be on the lookout for signs such as verbal aggression; raised volume and pitch of voice; threatening and aggressive gestures; pacing up and down; quick, darting eye movements; prolonged eye contact.

Try to respond in ways least likely to provoke further aggression.

- Use listening skills, and appear confident (but not cocky).
- Keep your voice calm and at a level pitch.
- Do not argue.
- Do not get drawn into prolonged eye contact.
- Attempt to defuse the situation with empathy and understanding. For example, 'I realise you must be upset if you believe that George said that about you. I can see that you're very angry. Tell me about what happened.'

Be prepared to try a different approach if you find you are not getting anywhere. Always make sure that an aggressor has a way out with dignity, both physically and emotionally.

Remember

- Preventing abusive or aggressive behaviour is better than having to deal with it.
- Support may make all the difference to a person under stress.
- Only intervene directly if there is an immediate risk.
- Act assertively to stop any aggressive or abusive behaviour.

Protection of Vulnerable Adults scheme

One important way in which vulnerable adults in England and Wales are protected is through the Protection of Vulnerable Adults (POVA) scheme. This is a provision of the Care Standards Act 2000 and was implemented in July 2004. A similar scheme is currently being developed in Scotland.

The scheme currently covers staff of care homes, registered domiciliary care agencies and adult placements, and provides for a ban on unsuitable people working in the care sector. Employers have a statutory responsibility to check staff against a list of known abusers before they start work. Checks are made through the Criminal Records Bureau (CRB), so a POVA check also includes a criminal record check.

Employers are also required to submit for the list the names of staff who have been sacked or suspended because of misconduct which harmed a vulnerable adult or placed him or her at risk of harm. To be confirmed on the list, people will broadly fulfil the following criteria:

- their employment falls within the scheme
- misconduct occurred which harmed or placed at risk of harm a vulnerable adult
- the misconduct resulted in the person being sacked or suspended
- the person is unsuitable to work with vulnerable adults.

The POVA scheme began on 26 July 2004, and over 700 people are currently barred from working in regulated social care settings. At the end of June 2005, 155 people had been permanently barred from working with vulnerable people, and the names of 559 people were provisionally on the list pending further investigation. More than 2,000 referrals have been made to the scheme, and they come in at a rate of about 200 per month.

Research at Kings College, London commissioned by the Department of Health in 2005 showed that:

- just over a third of referrals concerned male workers involved in physical abuse, despite men forming only 5–15 per cent of the workforce
- the vast majority (87 per cent) of referrals were of front-line workers, care assistants and support workers, including 8 per cent who were registered nurses
- the top three reasons for referral concerned neglect, physical or financial abuse
- neglect and physical abuse were more likely to be found in residential settings, and financial abuse in domiciliary care
- 81 per cent of referrals came from residential services, despite the fact that in England and Wales 80 per cent of service users receive community-based services
- of the referrals from residential services, 94 per cent came from the independent sector, the vast majority of these from the for-profit sector; this does suggest that residential services are taking their statutory responsibilities seriously in referring wrongdoers to the list
- the police were involved in 40 per cent of referrals and seven staff have been convicted of offences
- many workers were referred for more than one type of abuse.

Test yourself

1 List some key methods of empowering vulnerable adults.
2 Why is it important to empower people?
3 How are 'whistleblowers' protected?
4 What are the underlying assumptions about mental capacity?
5 How are vulnerable adults protected against abusers entering the workforce?

HSC 335c Respond to and report on suspicions of harm and abuse

How to respond to concerns

You may find that you have concerns about a situation because of what you have observed, or because of what has been disclosed to you by a vulnerable person. In either situation, you must be very clear about the actions you need to take.

Some situations will be clear cut – for example, you may see a colleague involved in abusive behaviour. You must immediately report the incident to your manager, who must follow the procedures laid down for your workplace. This will involve immediately suspending the accused person from the workplace, calling in the police if necessary and starting the procedures for undertaking an investigation.

A similar process should be followed where a service user discloses to you that he or she has been abused by one of the professionals caring for him or her. This could be a colleague from your own workplace, or it may be another professional who is providing a different service. Your report to your line manager should set the procedures in motion for investigating the disclosure.

Confidentiality

In general, of course, the right of every individual to confidentiality is a key element in good practice. However, abuse is one of the few situations where you may have to consider whether it is possible to maintain this. You will always need to make clear, when someone discloses abuse to you, that you cannot promise to keep the information confidential.

This is not always easy; very often, when people first speak about abuse they have suffered they will start by saying: 'If I tell you something, will you promise not to tell anyone?' You cannot guarantee this. It is never acceptable to say one thing and do another, so you must make clear from the start what your responsibilities are, and that you may have to share what you are told with others. You can, however, reassure someone by saying: 'I can't promise not to say anything to anyone, but I can promise you that I will only tell people who will help you'.

You can also promise that although some information may have to be shared, it will be shared on a 'need to know' basis, and only among those agencies directly involved in any investigation.

However, vulnerable adults are not children, and if they absolutely refuse to allow you to share information, it is very difficult for you to do so – beyond the absolute necessity of sharing it with your manager. All efforts then have to go into trying to encourage the person to agree to sharing the information and pursuing an investigation – but if there is no question of lack of capacity (see page 82) you may have to accept that all you can do is to monitor matters carefully.

There can be circumstances in which it is necessary for you to break confidentiality. For example, if someone discloses that an officer in charge in a residential care home is systematically stealing from the people living there, you would be justified in breaching the confidentiality of one person in order to protect other vulnerable people. However, this must only be done in discussion with your line manager, and any decisions taken must be fully recorded, giving reasons why it is necessary. You must also make sure that the person concerned knows whom you have talked to and why.

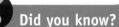

Did you know?

Recent research showed an average of almost 142 incidents of abuse of vulnerable adults are dealt with by each local authority in England every year. That means there are over 56,000 incidents of abuse in England each year.

Data protection

Any personal information held about anyone is subject to the Data Protection Act 1998. Under this Act, anyone processing personal data must comply with the eight enforceable principles of good practice. These say that data must be:

- fairly and lawfully processed
- processed for limited purposes
- adequate, relevant and not excessive
- accurate
- not kept longer than necessary

● *Personal information held on a computer must be password protected*

- processed in accordance with the data subject's rights
- kept secure
- not transferred to countries without adequate protection.

You therefore need to ensure that any written information is kept securely. Information about abuse or potential abuse is very sensitive, and it is important that people have their rights to privacy and confidentiality respected. Information must be kept securely, password protected if it is kept electronically, and locked in a cabinet if in hard copy. Make sure that no more information than necessary is kept, and that it is used for the service user's benefit and in his or her best interests.

Active knowledge

Check out the ways in which the organisation you work for keeps information relating to suspected or actual abuse. Find out whether it is stored or accessed in a different way from other information – if so, try to find out why this is. Look at your organisation's policy on confidentiality – do the storage and access arrangements comply with this?

What happens next

Priority 1 – Protect

The first and most important concern when abuse is found or suspected is to ensure that the abused person is safe and protected from any further possibility of abuse. Make sure that any necessary medical treatment is provided, and give plenty of reassurance and comfort so that the person knows that he or she is now safe. Even if the abuse happened a long time ago, or has been going on for a long period, the process of disclosing it can be very distressing as well as being a huge relief, so plenty of warm, kind and caring support is vital.

Priority 2 – Report

You must report any abusive situation you become aware of to your line manager, or the person named in your workplace procedures for the protection of vulnerable adults. You may have formal reporting procedures in place in your organisation, or you may simply make an initial verbal referral. However, it will be essential that you make a full, written report as soon as you can after the event. The following checklist may help you to recall details you will need later, and make sure that you have done everything you need to.

Checklist

Disclosure/observation made by ....

Date ....

How? ....

To whom? ....

Action taken by ....

What action? ....

Reasons if no action ....

Vulnerable adult seen? Yes/No

When seen (date and time) ....

Who saw the vulnerable adult? List all ....

....

Consultations/information sharing/notification – health

GP? Yes/No

District nurse? Yes/No

CPN? Yes/No

Consultations/information sharing/notification – Social Services

Community team? Yes/No

Hospital team? Yes/No

Police? Yes/No

Housing/supporting people? Yes/No

Provider agencies? Yes/No

Other ....

Medical examination? Yes/No

When? ....

Where? ....

By whom? ....

All action recorded? Yes/No

Reasons for non-action recorded? Yes/No

Telephone conversations confirmed in writing? Yes/No

Strategy meeting? Yes/No

Date of meeting ....

Priority 3 – Preserve

Preserve any evidence. If this is a potential crime scene, you must be very careful not to destroy any potential evidence. If an incident of physical or sexual abuse is recent and there is likely to be forensic evidence, you must preserve it carefully until the police arrive and take over. For example:

* do not clear up
* do not wash or clean any part of the room or area in which the alleged abuse took place
* do not remove bedding
* do not remove any clothes the individual is wearing
* do not allow the individual to wash, shower, bathe, brush hair or clean teeth
* keep other people out of the room or area.

If financial abuse is disclosed or suspected, ensure that you have not thrown away any papers or documents that could be useful as evidence. Try to preserve as much as possible, in order to hand it over to those investigating the allegations.

The evidence for other types of abuse is different. Sadly, neglect speaks for itself, but it will be important to preserve living conditions as they were found until they can be recorded and photographed. Bearing in mind Priority 1, however, any treatment or medical attention that the individual needs must be provided immediately. Make sure that you explain to any doctor or paramedic that the situation may result in a prosecution, so that he or she carefully records any findings in case of being required to make a statement later.

Psychological or discriminatory abuse is likely to have witnesses and/or disclosure from the abused person, rather than physical evidence.

Priority 4 – Record and refer

Record what has happened. This is vitally important; you may need at some stage to make a formal statement to police, or other investigation team. Initially, make sure that you have recorded all the key details for your own organisation. You may also need to make a referral to another agency, for example the police or social services. You will need to record all the information carefully, including a detailed account of what happened, what you saw or were told, and who said or did what.

Be careful that you do not mix fact and opinion, and make sure that you distinguish clearly between what you know because

● *Record all information carefully, keeping to the facts*

you have seen or heard it yourself, and what you have heard from others – this is hearsay, or third-party evidence, and it is important that investigators are able to judge how reliable your information is. For example, 'Mrs J was crying when I arrived' is a fact. 'Mrs J should not have been living there with him – everyone is aware of his bad temper' is an opinion. 'Mrs J had been upset earlier in the morning when her neighbour visited' is hearsay from the neighbour, and not a fact that you have witnessed first hand. This type of information can be useful in a report, but you must describe it factually: 'Mrs J's neighbour, Mr S, told me that she had been upset earlier in the morning when he had visited'.

If you have to make a formal statement, or produce a report that will be used in court, you cannot include any hearsay, and must report only facts that you know because you have seen or heard them for yourself.

If you need to make a referral to another agency, you should include all the following information.

Referral information
Details of abused person
- Name
- Address
- Telephone number
- Date of birth
- Gender
- Ethnic background (including principal language spoken)
- Details of any disability (including any communication needs)

GP

Details of carers and any significant family members, neighbours, friends

Details about home/accommodation

Reasons for concerns with details of any incidents, etc.

Details of alleged abuse including information about suspicions, specific information

Details of any immediate action taken to make safe and protect

Details of any medical examination/treatment

Whether the person has agreed to/is aware of referral being made

The mental capacity of the individual – how this has been decided

Details of any other professional/agency involved

Details of other agencies copied in to referral (Commission for Social Care Inspection, police, primary care trust, hospital trust, etc.)

Details of the alleged abuser

Background information or history

How to deal with abusive behaviour

Most of the time, your role in dealing with abuse will be the vital one of being aware of the possibility of abuse, reporting and recording any concerns you have, or reporting any disclosure made to you.

However, there may be occasions when you have to intervene in order to prevent an abusive situation developing. The abuse can be physical, verbal or behavioural. This is most likely to happen in a hospital, residential or day-care setting between patients or service users. If you work in the community, you could be in the situation of having to deal with abusive behaviour from a carer. If you do have to act directly to prevent abuse, remember the following steps.

- Always prevent an abusive situation from arising if you can. If you know, for example, that two people regularly disagree violently about everything from politics to whether or not it is raining, try to arrange for them to be involved in separate activities and, if possible, have seats in separate lounges! Alternatively, you may decide to deal with the situation by talking to them both, and offering to help them try to resolve their disagreements.
- Deal with abusive behaviour in the same way as aggression – be calm and clear. Do not get drawn into an argument and do not become aggressive yourself, but make it very clear that abusive behaviour will not be tolerated.
- Intervene directly only if there is an immediate risk. You will need to use your communication skills to ensure that you handle the situation in a way that does not make things worse, and will ensure that you protect the person at risk.
- If there is not an immediate risk, report the incident and get assistance as soon as possible.
- If you have to intervene in an abusive situation, behave assertively. Do not shout, panic or get into an argument. State firmly and clearly what you want to happen – 'Mary, stop hitting Enid now!' You can deal with the consequences a little later, but the key action is to stop the abuse – 'Lee, stop calling Mike those names and move away from him now!' There must be no mistake about what has to happen. This is not the time to discuss it, this is the time to stop it. The discussion comes later.

Remember

The basic rule is to follow the policies of your workplace in dealing with the particular behaviour, but do not be concerned about trying to resolve a problem until the situation is calm enough for discussion to be possible.

- Remember that in the case of an act of abuse which may constitute a criminal offence, you should *not* remove any possible evidence until the police have examined the scene.

Evidence indicator

Think of a situation where you have had to act to challenge aggressive or abusive behaviour, or intervene to prevent such behaviour when it seemed likely to occur. Make a note of how you handled the situation. Could you have dealt with it in a better way? What else could you have done? Would it have turned out differently?

If you have never had to act in such a situation, ask an experienced colleague to tell you about an incident he or she has had to deal with. Then answer the same questions, based on what your colleague has told you. Remember, your colleague may not want to hear the conclusions you draw! Keep your notes for your portfolio.

The process of dealing with abuse

All organisations will have their own procedures to be followed in abuse cases, but they are likely to be along the following lines.

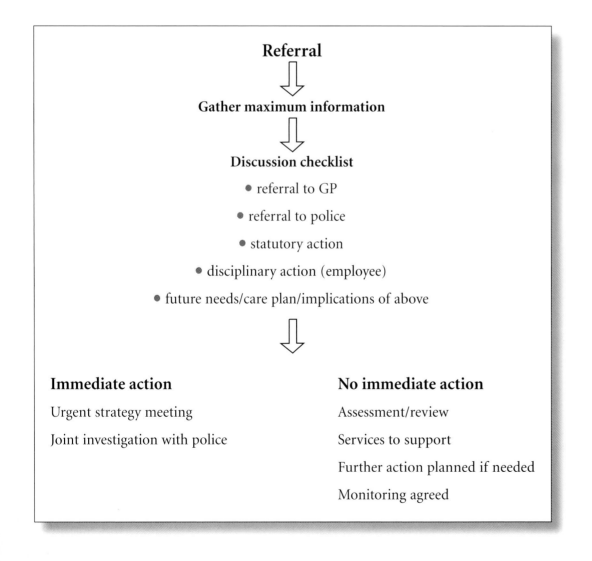

Referral

⇩

Gather maximum information

⇩

Discussion checklist

- referral to GP
- referral to police
- statutory action
- disciplinary action (employee)
- future needs/care plan/implications of above

⇩

Immediate action

Urgent strategy meeting

Joint investigation with police

No immediate action

Assessment/review

Services to support

Further action planned if needed

Monitoring agreed

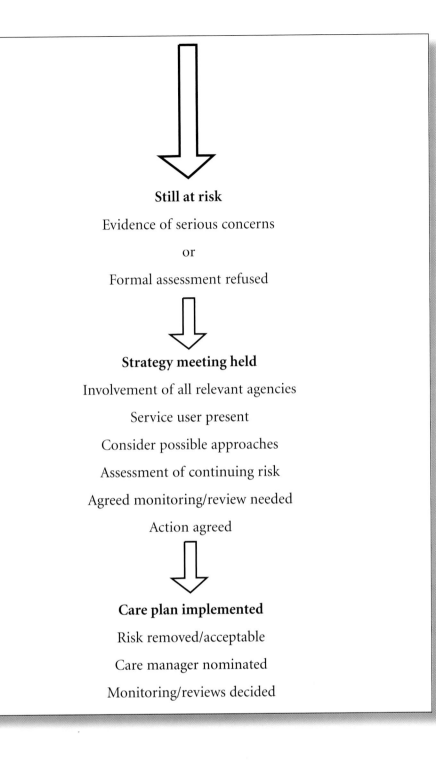

Still at risk

Evidence of serious concerns

or

Formal assessment refused

Strategy meeting held

Involvement of all relevant agencies

Service user present

Consider possible approaches

Assessment of continuing risk

Agreed monitoring/review needed

Action agreed

Care plan implemented

Risk removed/acceptable

Care manager nominated

Monitoring/reviews decided

Remember

Following the review and all discussions of an incident, complete accurate records about decisions taken and actions that are recommended for the future, and store your records according to workplace requirements.

Overview

Working through this unit may make you feel as though abusive behaviour is all around you and that vulnerable people are being hurt and frightened by carers all the time. Thankfully, the majority of carers do not abuse, but provide a good standard of care, and most vulnerable adults are not subjected to harm. However, while that may be comforting to know, it is vital that you are alert to any risks of abuse. As more professionals develop understanding of abuse and are aware of how to recognise and respond to it, the less likely it becomes that abusers will be able to continue to harm vulnerable people.

Test yourself

1 Why is it important to record information about suspicions of abuse?
2 What should you do if an individual asks you not to tell anyone about abuse he or she has experienced?
3 What type of information is protected by the Data Protection Act 1998?
4 What is hearsay evidence? Why should it be carefully identified as such?
5 What evidence might be available in a case of financial abuse?

HSC 335 UNIT TEST

1 What is the direction of current thinking about protecting vulnerable adults?
2 What is POVA, and why does it help to protect people?
3 List three items you would need to make a record about if you were involved in an abuse disclosure.
4 What are the key steps to ensure that you do not destroy potential evidence?
5 What are the ways in which organisations can be abusive?
6 How would you go about reporting concerns about a colleague's abusive behaviour?
7 List the key indications of each of the different types of abuse.

Plan, agree and implement development activities to meet individual needs

Activities are important for everyone and can serve a different purpose for each individual. Well-planned and supported activities are about much more than giving people something to do; they can provide a valuable way for individuals to promote various aspects of their development which may have been impaired, delayed or interrupted.

There are several key stages to providing development activities: first, it is important to support people to find out which are appropriate activities for them and which are best going to meet their needs. Then it is necessary to help to plan activities and provide support if needed, and finally to evaluate the effectiveness of the activities you have been involved with.

Working alongside individuals involved in activities, whether by themselves or in a group, can be thoroughly enjoyable – depending on the activity, of course! It gives you a really good chance to get to know people and enables you to build and develop relationships as well as supporting individuals to further their own development.

What you need to learn
- Assessing people's needs
- Ways to identify needs
- Putting individuals in control of assessments
- How to record information about pre-activity assessments
- Development activities
- How to plan for activities
- Preparation for activities
- Establishing consent
- Ways to give feedback and encouragement
- Staying safe
- How to measure progress towards goals
- How to share information with the care team

HSC 351a Identify and agree development activities to meet individual needs

Assessing people's needs

Before any activities can be planned or undertaken, first you have to work with people to find out exactly what they need, what they can already do, and what they want to achieve. The process of working with people to assess what they need is a key part of planning an activity programme that is intended to improve people's development and increase their self-esteem.

To plan a series of development activities without carrying out an assessment of what was needed would be to risk making arrangements for something that turned out to be inappropriate or unnecessary. No matter how well it is planned, prepared, or administered, something that is not the right activity or not pitched at the right level of development will be a failure.

Getting the level right is vital. Think about any new activity you might undertake, for example learning to ride a horse. If you had never ridden a horse before, it would be counterproductive for you to be given the largest or friskiest horse and be told to ride over a series of jumps. You would simply fall off and not learn anything! On the other hand, if you were a highly skilled and experienced chess player, you would not learn much from playing in the local 'Chess for beginners' class.

Measuring development

Assessment of need is important because it allows individuals to look at their own development needs using objective criteria linked to their own wishes and desires. Regardless of who you are working with, it is always important to measure and record progress. Measuring development and recording the data for an individual makes an important contribution to the assessment and identification of needs.

Remember

Measuring is different from finding out about needs, or how much support someone needs. In order to measure anything, there must be something to measure against – an objective criterion. The most obvious example is measuring length or height, which cannot be done without some form of measuring instrument. The instrument can be as simple as a ruler or tape measure or as complex as a fine electronic device used by engineers. But if measurements are not accurate, all kinds of problems can develop.

Active knowledge

Make a list of the types of things you measure frequently, for example the ingredients for a recipe, how tall your children are, or your weight, all of which are measured against agreed and accepted scales. You can easily obtain the tools you need to make these types of measurements, such as scales, rulers or tape measures, and they will enable you to measure against an agreed scale so that your results are meaningful.

What needs to be measured

People may want to measure a range of abilities, depending on their own circumstances and what they want to achieve. This can also depend on the services they want to access. Some services may carry out measuring and assessment as part of their work – many health-based services may do this.

For example, an individual may need to measure the degree of sensory impairment he or she has in order to make a decision about the type of development activities that are likely to be of most benefit. This can be done by looking at the results from a range of different tests and observations that have been carried out by the relevant professional, or an individual may want to carry out some of the measurements and observations for himself or herself.

Ways to identify needs

Many assessment programmes and tests have been devised to measure specific conditions; doctors and psychologists, for example, use a wide range of tests to measure conditions ranging from cerebral palsy to autism, and from dyslexia to sensory impairment. These are called **standardised tests**, because they measure against an agreed standard, so the results are comparable for all those being assessed.

Formal assessments are usually administered by the relevant professional for the condition being assessed, and will provide a clear set of measures and a system for making judgements – often using a scoring system. Well-known examples of formal assessment are:

- IQ tests, which are usually administered and scored by psychologists, or occasionally teachers, and ask a series of questions or give problems to solve; the results are measured against a scale, and an IQ score is given
- eye tests, such as the basic test of reading letters on a screen. This provides an optician, or a doctor, with some basic information about the individual's sight, and they can go on to find out more by using a series of other tests.

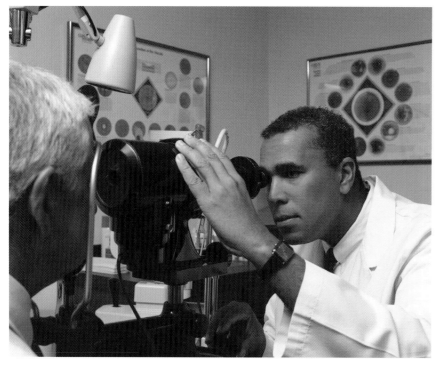

● *Eye tests are an example of formal assessment*

You may also know about other tests, such as the following.

- Portage workers undertake an assessment of a child, along with the parents, using a checklist. This checklist is used to measure a child's abilities in six areas: infant stimulation; social development; communication, speech and language; self-help; cognitive development; and motor development.
- Health visitors can carry out a preliminary test called CHAT (Checklist for Autism in Toddlers) which can identify potential autism in toddlers as young as 18 months. This is a questionnaire asked of parents, followed by observations which the health visitor or other primary care worker (such as the GP) needs to make. Both sections of the test are scored against

a standard system and the results give an indication whether the child may be at risk of developing a social-communication disorder such as autism. The questionnaire asks a series of questions such as: 'Does your child ever *pretend*, for example to make a cup of tea using a toy cup and teapot, or pretend other things?' and 'Does your child ever use his/her index finger to point, to indicate *interest* in something?'

Observations also need to be made, such as:

- Get the child's attention, then point across the room at an interesting object and say 'Oh look! There's a [name of object]!' Watch the child's face. Does the child look across to see what you are pointing at?
- Get the child's attention, then give the child a miniature toy cup and teapot and say 'Can you make a cup of tea?' Does the child pretend to pour out tea, drink it, etc.?

Say to the child 'Where's the light?', or 'Show me the light'. Does the child *point* with his/her index finger at the light?

Sometimes assessments will need specialised equipment, for example testing someone's fine motor skills. This may involve the individual being asked to pick up and move small objects, or to draw, or to fill in drawn outlines. Standardised psychological tests will have scoring charts and documentation to interpret the results. Tests designed to measure sensory impairment are likely to use advanced technology, as will many of the tests designed to measure physical levels of functioning.

Informal assessment

Informal assessment does not use a system of scoring results against a set of agreed measures in the same way as standardised tests. It involves supporting an individual to make judgements based on what you have learned from observations, simply talking to the individual or using a checklist.

For example, you may have a view about the extent to which someone with a learning disability is likely to benefit from an activity you are planning around using ICT as an aid to daily living; or you may consider that a group of people you support who have poor concentration as a result of depressive illnesses will benefit from a memory game designed to improve concentration. You should share your views with those you are supporting, if they ask for input from you. You should be particularly ready to contribute ideas if they express a wish to embark on an activity that you feel may not provide much benefit for them – you should suggest alternatives that may be more appropriate.

An important part of the assessment process is to identify the resources needed for any planned activities, and ways in which gaps in resourcing can be addressed. Any conflict between what the individual wishes to embark upon, what you feel would be beneficial, and the resources you have available, will need to be resolved sensitively by reference to your line manager if necessary.

Identifying and agreeing

In your workplace, you may have drawn up a checklist of factors you will encourage individuals to take into account before decisions are taken as to whether they will benefit from an activity. If not, you will need to work with other members of the care team to develop one. Your checklist will, of course, be specific to your workplace and the particular group of individuals you support. The checklist for a technology activity is likely to include the following areas for consideration:

- familiarity with technology
- ability to follow instructions
- ability to retain information and repeat actions
- likelihood of direct benefit from using technology
- problem-solving skills
- interest in technology.

If you were working with someone who was very keen to be involved in working with technology, then you would have to give a great deal of weight to the last factor on this list, as it may well prove to outweigh any concerns about other factors. Discussions about possible activities and their likely benefits are very important and also give you the chance to deal with any questions or concerns individuals may have.

For an individual you work with regularly, you will have other valuable insights to support the identification of suitable activities. For example, you will know whether there are family members or friends who are likely to be supportive and interested in the activities, and you will know the individuals' previous responses in situations involving a new experience or skill.

Evidence indicator

Check out the arrangements in your workplace for identifying development activities. Look at the different factors that are taken into account for different types of activities. Make a list of activities and note down one particular factor you would take into account for each activity on your list.

Observation

Observation is an important skill, and forms a key part of identifying what is appropriate to meet the needs of a particular individual. Observation is about much more than simply looking at someone or something. In order to observe, you will need to know in advance what you are looking for, and to watch carefully and note down details of the relevant points.

For example, you may decide after careful observation of someone who has been depressed that he or she seems to respond better to some people in the group rather than others. The information gained from this observation could be useful if you are designing activities that involve interacting with others. In another case, you may have observed that a particular individual with learning difficulties has a noticeable improvement in motor control when he or she is absorbed in the task of transplanting small seedlings. This could be valuable information if you are thinking about the types of activities that could improve this individual's motor skills, and you could try developing more activities connected with plants or gardening.

Good observation is a key part of assessment. Although observation can be a planned assessment tool, it can also be spontaneous and part of your everyday work.

✔ Keys to good practice: Effective observations

✓ Be unobtrusive – do not sit and stare!

✓ Always be alert to what is happening around you.

✓ Observe details such as people's body language and non-verbal communication.

✓ Look at people's reactions to their environment and others around them.

✓ Make notes about what you observe – you will not remember the detail.

● *When making observations it is important to be unobtrusive*

Putting individuals in control of assessments

Remember that an individual's assessment is about him or her as a person, and that the individual is the most important person in the process. It is essential that people feel they are involved and not that the assessment is something that is being 'done to' them.

This is not always easy, particularly if the assessment is a standardised test or a formal process. These are usually not designed in a way that encourages people to feel they are gaining something from the process. It is easy for people to feel they are being tested or experimented on, like a laboratory animal. So it is your job to make sure that anyone you are working with is clear about:

- what is to happen
- why it is happening
- how it will be carried out
- what they need to do
- how to stop it if they are unhappy.

Needless to say, you should make sure that people are able to communicate in their preferred way. For example, if someone uses sensory aids you need to check that these are available and can be used if necessary. You should always check that devices such as hearing aids are working correctly.

It is important for any assessment that all sensory and other equipment is in working order, otherwise there is a risk of not getting an accurate picture of development needs. For example, if you attempted to undertake an assessment for someone who normally wears glasses, but did not ensure they were worn for the assessment, you are likely to end up with an inaccurate picture of the extent to which activities based on visual participation will be of value.

✔ Keys to good practice: Sensory aids

✓ Check glasses and clean them if necessary.

✓ Check batteries in hearing aids, and clean the aids if necessary.

✓ For speaking aids, such as voice synthesisers, check and obtain technical help if necessary.

✓ Check any prostheses.

✓ Check any implants related to mobility or sensory function.

✓ Check mobility aids.

In order for people to be in control of any assessment and to be able to get information to help them identify their needs, they need to be clear:

- why the assessment is being done
- what exactly is going to happen

- what you have found out when the assessment is complete
- what the results mean in terms of the activities that will follow.

Obtaining agreement

Only by carefully explaining the purpose and process of the assessment and the recommendations for development activities can you ensure that the individual fully accepts the activities you have identified. People must be able to make an informed decision. Provided that the purpose of the assessment and activity programme is understood and that an individual, or his or her advocate, can see how the assessment and subsequent activities are linked to the agreed plan of care, you are unlikely to experience any difficulties with obtaining agreement.

However, if agreement is refused, it is not possible to proceed. You will need to re-think and come up with an alternative way of identifying and fulfilling needs.

Your workplace will have a protocol relating to consent for assessments of needs. It is unlikely to involve the signing of a written consent form, as these are not usually invasive or risky procedures, but there will be a procedure in your workplace for obtaining consent. It is most likely that a verbal indication of agreement is sufficient.

Active knowledge

Find out your workplace protocol for obtaining consent for assessment – does it vary depending on the type of activity? Is it always verbal, or always written? Check how this relates to the overall policy regarding consent for other procedures. Is there a difference? Try to find out the reason and justification for the difference.

How to record information about pre-activity assessments

Recording both the process and the results of assessments is important in the overall care of the individual. If you are using a formal assessment method, the process is likely to include a scoring or record sheet. This will need to be completed in order to obtain the results of the assessment, and is then usually kept in the person's records for future reference.

If you have carried out an assessment based on more informal methods, such as observation or interviews, you will need to make sure that you have recorded the results in the notes in the normal way. This will provide useful information for other members of the care team, and will mean that future use can be made of the assessment results you have obtained. Make sure all records are clear and readily usable by others. In order for assessment records to be of the maximum possible use, they need to include:

- the date, time, duration and place of the assessment
- the purpose of the assessment

- who was present
- the methods used for the assessment
- the individual's view of the assessment
- the results
- the implications of the results
- the activities that are planned as a result of the assessment.

They also need to be readily accessible and not be too long, or include too much detail.

Test yourself

P is 27 years old. She lives with her two children aged 3 and 5. She has a hearing impairment for which she is supposed to wear a hearing aid, but doesn't wear it as she says she never sees anyone, so there is no point.

P has hardly been outside the house since her younger child was born, and she has suffered severe post-natal depression. P does not have a partner – he left because he was unable to cope with her depression. Transport is provided to take the children to nursery and school. P does most of her shopping from the mobile shop, and has a friend who does other shopping for her.

If P attempts to leave the house, she experiences severe panic attacks. These have distressed her so much that she is now afraid to go out. However, P recognises that she needs to address some of the issues around her fears of going out, and has been working with a counsellor. She is keen to become involved in any activities that may help her.

1   What factors need to be taken into account when identifying development activities for P?
2   How would you go about supporting P to identify her needs?
3   What issues would you expect to arise in gaining P's agreement to development activities?

HSC 351b Plan and implement development activities with individuals and others

Development activities

Any activities carried out for the specific purpose of improving an individual's health or well-being can be classed as development activities. It is the **purpose**, not the **type**, of the activity that determines whether it qualifies as a development activity.

For example, a commercial artist painting a picture because he or she has been commissioned to do so is pursuing a different purpose from the person who has mental health problems and is using the medium of painting as a therapeutic way of expressing the complex feelings he or she is attempting to deal with. A group of older people chatting about the good times they remember from their youth and the way life has changed are different from a group of older people being encouraged to reminisce in order to help them to communicate, or where reminiscence is being used as part of life-review therapy for those who are terminally ill. The activity is the same, but the purpose is different.

Active knowledge

Think about activities you undertake in your own life which may be repeated, but have a different purpose. For example, reading a magazine to look at the latest bathrooms or hairstyles or cars is different from reading a magazine article that your NVQ assessor has asked you to read by tomorrow.

Now think about activities you carry out in your workplace. When does talking to someone stop being just chatting or communicating, and start being a development or therapeutic activity? Discuss this with your supervisor or assessor.

A wide range of activities can be carried out with the purpose of promoting the development of an individual. Some of these may be undertaken by a specialist professional such as a physiotherapist, occupational therapist, art or music therapist. Other activities may be carried out by the individual alone, or with support from professional carers in the care setting.

You could be involved in planning and preparing for many different activities depending on the group you work with and their identified needs. The types of activities you may be involved in planning and carrying out could include those in the following table.

Type of activities	Possible development objective
Social activities – e.g. birthday parties, social events, joint events with local community, visits to places of interest, luncheons, family outings	Preventing isolation, opportunity for variety of experience, promoting happiness, providing support or companionship, improving health and well-being, helping meet emotional and social needs, maintaining contact with outside activities, providing opportunities to maintain/increase social contacts, providing interest and stimulation
Intellectual activities – e.g. word games, chess, following current events, using the Internet and other IT, academic classes, health care groups, etc.	Helping to improve verbal ability, stimulating thought processes, stimulating those with cognitive impairment, providing intellectual challenges, maintaining contact with the outside world, helping orientation level, maintaining intellectual/cognitive level

Type of activities	Possible development objective
Spiritual activities – e.g. attending religious service, attending prayers, involvement in nature's sounds and sights, etc.	Meeting need for pastoral/spiritual care, improving comfort level, maintaining religious/cultural beliefs, helping with mood and behaviour, self-esteem, providing opportunities to socialise
Specialty activities – e.g. sensory integration, re-motivation, 24-hour reality orientation, handwriting classes, etc.	Maintaining or increasing alertness, decreasing anxiety, improving or maintaining orientation, increasing motivation, helping with mood, maintaining or improving skills, preventing withdrawal/regression, increasing attention span, increasing independence
Creative activities – e.g. resident council, craft/art/poetry/ creative writing classes, knitting, needlework, woodwork, etc.	Maintaining or improving cognitive skills, improving self-esteem, improving motor control/co-ordination, providing intellectual stimulation
Physical activities – e.g. walking, exercise programmes, competitive sports, swimming, gardening, golf	Maintaining or improving cardiovascular fitness, toning muscles, promoting feeling of well-being, improving self-esteem, maintaining/improving mobility

● *Swimming is an excellent form of exercise for many people*

How to plan for activities

Planning for the individual

In the first part of this unit, you looked at the ways in which assessments are undertaken and needs are identified. The planning of activities is the next step and is always based on the results of the identification and assessment process.

The examples in the table on pages 111–112 show some of the activities that may be implemented in your workplace, with some general suggestions about the developmental value they may have. However, the value is only realised for each individual if the activities are planned in response to the identified and assessed needs of the particular individual. An exercise programme that would provide a first-rate cardiovascular workout for a fit and active 65-year-old could have dire consequences for an overweight, unfit 40-year-old!

Depending on the type of activity, the planning may be undertaken by the relevant professional – for example, a programme of muscular exercises for someone recovering from a stroke may be planned by a physiotherapist, or a programme of activities to support speech improvement may be planned by a speech therapist. Alternatively, professional carers supporting an individual may need to develop a programme of activities designed to promote and meet social, intellectual or emotional needs. These could include:

- discussions
- outings
- games
- exercises
- relaxation
- work experience.

The planning process

In order for planning to be effective in promoting development goals, it needs to be about far more than just making sure that the timetable works or that you don't forget a vital piece of equipment. Of course these things are important, but good planning plays as important a part in the final benefit as the activity itself.

Planning is part of a process which begins with assessment and identifying needs, and the two are closely linked. The assessment will have helped the individual to identify needs and to make a judgement about his or her own ability to participate in a development activity. An assessment will also have identified the activities that are likely to be appropriate and benefit the individual. The plan is a means of meeting the identified needs.

Setting goals, targets or aims and objectives

All plans must aim towards a clearly identified goal, or goals. Otherwise, a plan becomes just a list of actions without a focus or direction. Imagine a football team taking to the field without a game plan – everyone would be running around without any clear idea of what they were doing. Something similar can happen to a care team who work without clear goals!

Goals can take many forms, depending on the needs of the individual. There will be an overall aim for the individual, which he or she will have identified and which will have been agreed by all involved. The goals that are set must all contribute to the overall aim – see the example in the case study on the next page.

● *Goals must be clearly identified and contribute to the overall aim*

CASE STUDY: Promoting independence

J is 27 years old. She has Down's syndrome and has always lived with her parents. J has attended a local day centre since she left school, but has always been very dependent on her parents and reluctant to meet new people or to try new experiences. She has always got on well with older people, however, and seems to have a real rapport with them.

Her support worker has arranged for J to spend time as a volunteer at a local residential care home. Although shy at first, J has recently been increasing the time she has spent working as a volunteer. She makes tea and lays tables for the residents, enjoys talking with them and now wants to learn how to improve her skills. J is hopeful that she may eventually be able to get a job at the residential home and is now asking for information about how she can increase her independence by moving into supported accommodation.

J's parents are now approaching their seventies and have always been concerned about what will happen to J if they can no longer care for her. They are supportive of her wish to become more independent, and have requested that the care team look for ways to encourage J to be more independent.

Q: What is the overall aim for J?
A: To increase her ability to live as independent a life as possible.
Q: What are the goals for J?
A: The goals are:

● to increase her confidence
● to gain some employment experience
● to consider more independent living options.

Q: How do the goals relate to the overall aim?
A: If J gains in confidence she is more likely to consider living a more independent life. If J has some employment experience, she can decide if she wants to find employment.
Q: How are the activities related to development?
A: They are aimed at improving J's social development.

Setting the criteria for success

There is no point in setting goals and targets unless you know when you have achieved them. You know when footballers score a goal because there is an accepted criterion that the ball has to go into the net – if it misses, it is not a goal, and everyone is clear about that.

With a development activity programme, you need to know:
- what the overall aim is
- what the goals are along the way.

You now have to agree what the criteria are going to be so you will know whether the goals have been achieved.

Think about goals as steps on the way to achieving the overall aim of the individual. In order for individuals to be able to achieve the goals they have agreed with you, the goals must be realistic and achievable. There is no quicker way to demoralise and demotivate an individual than to set unrealistic expectations which he or she constantly fails to meet. Goals work better if they are small and achievable rather than large and out of reach.

Goals must be related to an assessment of both need and ability. For example, someone who has a panic attack every time he or she leaves the front door is unlikely to achieve a goal of coping with a Saturday afternoon shopping in London's Oxford Street! However, a goal of being able to walk as far as the front gate, or the bus stop, may be something that can be managed. All of your communication skills may be needed as you tread the fine line between aiming too low and contributing to a feeling of worthlessness, and aiming too high and setting a person up to fail.

Setting the pace

The timescales and the pace of activities are also an important part of planning. As with the setting of goals, the speed at which goals are expected to be achieved is a key element in how realistic the plan is for the individual concerned.

As always, the individual should be the one setting the timescale for the achievement of goals. You may find that you need to encourage and support individuals in thinking about what is realistic for their own circumstances. For example, someone with a long history of stress-related illness may decide that he or she wants to be off medication and back in full-time work in six weeks. However, a more realistic timescale may be six months, or even 12 months. This is a long period of time, so smaller, interim goals that can be achieved over relatively short periods are more likely to be appropriate.

Remember, nothing succeeds like success – achievement makes people grow in confidence and therefore become more likely to go on achieving.

Planning as a shared process

Making sure that individuals are a part of the planning process is one of your most vital roles. People have a right to decide what they want to achieve and how they can go about it to the best of their ability. They should be taking control of the planning process to whatever extent they wish. Individuals should also be able to delegate the planning process to others if they wish.

The methods you use to encourage participation will vary depending on the setting in which you work and the wishes of the individual concerned. If you work in a residential setting, participation could be on two levels: the individual may decide his or her own programme of activities, and a residents' group may also have an overall plan for group activities for the setting as a whole.

It is important to challenge any discrimination or stereotyping that you find when planning activities – for example, assumptions that people who fall into a certain group will be incapable of particular activities, or will prefer to be involved in certain other types of activities. Remember, everyone is an individual!

Any of the following methods could be helpful in encouraging participation:
- one-to-one planning
- involvement in the review process
- discussions with significant carers, relatives or friends
- preparing written plans for comments
- taking someone to see activities to provide examples and ideas
- asking an individual to prepare his or her own plans.

Evidence indicator

Find out the method in your workplace for agreeing and recording goals for individuals. Check whether decisions about activities are made by the individual or by a group, and what is the process for involving the care team or key workers. Discuss with colleagues the basis for the procedures that are in place, and make notes.

Preparation for activities

Preparing for your role

You could be supporting, organising or participating in a wide range of activities and your role will be different depending on the individual involved and the identification of his or her needs and abilities. The extent to which you are directly involved or participate in the activity is also likely to vary, depending partly on the activity, but also on the individual's needs.

In some activities you may be taking part alongside the individual; in others you may need to demonstrate what needs to be done, and sometimes you may only be needed in order to set up the activity and give any advice and support.

Examples of types of activities and your likely roles are set out in the table below.

Type of activity	Likely role
Swimming	Participation/demonstration
Assertiveness group	Participation
Relaxation	Advice and instruction
Outings and visits	Participation
Art/craft group	Demonstration
Gardening	Demonstration/participation

Preparing equipment

Depending on the activity, you may need to have equipment or materials ready. Nothing is more likely to make people become frustrated and demotivated than equipment being missing, or constant interruptions to search for missing items.

As part of the planning process, it is useful to make a list of any materials or equipment you will need and to make sure that it is ready, working and available. For example, if you are planning to run a relaxation session, you will need relaxing sounds or music on CD or tape – and something to play them on. Your checklist may look something like this:

Checklist of items

❑ Numbers participating

❑ Music CD

❑ CD player

❑ Check location of power socket

❑ If no power socket – use batteries

❑ Spare batteries

❑ Check room temperature

❑ Individual mats or towels

❑ Soft and warm floor covering

❑ Check lighting – use lamps if general lighting is too harsh

❑ Privacy – curtains/blinds

You can add tick boxes like the above to your checklist and tick off the items as you collect them together. Your checklist for a visit to a theatre or gallery, designed to promote social and intellectual development, will include items such as tickets, guidebooks or programmes and transport arrangements.

If the activity is a craft session designed to develop motor and intellectual skills, such as making a collage, you may need to prepare some materials in advance. You could cut up pieces of material and tear out magazine pages. Your list of materials in this case may be lengthy and will need to include items such as glue, scissors and paper. Access to water for cleaning up afterwards will be important, as will good lighting and sufficient tables and chairs – all things that need to form part of your checklist.

If you are preparing for a board games session with a group, in order to improve concentration, intellectual and communication development, you will need to think about the games you are going to use and check that they are all available and are complete. Scrabble with half the letters missing, or Monopoly without dice or Park Lane is not much fun!

● *If planning to use board games, check that they are complete*

As with all the planning and preparation process, the needs of the individuals you are supporting must take priority. There is little point in planning a relaxation session which involves lying on the floor with a group of people who will have difficulty getting up and down! Similarly, material and equipment you are planning to use for your activities will need to be suitable for the group or individual for whom the activity is designed. Some examples are shown below.

● If you are planning a craft session involving glue, can the handles of the brushes be gripped by the individuals who will be participating?
● If you are planning a games session, can everyone in the group see to read the cards and dice?
● If you are planning a discussion group, does anyone in the group need support in hearing what is going on?

M works at a busy day centre for people with mental health problems. He has only been working in the job for six months, but he loves it and is starting his NVQ.

He was asked to organise a small group for people who wanted to discuss employment issues. All those who were participating had previously had problems with working, either because they presented challenging behaviour in the workplace or because they found workplaces threatening or stressful. Group members were all at the stage where they wished to get back into work, but wanted support and the opportunity to discuss concerns and fears in a group.

All the group rooms were in use on the day allocated for the first meeting, so M decided to use a room in the nearby council building. He left a message on the voicemail of the person responsible for booking rooms. Prior to the meeting M collected up-to-date information about employment opportunities and possible opportunities for work experience. He explained the aims of the group to the local job centre and agreed to keep them informed of developments.

On the day of the group meeting, everyone was ready and sitting in the main coffee lounge, and M explained that the meeting was to take place in the council building down the road. When they arrived, the receptionist had no record of the room booking, but a room was available and after about 10 minutes of negotiation M was able to book it. The room needed to have extra chairs brought in, which made everyone a bit hot and squashed, but the group did eventually get started.

1   What was M's first mistake?
2   What should he have done?
3   What preparation did he miss?
4   What preparation did he do well?
5   How do you think group members were feeling by the time the group began?
6   What does M need to do next?

Establishing consent

Gaining the individual's consent is as essential for joining an activity as for a medical procedure. Be wary of assuming that a person is willing to participate without asking him or her. Because the individual has been involved throughout the process of assessment and planning, it could have slipped your attention that no one has actually asked the individual if this is something he or she wishes to do!

Consent may not always have to be formal, such as signing a consent form, although some activities may require this. Your workplace will probably have clear policies about when specific consent is required – for example, if you were planning to take someone hang-gliding or hot-air ballooning you would be likely to need written consent. On the other hand, if you are going for an outing to the local supermarket with someone who is about to move into semi-independent living, you are unlikely to need to have any forms signed.

Active knowledge

Look at your workplace's policy on obtaining consent for activities. See if you can work out the basis for the policy. Is it based on the potential risk of the type of activities? Or is it based on cost or level of involvement? If you are unsure, ask your line manager.

If there are no requirements for formal consent for the activity you are planning, then you should still ensure that the individual is a willing participant by asking directly. You will need to explain exactly what is planned, what will happen and the reasons for the activity so that you can be sure that he or she is giving informed consent. It is not enough to say merely 'We'll go for a swim tomorrow, OK?', unless this is a regular part of an ongoing programme that someone has already consented to. It may be useful to consider using a 'contract' or working agreement, so that everyone is sure about what has been agreed and who is going to do what.

Ways to give information about activities

You will need, generally, to give plenty of information, such as: 'You remember you said at the last planning meeting that you wanted to take more physical exercise? Well, I've checked out the times at the new pool and they have an adults-only session at 10 am tomorrow. That means that it should be fairly quiet and not too much splashing. If you would like to go, we could get there at about 10 and stay for about half-an-hour. Allowing time to get changed, that should get us back here for about 11. Would that suit you?'

Information can be provided verbally, as in the example above, or it could be in a written format giving details of the plans. This could be an individual note or, if it is something undertaken regularly, there may be a leaflet or poster giving information.

For some individuals, it may also be appropriate to provide information to their carers – with the person's agreement, of course. This may be particularly relevant where an individual has a poor memory or where the carer is likely to be involved in the activity or the consequences of the activity. For example, if someone is participating in a basic computer skills group and is likely to have some 'homework' to do, the carer may need to provide support at home. It is also essential to involve carers in all aspects of care, including development activities. Where there is agreement, carers should be a part of the process throughout.

Ways to give feedback and encouragement

Nothing is more discouraging than doing something, especially something new or that you are unsure about, and getting no information about how well you are doing. Many people will remember that one of the most difficult aspects of a driving test is that you have no feedback while it is going on; you only find out at the end how well (or badly!) you have done. So throughout activities, make sure that you provide feedback and encouragement.

Feedback should always be constructive. If you need to offer criticism, it should always be positive and offer some ideas for improvement. Negative feedback is very destructive and demotivating. For example, you could say:

- 'Leilah, you are relaxing much better now – if you keep going on the breathing pattern you'll find it will work even better.'
- 'Frank, that spreadsheet is so good – I think we could use it in the office if there was a date column added.'
- 'Liz, the way you have made contributions in the group recently has been fantastic. I'd love to see how well you can use your listening skills to help others to join in.'

These are all in fact positive ways of saying:

- 'Leilah, you won't ever relax properly unless you get your breathing right.'
- 'Frank, you've missed out the date column.'
- 'Liz, you need to talk less and give others a chance to get a word in edgeways.'

Active knowledge

Think of occasions when you have been put down by negative criticism. Try to remember how you felt.

Make a list with two columns: one for negative and one for positive feedback. Look at the examples in the bullet lists above and add to them. For each feedback give a positive and a negative version. Over a period of about a week, make a note each time you express a criticism of how you could have done it more positively.

Staying safe

Some development activities will have health and safety implications. In line with legislation and your organisation's policies, you must carry out a risk assessment before undertaking some development activities. Those which involve physical activity or going off site will definitely need a risk assessment. Holding a discussion group, or playing a board game may not – but an exercise group or a dancing class may. If you are in doubt and your organisation's risk assessment policies are not clear, check with your line manager.

● *Risk assessments will be necessary for physical activities*

HSC 351c Evaluate and review the effectiveness of the development activities

How to measure progress towards goals

The goals that were set during the planning process are the basis for evaluation. You will need to measure progress towards these goals.

Some goals are easier to measure than others. If, for example, the goal was to walk unaided to the end of the corridor, its achievement, or progress towards it, could be measured and recorded. This type of information is 'quantitative', which means it can be measured against known criteria. The criteria will have been set in advance, when you were planning the activity; you will have jointly agreed what the criteria for success would be. In the above case, the criteria are about distance ('to the end of the corridor'), and the amount of support needed ('unaided').

John walked two-thirds of the way along the corridor unaided. He feels that this is excellent progress towards his goal and is keen that the exercise programme should continue.

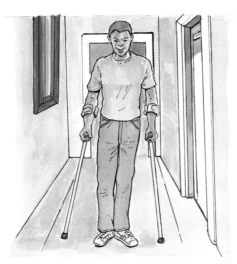

You could decide to have a progress chart or map to show how well an individual is doing. This can be very helpful in keeping someone motivated. If you do this, you will need to convert your criteria into a scoring system; for example:

- Achievement of the goal is 100 points.
- Walking unaided past the first two doorways on the corridor is worth 25 points.
- Walking the full length of the corridor with help is worth 50 points.

Active knowledge

Take any activity you do that can be measured easily by quantity; for example, making beds, mopping floors, going for a run, walking round the park, swimming lengths and so on. Write down some criteria and a scoring system so you can measure when you are part-way through, when you are half-way through and when you have achieved your goal. Think about whether knowing how well you were progressing made the achievement any easier.

If, on the other hand, the goal was to become more assertive, that is more difficult to measure because it is largely about how people feel and behave. However, some examples can be used to illustrate progress. It is still possible to measure and record this, but the information will be 'qualitative', which means it is based on people's feelings or opinions rather than measurable facts.

Asher feels that the assertiveness group has helped him in changing his behaviour. He explained to his colleague this week that he was not able to do any extra work to cover for her again, as he needed to leave work on time that day. He also sent back a meal at a restaurant because it was not what he had ordered.

Key terms

Quantitative: Relating to quantity (such as size, number or amount) and its measurement.

Qualitative: Relating to quality (such as conditions, opinions or feelings) and its measurement.

The judgement about the extent to which goals have been met must be made by the individual, supported by the care team. In many cases it is the individual's feelings that are being measured, and while this can be more difficult, there are ways of doing it. The best way is to decide before you start the activity what the criteria for success will be; so you may decide that John will record how confident he felt about walking along the corridor. If he felt very confident, you could record a considerable success. You would normally suggest that John rate his feelings – either by using a scale (such as 1 to 10 with 10 meaning supremely confident), or by using a series of statements such as 'not confident', 'fairly confident', 'confident', 'very confident' or 'supremely confident'.

Moving the goalposts

Sometimes, the evaluation process can identify that goals should be changed. For example, someone may have wanted to live independently and move out of his or her parents' home. However, after developing more assertive behaviour, he or she may have found there was a change in the relationship with the family which means that there is no longer a need to leave.

Goals may also be reviewed and changed if appropriate to make them more demanding and to meet the next challenge. Someone whose previous goal was to be able to leave the house without having a panic attack may now want to move the goal on to planning a visit to the supermarket. This is real progress and should make the individual feel very positive and increasingly confident.

Identifying the questions

A list of questions can be useful in supporting individuals to think through what they have achieved and what they are looking for next. Each work setting will be different, and everyone will need his or her own list. However, something like the following may help.

List of questions on achieving goals

1   What did you want to achieve?

2   Did you achieve it fully, partly, not at all?

3   How do you feel about your progress?

4   Has your goal changed?

5   If so, what is your goal now?

6   Do you think the way you set about achieving your goal worked?

7   If not, why not?

8   What do you want to do next?

9   How will this help towards your goal?

Depending on their circumstances and personal choice, individuals may prefer to think about this independently. Some may wish to work through it with their carer, family or friends, and others may want their key worker to work with them. Whatever method they choose, you will also need to share your own evaluation of progress towards the agreed goals and the effectiveness of the activities and approaches chosen.

Did you know?

According to findings from the 2003 Health Survey for England, 81 per cent of men and 87 per cent of women aged 55 years and over do not reach the recommended levels of physical activity to benefit health.

There is a sharp decline in activity levels with age: 32 per cent of men aged 55 to 64 years were reaching the recommended levels of physical activity. This figure decreased by 15 per cent for men aged 65 to 74 years and a further 9 per cent for men aged 75 years and over.

The 2000 Health Survey for England found that 86 per cent of women and 78 per cent of men who were residents of care homes were classified as inactive.

How to share information with the care team

Other members of the care team will need to be able to participate in the evaluation process, either because they have their own contribution to make, or because they have an interest in the progress of the individual.

The most obvious time to discuss and share progress reports and evaluations is at a regular review meeting. Depending on your work setting these may be held at set intervals, or whenever there is something to discuss. The process will usually include the individual, all the professionals involved with that individual, and his or her carer.

Other workplaces may not operate in quite the same way and evaluation may be on a smaller scale, and just involve the key worker and individual, along with carers or family, if appropriate. Then the information may be passed on to the other members of the team.

Review meetings give an excellent chance for everyone to make a contribution and develop the next stage of any care plan or programme. The review meetings to discuss progress are similar to any other review process, and you should make sure that the individual, carers and significant people are aware and able to attend. Everyone should have the opportunity to contribute, using advocates if necessary, and everyone should try to reach agreement on the next steps. However, ultimately it is the individual who must direct what the next steps should be. Your role is to ensure that he or she has all the information needed to make a clear decision.

It is important that all evaluations or progress are recorded and any changes are clearly noted in the individual's care plans.

Be sure to remember the rules of confidentiality and the provisions of the Data Protection Act 1998 when storing and sharing records about individuals.

Evidence indicator

Prepare a report of a review concerning an individual's progress towards an agreed goal, or set of goals. The report can be based on an individual you support, or have supported previously, or it can be entirely imaginary. If you do write about an individual you work with, make sure that he or she agrees to your use of the information and that the person cannot be identified from what you write.

Your report should include:

- information about the individual's circumstances and background
- the goals or targets, and the reasons for them
- the development activities and why they were chosen
- the criteria agreed to measure success
- the results of the development activities
- the results when measured against the criteria
- a judgement as to how successful the activity has been
- a proposal for the next steps.

Test yourself

1 List two ways in which you could measure progress towards goals.
2 Why is it important to involve individuals in the evaluation process?
3 How are criteria used to measure success and/or progress?
4 What is the difference between criteria and a scoring system?
5 Suggest ways to support people to keep motivated during an activity programme.

HSC 351 UNIT TEST

1 Why are development activities important?
2 List at least three purposes of development activities.
3 What types of activities can be useful for improving development?
4 What are the important aspects of planning?
5 Why is careful preparation important?
6 How can you support individuals during activities?
7 What are the most effective ways of giving feedback?
8 Why is evaluation important?
9 How can you share information with the care team?

Contribute to planning, monitoring and reviewing the delivery of service for individuals

Making sure that individuals are supported to receive the right services, at the right time and in the right way, is a key part of your role as a care worker.

This is the next stage on from care planning. It is about making the care plan into a reality by delivering the services identified in the plan and ensuring that they meet the needs they were intended to meet.

You may be involved with service delivery in different ways depending on your job role. Planning, monitoring and reviewing services could be about the services for one person or a group of people, depending on what you do.

Current thinking recognises the importance of empowering people in relation to choosing and using their services, so one of your most important roles is to make it possible for the individuals you support to be in control of the services they use. Recent changes in thinking can mean big differences in the way services are delivered; you will need to make sure that you have the knowledge and skills to work with these changes.

What you need to learn

- New structures to deliver new services
- Inputs and outcomes
- Making an assessment
- Direct payments and individual budgets
- Inspecting planning
- Commissioners and providers
- Planning for delivery of services
- Monitoring
- Involving individuals, families and carers
- Reviews
- Evaluation
- Your role

HSC 329a Contribute to planning the delivery of service for individuals

The government Green Paper 'Independence, Well-being and Choice', which was published in 2005, and the White Paper 'Our Health, Our Care, Our Say', set out a new approach to the way that services are delivered to adults in England. This reflects similar thinking in other parts of the UK. Scotland's '21st Century Social Work Review' has similar proposals, and the thinking is also evident in the 'National Service Framework for Older People' in Wales, and the reviews that have been undertaken in Northern Ireland.

New structures to deliver new services

One of the main proposed changes is that all local authorities will have a Director of Adult Social Services, who will be responsible for the delivery of services for adults through working in partnership with primary care trusts, the independent and voluntary sectors. This is very similar to the structures now in place in England for the delivery of services for children and young people, and it is possible that this type of integrated service delivery may be adopted in other parts of the UK too.

The intention is that this type of structure should provide better services because they will be more integrated and 'joined up'.

Active knowledge

Get hold of a copy of the latest document about the future of adult social care services in your area of the UK. Your employer will probably have a copy, or you will be able to download it from government websites. Read the executive summary, then make some notes about how each of the proposals is different from what you do now.

Inputs and outcomes

One of the key changes is that instead of structuring services around what we, as the social care work force, do in order to ensure that individuals receive services, the new structures will be structured around **outcomes**, in other words what is achieved by the people receiving the services.

Think of it like this. Imagine you spend three hours taking Emily on a shopping trip. You have worked with her to plan the trip, as she has not been out of the house since she had a bad fall six months ago. You accompany her to the local shops, spend time while she chooses her shopping, and go home with her. Then you talk through the experience with her and discuss what went well, and any areas she was not confident about. Finally, you discuss plans for the next outing with her.

Your three hours, and everything you do during that time, is your **input**.

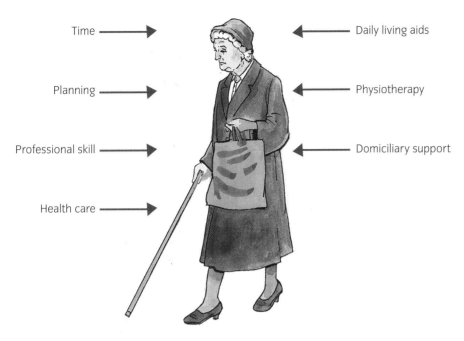

Time ——→

Planning ——→

Professional skill ——→

Health care ——→

←—— Daily living aids

←—— Physiotherapy

←—— Domiciliary support

● *Some possible inputs for Emily*

In order to find the **outcome**, you need to look at what Emily has got out of this. The trip has helped to increase her confidence, raise her self-esteem and increase her general well-being; it has helped her to achieve some physical exercise and improved her mobility. It has also contributed to increasing her independence. These are the achievements that have resulted from your input, and these achievements are called **outcomes**.

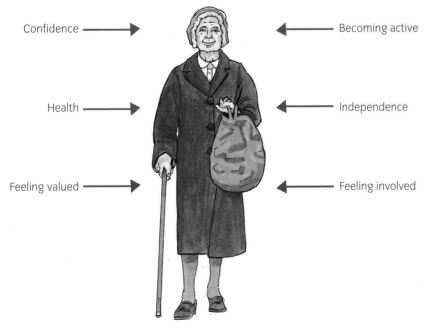

Confidence ——→

Health ——→

Feeling valued ——→

←—— Becoming active

←—— Independence

←—— Feeling involved

● *Some possible outcomes for Emily*

This means that when we plan for the delivery of services, we need to think about the outcomes the individuals want to achieve, and work with them to make sure that the services are helping to achieve these outcomes. Remember that an individual's relationships and support network are vital in promoting his or her well-being, and all factors must work together to achieve desired outcomes.

Remember

Think of the inputs and outcomes involved in baking a cake. You need all the ingredients: flour, butter, sugar, eggs; all of these are inputs. But unless you are clear about what your outcome should be – a light, fluffy sponge cake, for example – you won't know how to use your ingredients (inputs) in the best possible way. You could spend a lot of time thinking about ways to get all the ingredients together at the same time and in the same place, but if you don't have a clear idea of your intended outcome you could instead end up with pancake batter, a Yorkshire pudding, fudge, shortbread or scones!

The approach to service provision which is all about inputs is called **service-led** provision, and the approach that focuses on outcomes is referred to as **needs-led** provision.

Outcomes for everyone

Outcomes are a key part of the approach to adult services. The proposed outcomes for all adults, which have resulted from consultation, are as follows.

- **Improved health:** Enjoying good physical and mental health (including protection from abuse and exploitation); access to appropriate treatment and support in managing long-term conditions independently; opportunities for physical activity.
- **Improved quality of life:** Access to leisure, social activities and life-long learning and to universal, public and commercial services; security at home; access to transport; and confidence in safety outside the home.
- **Making a positive contribution:** Active participation in the community through employment or voluntary opportunities; maintaining involvement in local activities; being involved in policy development and decision making.
- **Exercise of choice and control:** Maximum independence and access to information; being able to choose and control services; managing risks in personal life.
- **Freedom from discrimination or harassment:** Equality of access to services; not being subject to abuse.
- **Economic well-being:** Access to income and resources sufficient for a good diet, accommodation and participation in family and community life; ability to meet costs arising from specific individual needs.
- **Personal dignity:** Keeping clean and comfortable; enjoying a clean and orderly environment; availability of appropriate personal care.

These aims mean that all services for adults will be focused around achieving the outcomes, and services will have to be able to show how they have made a contribution towards each of the outcomes.

Making an assessment

In developing a plan for an individual, an assessment will have been carried out, working with the individual and his or her carer to reach an agreement about what services can be provided. You may have become involved at the stage of making the assessment, or of making the care plan happen. Regardless of when your role begins, you need to be clear about the assessment process.

In England, the Community Care Assessment Directions of 2004 provide the legal basis for good practice in making assessments. This means that:

- the individual and his or her carer should be fully involved in both assessment and planning
- the full range of needs (physical, intellectual, emotional and social) must be taken into account
- information must be available in a variety of formats
- separate assessments must be offered to carers – this is laid down in the Carers and Disabled Children Act 2000, and extended by the Carers (Equal Opportunities) Act 2004
- individuals who lack the capacity to participate in the assessment and planning process should have their carers as fully involved as possible
- disagreements between individuals and their carers about the assessment process and outcome should be handled sensitively, with consideration given to the interests of both; using an advocate should be considered.

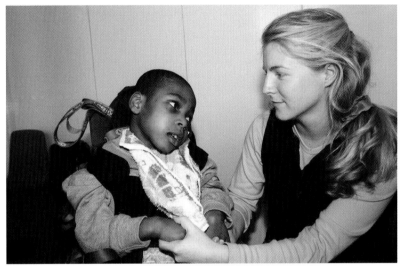

● *Separate assessments must be offered to carers*

The directions contain general statements about good practice in assessment and planning, which is required wherever you work.

Single assessment

In order to develop integration of services and to ensure that people are not having to answer the same assessment questions repeatedly, older people are now assessed for health and social care services using a single assessment process, referred to as SAP. In theory, this means that health and care professionals share assessment information, with each of the professionals adding their own area of expertise without having to repeat the same basic questions.

For example, if a person's first contact with health and care services was with a physiotherapist, the basic assessment would be done. If Social Services then became involved, staff would use the information from the first assessment and focus on the social care needs, without having to go over all the basics such as medical history, family history and personal circumstances.

Evidence indicator

Find out how the single assessment process is used in your workplace. If you are not already familiar with the assessment documents, make sure you get hold of one and read it through. Think about the different professional areas that could add to the initial assessment. Make notes on your findings.

Empowering people

One of the key changes in approach is about giving people direct control over the services they receive. This is about much more than choice; it is about empowerment. There is a real difference between choice and empowerment:

• *Choice*

• *Empowerment*

If you think about the example in the illustration above, you will see that choice is something that is limited by the control exerted by people who hold power. Where power is held over an individual, there is always the risk that it can be abused, for example by coercing the individual into accepting particular options. Empowerment means that much of the power is handed over. For example, the girl in the shoe shop in the right-hand picture above has the freedom to decide to buy a cheap pair of shoes and keep the change, buy a more expensive pair and put in the difference herself, or not buy any at all. Empowerment promotes people's self-esteem, and helps them to cope with change in a positive way.

Direct payments and individual budgets

Until quite recently, there was little choice for people who received services. The local authority carried out an assessment and then contracted with various agencies to provide services.

The introduction of the **direct payments** system changed all this. Direct payments are made by Social Services departments directly to the individual concerned, who then becomes responsible for contracting and managing his or her own service provision.

The take-up of direct payments is increasing throughout the country, and its use is being encouraged. Most local authorities provide support for those who decide to take up direct payments, offering advice and guidance about how to go about becoming an employer and contracting for the provision of services. The training and support on offer can cover advertising, employment law, contracting, and monitoring and maintaining quality.

Many of the people taking up direct payments are disabled people who report that they have been able to change their lives by employing personal assistants to provide support and access to employment and social life. In other situations, carers have taken up direct payments in order to organise a package of support to meet the needs of the individual they are caring for.

Where direct payments are made, individuals will be responsible for arranging their own package of care. They may choose to contract with services with whom the Social Services department or health authority already has arrangements, but if they wish they can advertise, recruit and employ their own carers and establish their own package of care as they see fit.

Did you know?

Currently, over 24,000 people are in receipt of direct payments, and this figure is growing rapidly.

This level of responsibility is not for everyone, so one of the ideas currently being piloted is **individual budgets**. This works a little like direct payments; people are told the amount of money available to provide the care they have been assessed as needing, and they can then choose how to spend the money. The local authority still deals with all the contracts and payments, and the individual does not have to employ the staff providing the services. This means that they are empowered to choose their own package of services, but do not have the responsibility of organising everything themselves. This may be the way forward for service provision in the future.

Inspecting planning

The Care Standards Act 2000 provides the legal basis for the inspection of all social care provision against a set of national minimum standards. Regardless of whether the provision is residential or domiciliary or day care, and whether it is for older people, people with a learning disability or people with complex needs, the standards include a criterion about assessment of needs and planning to meet those needs. All services must be able to meet the national minimum standards and plan services effectively to meet the needs of each individual.

CASE STUDY: Direct payments

B has multiple sclerosis. She is 25 years old and is a qualified accountant. As her condition deteriorated, she began to rely on support by carers who came in throughout the day. A package was arranged whereby carers would come first thing in the morning, at lunchtime and again in the evening.

B was finding this difficult because the carers would often change and, as she continued her accountancy practice from home, she needed people who were familiar with her routine. There had also been a couple of occasions where problems arose because carers were asked to carry out tasks to support B's professional activities. One or two carers had felt that this was not their role.

B decided that direct payments would be a good option, and she now employs a team of personal assistants, who are able to support both her personal and professional needs. She finds that this process works well and she is much more confident that she can work and maintain all the support she needs to manage her condition.

1　Why do you think that direct payments worked for B?
2　Were there any other alternatives that could have been considered?
3　Are there any factors in B's situation that make it easier for direct payments to work?
4　What are the risks to B of moving to direct payments?

Commissioners and providers

All social care services are provided either by the local authority, an independent services provider, or a voluntary sector provider. Health services are normally provided through the National Health Service, either through primary care (in the community) or secondary care (in a hospital), and some health services are provided through the private sector. Depending on your job role you may work for any one of these types of providers.

However, services do not appear out of the blue! All health and care services have to be commissioned – which basically means ordered – and this is done by the body that will pay for them. This can be the local authority or the primary care trust – or very soon, a GP practice.

Most social care services are commissioned by the local authority. This means that sometimes the local authority can be both the commissioner and the provider, where in-house services are used such as residential care homes or domiciliary services. Examples are shown in the table below.

Service	Commissioner	Provider
Home care	Local authority	Private sector Not-for-profit sector Local authority
Residential care	Local authority	Private sector Not-for-profit sector Local authority
Geriatric medical services	Primary care trust	NHS hospital trust

Commissioning is about ordering services; the purchasing (agreeing prices and payment) and contracting (putting it all in a legal framework) is usually carried out by a contracting unit within the local authority. Under the new pilots of individual budgets, people will be able to contract directly with a service provider if they wish. Unless you are part of a commissioning team – care manager or care team support worker – you will work for a service provider, and the work you do will have been commissioned by someone.

Did you know?

According to the Royal Commission on Long-Term Care, there are now twice as many people over 65 years of age as there were in 1931, and people over 100 years of age are the fastest growing group.

Planning for delivery of services

The care plan will have identified the services that the individual and carer have decided are necessary. At this point, the services have simply been agreed, not yet delivered. This is a vital stage, and if the planning for this is not done carefully, it can result in a very unsatisfactory outcome.

A step-by-step checklist is always useful if you are a key person, working with the individual and his or her carer to deliver services. Your role could be:

- the commissioner of services, so that you are the person carrying out the wishes of the individual
- a provider of services, so you will be involved in the planning process to ensure that the service you provide meets the needs of the individual.

Current thinking recognises that in order to empower people who use services, their hopes, needs and wishes must be the basis for the commissioning and delivery of services. This is called **outcome-based commissioning** and is replacing **block commissioning**, where local authorities contracted with just a few providers for pre-agreed quantities of a particular service. This meant that everything was controlled by those commissioning the services, and almost nothing was in the hands of the people using them.

Regardless of the role you are working in, the key task is to play your part in making sure that the right services are delivered to the right person at the right time, and in the right way.

Step 1

Check that the services agreed in the care plan are still what the individual wants. Even if the care plan is fairly recent, people can have second thoughts, or their condition can change. It is always good practice to check, so that no one feels that he or she is being pushed into accepting an unsuitable service.

Step 2

Check that all of the information needed in order to deliver the services has been collected and given to the right people. Information will have been gathered as the care plan was developed, and the single assessment process (SAP) documentation should contain all the basic information. However, different people in the process of delivery need different information, as shown in the following table.

People	Information
Individual and family	Provider background, history, reputation, inspection reports, quality assessments, references and experience.
	Exactly what will be delivered, when, how frequently, for how long and by whom.
	Cost – overall, and how much of this they have to meet.
	Contact details for you, an emergency contact, the provider, your manager, complaints and the inspectorate.
	Care plan, delivery plan, outcomes, monitoring and review process.

People	Information
Provider	SAP documentation, care plan, delivery plan, outcomes, monitoring and review process.
	Agreed funding process, payment process.
	Resolution of complaints process.
	Contact details for you, your manager, the individual, key people, contracts unit, finance unit.
Contracting/ commissioning unit	Individual details, provider details, agreed service levels, monitoring process, review process.

Step 3

Check that everyone is aware of any issues and concerns regarding the provision of services, and that people who want to explain or identify issues, concerns and problems can do so.

For example, someone may be unsure whether it is possible to get him or her out of bed, washed and ready for breakfast in the time allocated. You may need to ask the individual and the provider to go over the plan in detail, so that the individual is reassured. Alternatively, a provider may be concerned because an individual does not want a particular type of equipment to be used. This will need detailed discussion, and the provider will need to be reassured that the service can be provided without the equipment in question.

Step 4

Check that everyone is clear about the nature and purpose of the particular services and the reasons for providing them. This may sound obvious, but sometimes it is useful to check that everyone, particularly the individual concerned, understands why the proposed service is being provided rather than a different service. It is also essential that everyone is clear about what the service is for and what it includes. This helps to reduce any misunderstandings about what is, and is not, part of the service and reduces the risk of any unrealistic expectations about what the service can provide.

Step 5

Ensure that everyone is aware of the outcomes the individual wants to achieve. This is a vital part of the service. The process of monitoring and evaluation, and perhaps the actual contract, will be based on the outcomes that are planned and agreed.

It is important that these are realistic; there is no point in agreeing an outcome stating that someone who is recovering from a fractured hip, who is 87 years old and has severe arthritis, will be fully independent in six months. However, it may

● *Outcomes may be as simple as making a cup of tea unaided*

be realistic to state that she will aim to go into the kitchen and make a drink in eight weeks, and get herself undressed for bed after 12 weeks.

The outcomes must be those the individuals want to achieve. You may have to try to encourage them to be realistic, but the outcomes must belong to them. Outcome-based commissioning is built around the outcomes desired by the individual, not the commissioner.

Step 6

Involve individuals, carers, key people, providers and commissioners in agreeing a plan for achieving the outcomes. This needs to be detailed and clear, so that everyone understands how the outcomes will be achieved. For example, if the agreed outcome is to go to the kitchen and make a drink after eight weeks, everyone needs to know how this will be done, and the stages involved. This way, the individual, carers, family and service provider can all see how much progress is being made, and whether any changes need to be made along the way.

Step 7

Make sure that financial information is accurate and that you have information about all the relevant costs and how they will be met. This will involve checking the funding available to commission the service, checking the charges with the provider, and remembering to include any additional costs that may need to be taken into account.

You may need to either undertake, or check, a financial assessment for the individual in case he or she is required to make a contribution to the cost of the services received.

Step 8

Work alongside the individual and his or her carer to look at any potential problems or risks with the agreed services. Very few situations are without any risks or difficulties, and it is no use pretending they don't exist, or will go away if you ignore them – they won't.

Individuals and families must be aware of any risks associated with the plans for service delivery. Use your organisation's risk assessment procedures and discuss the issues with the people involved. If an individual is going to be working towards making her own drink in the kitchen, for example, there are risks that she may fall, risks that she may scald herself and risks that she may fail and become disheartened. All of these possibilities need to be discussed, including the likelihood of each occurring, the consequences if it did occur, and what steps will be built into the plan to reduce each particular risk. Managing risk is part of everyday adult responsibilities, and individuals should be encouraged to contribute to these discussions as much as possible to promote their self-esteem and development.

If you spend time carefully working through each of the steps, it is far more likely that service delivery will be effective in achieving the outcomes, and that individuals and families will feel that they are achieving what they wanted. The service provider, too, should find fewer problems in delivery as a result of thorough planning.

Test yourself

1 Give an example of the difference between choice and empowerment.
2 How can outcome-based commissioning help to empower people?
3 List three ways in which direct payments could change someone's life.
4 Why is planning service delivery important?
5 Think of three possible results of a failure to plan for service delivery.

HSC 329b Contribute to monitoring the delivery of service for individuals

Monitoring

Monitoring services is a process of regular checks against an agreed set of criteria in order to make sure that the service is still reaching the expected quality, still meeting needs, and still achieving the outcomes that it was set up to achieve. It is also important to continue to monitor whether the needs of the individual have changed since the service began.

You will need to be sure that any monitoring process is covering each of these different aspects of service delivery:

- agreed outcomes (or agreed inputs, if your organisation is still working with service-led provision)
- individual needs and circumstances
- quality of service delivery.

Outcome-based monitoring

The key area of monitoring is checking that all the agreed outcomes are being met, or that progress is being made at the expected rate.

Monitoring the performance of service providers is very important, and it is likely that your organisation has developed systems and criteria to be applied to all service providers with whom they work.

Contracts based on outcomes or results, rather than inputs or descriptions of tasks, provide useful measures against which service providers or contractors can be judged. For example, a contract that simply says that 'the Fairways Day Centre will provide day-care facilities on five days per week for Mr J' is much more difficult to monitor than a contract that states:

> The outcomes that will result from this contract with the Fairways Day Centre are:
>
> - Mr J will develop greater confidence in participating in activities with others.
> - Mr J will take part in two group activities during his initial six weeks at the centre.
> - Mr J will develop his literacy and numeracy skills. Tuition will be provided and regular feedback will be given.
> - Mr J's motivation to complete the learning programme will be maintained.
> - Mr J will continue with his present medication, and will be able to maintain his medication without support by the first review after six weeks.

This form of contract identifies clear outcomes that will give a starting point for monitoring. Each of the outcomes that the service provider has to achieve is clearly stated in the contract. The individual, family and care manager will be able to monitor whether these outcomes are being achieved.

Obviously, some of the outcomes will be subjective and based on the feelings of the individual (does he feel more confident?). Others are more objective (has he joined in two activities with others? Is he taking his medication without support?).

Service-led monitoring

The criteria for monitoring service-led contracts will be different. For example, for Mr J, it could be: 'Day care is provided five days each week'.

Did you know?

There are 120,000 adults of working age, and 25,000 older people, with severe and profound learning disabilities in the UK. Estimates suggest that there are over 1.2 million people in England alone with mild or moderate learning disabilities.

This would then be monitored by checking attendance records at the day centre, but this does not give any indication of what Mr J wants to get out of his time at the day centre. It is quite likely that the day centre will encourage and support him to take his medication and become involved in group activities, but there is no check on whether they do – only on whether day care is provided.

There is also less opportunity for Mr J to be involved in the monitoring; he only has to confirm that he is going to the centre.

CASE STUDY: Achieving desired outcomes

E has a learning disability. She attends a day centre, and is very keen to get a job, as several of her friends have done.

A local residential care home offered her a job helping with the preparation and serving of meals, provided that she learned some basic hospitality skills such as how to set out a tray, how to serve meals and how to clear away. They offered to teach her basic food hygiene skills.

The requirement to learn hospitality skills was built into the contract for the day centre. The centre staff showed E the basic skills and allowed her to practise by serving tea and meals to staff and other day-centre users.

After a few weeks, at the review E was confident enough to want to show her new skills to the review meeting, and told everyone that the centre was really helping her to learn. Shortly afterwards she went to the residential care home, and was given the job. E was delighted.

1 What would outcome-based monitoring be looking at in E's case?
2 What would service-led monitoring be looking at?
3 What might the disadvantages of service-led monitoring have been for E?

Involving individuals, families and carers

In the process of monitoring, it is essential to involve all those concerned with any service provision. The relationship between the commissioner and the service provider is likely to be relatively straightforward, although the introduction of individual budgets will shift the power away from the Social Services department or primary care trust and into the hands of individuals, their families and carers.

The monitoring process is directly between the individual and the service provider, although the organisation paying for the service will also need to be involved, even if only to receive information on the performance of the provider.

Regular monitoring and feedback should cover the needs of carers, to make sure the provisions are still meeting their needs. This means that the individuals receiving the service and their carers are the most important people to be involved in the monitoring and evaluation process. One of your key roles is to identify any possible barriers to involvement.

You will need to explain the process clearly so that both individuals and their carers understand how the process works and their role in it, but you will also need to work actively to check out any possible barriers and make sure that they are overcome. The types of barriers that can prevent individuals becoming involved in effectively monitoring their own service delivery are:
* using jargon and complex professional language
* making the process complicated and difficult to understand
* having an attitude that intimidates and alienates individuals
* designing a monitoring system using methods that are not the preferred means of communication for the individual.

Individuals and their carers should be involved at every stage of the monitoring, review and evaluation of services. You should use a checklist at the different stages of the process to ensure that you have covered all the potential barriers and found ways to overcome them.

You will also need to ensure that information used in the monitoring process is gathered in such a way that is conforms to the rules of confidentiality and also to the relevant legal and organisational requirements.

Evidence indicator

How does your organisation make sure that individuals and carers are involved in monitoring services? If you cannot find the information easily, ask your manager. Make notes on your findings.

 **Did you know?**

There are over 6 million carers in the UK. Around 400,000 have an assessment of their needs every year.

Direct payments

The traditional method of Social Services departments and the National Health Service has always been to place the individual receiver of services in a position where the care manager has power over the individual receiving the services, because the managers have access to and control over resources. The development of direct payments has changed this situation dramatically.

Under this system, direct payments are made by Social Services departments to the individual concerned, who then becomes responsible for contracting and managing his or her own service provision. This approach is being used by many local authorities throughout the country, and its use is being encouraged and is on the increase. The current rate of increase is running at over 60 per cent each year.

Direct payments are not appropriate for everyone and not all individuals want to take on responsibility for their own services. However, the system has transformed the lives of many people and has enabled them to take control, very often for the first time, of the way in which their lives are structured.

Where direct payments are made, individuals are responsible for arranging their own services. They may choose to contract with providers with whom the Social Services department or primary care trust already has arrangements, but if they wish they can advertise, recruit and employ their own carers and establish a package of care as they wish. A care manager still has a responsibility to liaise with the individual to make sure that he or she is receiving all the care and support needed, and that needs as originally assessed are being met by the provision.

For many individuals in receipt of direct payments for the first time, the prospect of recruiting and managing their own service provision may be liberating and exciting, but also a little daunting. Training is often provided by the Social Services departments who are making the direct payments, covering matters such as advertising, employment law, contracting and managing the quality of provision. After undergoing this training, many individuals feel confident enough to take control of the way in which their needs are met.

Changes

Nothing stays the same, and there is no reason why anyone's circumstances will stay the same. As people's lives change, the kind of service they need also changes. An important aspect of monitoring is to check that the services which were meeting someone's needs six months ago are still doing so.

Many different aspects of people's lives change. Some changes can be predicted, such as the deterioration or improvement of a condition. Others cannot, such as winning the lottery, or a supportive neighbour moving away.

Active knowledge

Make two lists, one of predictable changes that may happen in the lives of the people you support, and one of unpredictable changes. Check the monitoring system in your organisation. Does it take account of changes in circumstances?

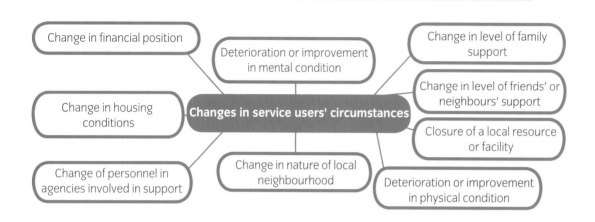

Quality

Some of the quality criteria against which service provision is measured may have been determined centrally within your organisation. Many local authorities have a 'preferred list' of providers who have already met the quality criteria. These providers are then the only ones with whom the local authority will set up a contract.

This may change, especially following the pilots of individual budgets, where individuals can choose to spend the funding in whatever way they choose. The government's response to concerns about the possibility of individuals contracting with poor-quality providers is that empowerment carries risks, and that everyone must be able to take risks in their lives.

Quality criteria are an essential tool for monitoring how well a service is being provided. Of course, all service providers are inspected – each of the four countries of the UK has an inspectorate, and the providers have to be able to provide evidence that they are meeting the national standards. National standards are a minimum requirement in order to be able to operate a service, but most organisations will have additional quality criteria for providers.

The quality criteria are a means of measuring standards. Criteria will vary depending on your organisation and the nature of the service, but indicators are likely to cover such items as:

- staff training and continuing development
- communication with individuals using the service
- quality of the care environment provided
- flexibility of response to change

- presentation of care staff
- quality of response to complaints or feedback from individuals.

Whether this process is undertaken by a central contracts unit, or through the individual monitoring and review process, it is important in helping service providers to continually improve the quality of the service they offer. If individuals are given the opportunity to have individual budgets, quality monitoring will become a very important tool for people in helping them to decide which provider to use.

Active knowledge

How often have you read reviews in consumer magazines, or newspapers, before deciding which product to buy? We do it with cars, computers, washing machines, and even holidays. Have you ever read Ofsted reports before deciding on a school for your child? All of these reports are about judging quality.

Find a review of an item or service in a magazine or newspaper (it doesn't matter if it is for a food mixer, a car or anything else). Read it through and identify the criteria the reporters used in order to rate the product.

Monitoring is important, but it is not complicated. Essentially, it is about two things:

- keeping a close eye on what is happening, so that any changes or problems can be identified before they get out of hand
- gathering information so that it is possible to make a judgement about whether the service is effective.

Test yourself

1 Why is monitoring important?
2 Name two aspects of service provision that should be monitored.
3 Who should be involved in monitoring?
4 What criteria would you use to monitor an outcome-based contract?
5 What criteria would you use to monitor a service-led contract?

HSC 329c Contribute to reviewing the delivery of service for individuals

Review and evaluation are the end result of a process of monitoring. The review is the process of discussion and examination of the information that emerges from the monitoring process. The evaluation is the final judgement made in respect of a care package, as to whether it is continuing to meet the needs of the individual in his or her current circumstances.

The evidence used to make the judgements is the evidence gathered from the process of monitoring and from the discussions held during a review.

Reviews

Reviews should be held as often as necessary, but at least every six months. Sometimes it is necessary to hold a review on a shorter timescale – for example, if an individual's circumstances change significantly, or if the service provision is new and it has been agreed to review it after an initial period of a few weeks.

What happens at a review

Reviews are meetings involving the care manager, the individual and any family or carers, and the service providers. This group should be able to review, on a regular basis, the effectiveness of the service currently being provided, and should make decisions about any changes needed.

The key people to be in control of the review are the individual who uses the service and his or her carer or advocate. They must be directly involved in the process of monitoring. Any changes proposed should come from the individual, or at least he or she must support any changes and clearly understand what is proposed.

Making changes

Individuals may want changes to the provision they currently receive. This can be because of changes in their lives and needs, because they have found out about alternative ways of achieving the outcomes they are aiming for, or because they have discovered information about other types of provision they wish to try. The review meeting is the ideal place to discuss these changes and to explore the ways they can be brought about.

It is important that reviews are conducted in an atmosphere where people can speak freely, and all proposals or questions are treated with respect and valued. Everyone has an important role to play. Ultimately, it is for the individual, carers and family to decide about the service provision that is right for them, but not everything is possible and the views and explanations of the care manager and service providers are essential.

Service providers, particularly, will have useful feedback to contribute about whether the service is being provided effectively and whether other approaches could be tried.

Changes by the funders

The process of change is likely to be easier if changes are a result of requests from the individual. However, there may be occasions when service provision has to be changed because of changes within an organisation, or a reduction in the availability of resources, which could result in a reduction in service. You will need to be clear about the procedures for reporting shortfalls in available resources to the appropriate authority.

Where it is impossible for resources to be made available, this needs to be explained to individuals and they may need to be supported to decide on plans for any alternative provision that can be put in place, or other support that can be used to make up for the shortfall in service provision. This can often be difficult for people to accept and understand, and they may feel that they have been let down by a service on which they have previously relied.

● *People may organise protests if they feel badly let down by changes to service provision caused by budget cuts*

You will need to use all your communication skills to manage such a difficult situation in order to ensure that everyone has plenty of opportunity to express their feelings about any changes in the service, and also that they feel able to ask questions. You should be ready to make suggestions as to how things can move forward in a positive way to maintain and support individuals in their present circumstances.

CASE STUDY: Changes to services

Mr K has been receiving domiciliary care support each morning and evening. He needs assistance to get up and dressed, and also to get into bed. During the day, he manages on his own with regular visits from neighbours and members of his local church.

Following a new tendering process, the service provider for Mr K's care has changed. Whereas the previous provider had always sent the same teams at the same times each day, the new one seems less well organised. The times of visits are variable. On some evenings, the team arrives at 8 pm in order to help Mr K get into bed; on other evenings, the team doesn't arrive until after 11 pm. When Mr K protested on one occasion, he was told that he had to fit in with everyone else.

Mr K has also found that he never knows who will be arriving, as the staff seem to change all the time, and he has to keep explaining his needs and preferences to new carers.

Mr K is very grateful that he receives a service that enables him to stay at home. A review is due shortly, but he is reluctant to criticise anything in case he appears ungrateful.

1 What should happen at the review?
2 Who should take the lead on raising Mr K's concerns?
3 Who should be involved in the review?
4 What needs to happen next?
5 Who needs to take responsibility for resolving the issues?

Recording the review process

As with all parts of the service delivery process, it is essential that any changes agreed at a review are recorded and copies are provided to all the key people. This should include the individual and anyone involved in his or her support, and all the service providers. This will reduce the possibility of any confusion or misunderstanding about the way in which the service should be delivered, or the nature and implications of any changes that have been agreed.

If there is a disagreement at a care review meeting, this is usually resolved by consensus following discussion. Normally changes to service delivery are agreed by all parties concerned, even if the discussion has been lengthy and lively. In the final analysis, the individual must be the person who makes the decisions about the services, but this can only be within the limits of the available budget.

It is the responsibility of the care manager to record review decisions and to briefly record the discussions that took place. This will need to be kept in the individual's records as well as being circulated to all those concerned, within confidentiality agreements and according to organisational requirements.

✔ Keys to good practice: Service planning and delivery

As someone involved in service planning and delivery, there are basic principles you should follow to provide individuals with the best possible service in order to meet their needs.

✓ Remember that the individual is the person who decides which services are wanted. He or she is the person in control of the services received.

✓ Always ensure that you are fully aware of all an individual's circumstances, using observation as well as assessment information.

✓ Make sure that you have the individual's agreement to use any of the information you have acquired.

✓ Ensure that all those who are involved in planning the service delivery have access to any information that is relevant to the service they are providing.

✓ Make sure that proposals made by health and care professionals meet with the agreement of the individual before starting any service delivery.

✓ Make arrangements to regularly monitor provision of the service.

✓ Set up arrangements for regularly reviewing the service, and make sure that the individual is in control of the process.

✓ Keep all the organisations who are involved in the programme of service delivery informed about any changes made.

Did you know?

According to the Royal Commission on Long-Term Care, by **2007** pensioners will outnumber children in the UK.

Records can be fairly short but they do need to include full details of any changes, the person responsible for implementing them, and the timescale for implementation. The form can vary depending on the organisation, but each is likely to identify the decisions that were made, the reasons behind any changes, and the people responsible for ensuring that changes are carried out.

Evaluation

Remember, evaluation is the judgement made following the review process. The steps to evaluation are very simple.

Step 1

Look at the criteria that the review group set out for monitoring.

Step 2

Ask whether those criteria have been met by the service delivery.

Step 3

If so, the review could reasonably make a judgement that the current package of care is effective and can continue.

Step 4

If not, the review should evaluate and decide which aspects of the care package have either been ineffective or do not meet any changed circumstances.

Step 5

Having established what needs to be changed, the review can complete the evaluation by identifying the changes and amendments needed.

Active knowledge

Think about a situation in your workplace where you have undertaken review and evaluation. Did you follow the steps outlined above? If you have not been involved in reviewing and evaluating a service, look at other situations where you evaluate progress or development for individuals. Think about the steps you take to complete the evaluation. You may be surprised at how broadly similar the evaluation process is.

Your role

You should always ensure that the individual and his or her family are aware of your role in the process of monitoring and evaluation. Depending on the way in which your organisation is structured, you may have a quite extensive role in relation to the monitoring and evaluation of service provision, and may deal with some of the broader, more strategic aspects of commissioning and contracting within your organisation.

Alternatively, you may have a role limited to the particular individuals with whom you work, where your information and feedback that could influence wider decisions is provided to your managers.

It is important that everyone is clear about the extent of your role so as to avoid raising unrealistic expectations. For example, an individual who provides feedback saying 'That day centre was hopeless – I hope you can get it closed down' will need to be advised of the steps you can take in informing the necessary inspection and quality monitoring teams within your organisation about any possible poor performance of a particular contractor, but that your ability to single-handedly close down a poorly performing facility is somewhat limited!

Evidence indicator

Write a report on a review you have been involved in. Remember to include all the important information:

- who was present
- the background and circumstances
- the services currently provided
- whether they are meeting current needs
- if not, why not
- what actions are to result from the review
- who is responsible for each action
- the time frame for each agreed action
- the date of the next review.

If you have never been involved in a review, write an imaginary one. You could make up a case or use someone you know, someone you work with, or someone from your favourite TV programme. Put the report in your portfolio.

Dealing with poor quality provision

Where it becomes evident from an evaluation that a contractor or service provider is not meeting expected standards or is offering a poor quality service, this information should be fed back to the relevant inspection body. Your organisation is likely to have procedures in place to ensure that this happens and you should check what they are and make sure that the necessary information is passed on accurately, clearly and without delay. If you have concerns about the quality of the service being provided you should make sure that you pass on:

- the name of the service provider
- the date and length of the contract

- the service they were contracted to provide
- the way in which your evaluation has identified a problem with their performance
- the circumstances under which they were delivering a service to the individual concerned
- your contact details for a further discussion
- a file reference where records of the review and evaluation may be obtained.

This is a general list only, and each organisation is likely to have its own provisions in place.

If planning, monitoring and reviewing services is carried out effectively, it not only ensures that vulnerable individuals are receiving services that meet their needs, but it also protects them from poor quality providers. Additionally, the process provides useful data for planning future services and helps decision makers at both local and national levels to identify the best ways of meeting the needs of individuals, their carers and families.

Test yourself

1 What is the difference between review and evaluation?
2 Why is it important to involve everyone in the review?
3 What information needs to be recorded from a review?
4 What types of changes could be considered at a review?

HSC 329 UNIT TEST

1 Who controls the process of planning, monitoring and reviewing service delivery now? Who will do so in the future?
2 What are the current changes designed to do?
3 Identify one advantage and one disadvantage of individual budgets.
4 Identify one advantage and one disadvantage of direct payments.
5 What steps can you take to make sure that individuals are able to participate in the process of planning, monitoring and reviewing services?

Provide frameworks to help individuals to manage challenging behaviour

Behaviour that presents challenges because it is aggressive, abusive or destructive is one of the most difficult areas of work in social care. This unit deals with behaviour that can be controlled or changed with help and support. It does not deal with challenging behaviour resulting from a physical or psychological condition or illness and which cannot be controlled, changed or moderated by the individual (although this is what is more usually understood by the term).

The key to supporting individuals to manage challenging behaviour is to provide understanding and insight in order to offer people ways to cope with their own behaviour. For many individuals and their families, this can be a life-changing opportunity. In order to do this effectively, you will need to understand some of the reasons why people behave in these ways, some of the triggers that can bring about challenging behaviour, and some of the ways in which people can choose to make changes to their own behaviour.

What you need to learn

- Challenging behaviour in context
- Why challenging behaviour happens
- Causes of challenging behaviour
- Facing up to consequences
- Theories on managing behaviour
- Deciding to manage challenging behaviour
- Dealing with challenging behaviour
- The impact on you
- Recording incidents
- Review and evaluation

HSC 337a Support individuals to identify the reasons and causes for, and the consequences of, their behaviour

How many times have you behaved in a way you were unhappy with and thought 'Why did I do that?' You may have snapped or shouted at a child or partner, or been totally unreasonable in your reaction to something quite minor. It happens to everyone sometimes. For most people, behaving in an unpleasant or aggressive way is the exception – we don't like ourselves very much for having done it, but it is a rare occurrence. There are some individuals, however, whose behaviour presents a challenge, both for themselves and for everyone else, on a regular basis.

Active knowledge

Think about a time when you know you behaved in an unacceptable way. Make some notes about what you did, how you felt at the time and how you felt afterwards. Particularly, try to remember whether you felt as if you were out of control. Can you think of any reason why you might have behaved like that?

Challenging behaviour in context

Regardless of the job you do, or the setting you work in, you are likely to come across challenging behaviour from the individuals you support. This may be directed at you, at the family or carers of the individual, or it may be directed at other individuals in the same care setting.

This unit does not deal with the type of challenging behaviour that results from a profound learning disability, a severe mental illness or a significant brain injury. People in these situations need to be treated with specialist skills and approaches, and some of the ones you learn in this unit will be relevant, but the basis for the behaviour is different, and other types of intervention such as medication and different therapies may also be appropriate.

You may come across challenging behaviour of a more general kind in people of all ages – being aggressive and difficult is not confined to one age group! You may experience behaviour that presents you with a challenge in a whole range of individuals, with a whole range of different support needs.

There may be a few people who enjoy being angry and behaving in an unacceptable way. However, most people want to be liked and accepted by others and do not want to continue behaving in a way that alienates and upsets other people. You can offer support and help so that individuals can understand why they are behaving as they are, and help them to learn some ways of dealing with it.

Essentially, you need to know two things:
- the likely reasons for the behaviour
- how to support someone to cope with it.

Defining challenging behaviour

There are various definitions of challenging behaviour. Most relate either to behaviour resulting from profound learning disability or mental health problems, or to challenging behaviour in the classroom. For our purposes we can define challenging behaviour as:

● *Most people want to be liked and accepted by others*

> Behaviour that places the individual or others in physical danger or a state of fear, results in damage to the immediate environment, or causes a period of disruption.

This could mean:
- aggressive or violent behaviour
- verbal aggression
- bullying
- shouting and using foul or abusive language
- damaging property or the immediate surroundings
- being disruptive, either through being noisy or by refusing to co-operate with others
- unacceptable sexual behaviour such as masturbating in front of others or showing pornography (there is a fine line between unacceptable sexual behaviour and sexual abuse)
- threats or intimidation
- refusing to wash or change clothes (if living in a communal setting).

These are examples. You may come across other types of behaviour that present a challenge, depending on the setting in which you work.

Refusing to wash or change clothes is not such a problem for someone who lives alone. It is not to be recommended, and will result in skin infections, but an individual can make an informed choice to live in that way. The matter is different if the person lives in a residential or supported living environment, where the impact of the behaviour will very soon be noticed by others and it will make the environment unpleasant in a fairly short space of time. This is behaviour that must be addressed.

Similarly, the behaviour of someone who is bullying and aggressive may not present quite as much of a challenge if he or she lives alone, but will need to be addressed if a group of other vulnerable adults is involved.

CASE STUDY: Encountering challenging behaviour

J lives in a run-down property in an area that has recently become more prosperous. He has lived alone since his mother died about ten years ago. He is very abusive towards anyone who approaches the house, and regularly shouts and swears at his neighbours for no obvious reason.

The property is in need of repair and the garden is badly neglected and overgrown. His behaviour is becoming increasingly aggressive and he has begun to come out of his house to shout at people parking in the street or walking past.

J has accepted some support and has a support worker. The same worker has been supporting J for about three years. She is used to his aggressive behaviour and is not concerned by it. She says: 'He's alright underneath it all. He's just angry at the world. I don't think he'll hurt anyone.'

When she was off sick recently, a new worker was sent. J was very angry and was so aggressive that the worker refused to stay, and reported the incident to her manager with a strong recommendation that help and support be provided for J to manage his behaviour.

1 Do you think that the worker who has known J for a long time was right not to worry about his behaviour?
2 What should happen now that the new worker has requested help?
3 What are the risks to J if he does not get help?
4 What are the risks for other people?
5 Who is responsible for getting help for J?

Stereotyping

When identifying challenging behaviour, you need to be clear that it is behaviour that is causing challenges, disruption and risk, and not behaviour that arises from being excluded or discriminated against. Always remember that people's behaviour can be a response to discrimination.

This is noticed most commonly in schools, where studies have noted that the behaviour of black young people can often be misinterpreted as challenging, when it is really the result of the fact that the curriculum does not provide culturally relevant teaching. This concern has been noted by many researchers including Ofsted, the schools inspectorate.

Always check, when you are dealing with behaviour that seems to present a challenge, that this is not because of your own prejudices and beliefs, and that you are not simply misinterpreting behaviour as challenging because it does not conform with your own views about how people should behave. Different behaviour can be culturally appropriate and acceptable within the peer group and culture in which people live.

Remember

As a professional in social care, your practice should always be guided by the Codes of Practice of the General Social Care Council, Scottish Social Services Council, Northern Ireland Social Care Council or the Care Council for Wales, depending on where you work. Each of these includes sections about respecting people as individuals as well as sections about respecting people's rights, but at the same time making sure that their behaviour is not a risk to themselves or others.

Why challenging behaviour happens

All of us become angry and distressed at some time; the causes are varied and the effects differ from individual to individual. An event that will distress one person will not concern another; a situation that can reduce one person to sobs or a temper tantrum will simply be shrugged off by someone else.

Do not confuse the **causes** of someone's distress with the **reasons** for distress. Causes can be a great many external factors, but reasons are a much deeper, psychological influence that affect the way different people respond in different circumstances.

All of us have a broadly similar process of emotional development, but as each person is an individual who has grown and developed in different circumstances, it is inevitable that the results will be different for each person. Psychologists have established, however, that there are some basic categories of behaviour that can be broadly understood and can explain some of the reasons why people behave in the way they do.

Bear in mind that the theories described below are for general application only. When working with individuals, make sure you are looking at behaviour in relation to the particular background of the person concerned, and that is it not the result of discrimination or stereotyping. Be sure you have consulted all relevant records and information about an individual. If you are clear that this behaviour is definitely a result of individual development, the theories about the reasons behind it can be useful in providing you with an overview.

Psychological theories

There is a range of psychological theories about why people behave in unacceptable and challenging ways. There has always been much debate about whether our emotional responses are inborn (or genetic) – that is, whether we have them by nature – or whether we learn them from our environment. This is known as the 'nature versus nurture' debate. The most likely explanation is that they are a combination of the two.

Most psychologists agree that there is an inborn response, which is evidenced through work with very young babies, examining their responses to sounds, pain or loss of support. As we grow and develop we learn to respond to different circumstances in different ways.

It is important to recognise that although these may be the basic stimuli to which humans respond, what you have to deal with when working in care is *how* humans respond, in other words what people do in response to anger and other emotions.

No one is expecting you to be a psychologist or therapist, but if you are to work effectively to support people in addressing their challenging behaviour, you will need to have some understanding of why people behave in the way they do. There are hundreds of theories about human behaviour, and you only need an overview of the broad categories under which most of the theories fall.

● At birth, babies show certain inborn responses to different experiences

Behaviourism

The theories of psychologists such as Ivan Pavlov and B.F. Skinner are based on the belief that human behaviour is modified in response to the consequences that result from it. So, if you drive your car past the speed camera at 90 mph, you will receive a fine and points on your driving licence, and you won't do it again!

This theory suggests that challenging behaviour develops because individuals have in the past been 'rewarded' for this type of behaviour. For example, if a child is always given what he or she wants after a tantrum of kicking and screaming, that child grows up learning that such behaviour is the way to get results.

● Behaviourist theories suggest that we learn to repeat behaviour that gets results

Developed by people such as Jean Piaget and Albert Bandura, this theory is about how individuals develop behaviour as a result of what they know and understand about the world. All of people's assumptions, attitudes and beliefs have an effect on how they behave.

An individual who has grown up in circumstances where violent and aggressive behaviour are seen as normal will understand that this is the way adults relate to the world. In a family where people behave in this way during a disagreement, or following a disappointment, children quickly assimilate this behaviour and it becomes part of their personality. Similarly, children who have been smacked when they are 'naughty' have been shown that the way to get people to do what you want, or to stop them from doing something you don't like – especially if you are bigger and more powerful than they are – is to hit them!

Humanism

Psychologists such as Carl Rogers and Abraham Maslow focus on feelings and emotions, and view challenging behaviour as the result of low self-esteem or difficulties in dealing with emotions. Humanists would argue that children who grow up not feeling valued, or having missed out on some of the basic building blocks of emotional relationships, or not having been able to develop a strong sense of who they are, will be unable to relate well to others when they are adults. This can result from parents being unable to put their child's needs ahead of their own, and so not providing the basic security children need. This is usually because they have not been adequately parented themselves.

Psychodynamics

Psychologists such as Sigmund Freud would argue that our unconscious and subconscious control our behaviour, and that we would all like to behave in a challenging way, but that psychological controls mean we conform to the norms and expectations of society. If people present challenging behaviour, this is a failure of part of their control mechanism, caused by a failed key relationship, or a failure to properly progress through all the stages of development. Freudian psychologists would also suggest that a traumatic event, such as abuse, may be the reason for the behaviour controls not being in place.

Systems theory

This approach views the family as a 'system' with rules and structures for how people relate to each other, how they express views and how they behave. As we grow into adults, we learn other 'systems' and ways of behaving. This is particularly relevant when people are living in a community, such as residential care, which also operates as a system, and all the parts of the system influence behaviour. This approach would look at all the aspects of the environment in which the individual lives, and assess the impact on behaviour.

Interactionism

Interactionists link the two sides of the nature–nurture debate and take the view that people do have particular types of personality, but that circumstances can make people with the same personality trait react in different ways. According to this theory, people tend to be one of a range of personality types including:

- extrovert or introvert
- agreeable or disagreeable
- emotionally stable or emotionally unstable
- conscientious or careless
- open to experience or closed to experience.

Circumstances can change people's normal personalities, however. For example, someone who is normally agreeable may become quite aggressive if threatened.

Early experiences

Most of these theories have one thing in common: they are about the experiences that people have early in their lives. There is little doubt that much of the way we behave is influenced by our upbringing, not only the emotional relationships with parents, but also the culture, environment and other relationships we experienced.

The formative periods in people's lives have a major impact on how they react as adults when they are faced with difficulties, disappointments and setbacks. Being able to cope with adversity is called **resilience**, and one of the key aims for those who work with young children is to support them to develop resilience. A child who is resilient will be better able to cope with uncertainty and difficult or traumatic experiences later in life. In order for children to develop resilience, they need to have experienced its three key building blocks:

- a secure base where a child feels a sense of security and belonging
- strong self-esteem
- a feeling of 'mastery' and control.

- *Young children need to experience the key building blocks of security, self-esteem and mastery*

Active knowledge

Think about someone you could describe as resilient. Choose someone who always seems to bounce back, no matter what life throws at him or her. Try to think about what makes the person like that. If it is someone you know well, you may already know about the sort of childhood he or she had. Otherwise, try to ask the person about his or her childhood. Note down the factors that have made him or her resilient.

Your role

You are not a therapist or a psychologist, so there is no need for you to try to explore the deep-seated reasons for someone's behaviour. You need to have a general understanding of the ways in which such behaviour can develop, but it is not your role to deal with the emotional history of the individuals you support. However, what you are in a position to do is to support people to look at the causes of their challenging behaviour and help them to find ways to deal with it.

Causes of challenging behaviour

Having looked at some of the reasons why people behave in a challenging way, we need to look at some of the immediate causes – the triggers for the behaviour.

Remember

Challenging behaviour is behaviour that places the individual or others in physical danger or a state of fear, results in damage to the immediate environment, or causes a period of disruption.

Naturally, every person is different, and will react to situations differently. Circumstances that will trigger challenging behaviour in one person will not do so in another, so it is important that you look at the causes for each individual.

The most effective way to approach this is likely to be in a one-to-one session, so that the person feels comfortable and able to discuss this difficult area with you. However, sometimes conversations develop spontaneously and you have to use the opportunity, even if it happens while you are helping someone to take a bath, or visiting the supermarket. The discussion will be just as useful – sometimes even more so, because it will have started naturally and the individual is ready to talk. You will need to use all your communication skills, including active listening, to make sure that the individual feels supported, respected and valued.

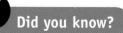
Did you know?

About 20 per cent of children and 15 per cent of adults with a learning disability show some form of challenging behaviour.

How to support people in identifying causes

It is helpful if you can encourage individuals to look at their behaviour by working with them to look at the most recent periods of challenging behaviour and to examine the events that led up to such incidents. Try to look at three or four incidents at least, and see whether a pattern is emerging.

Ideally, sit down with the person to make a chart, showing the behaviour, the incident, what happened immediately before it and the circumstances. An example is shown below.

Pete's behaviour chart

When	Behaviour	Who	Where	What	Mood prior
Saturday morning	Verbal abuse, very angry, kicked over coffee table	Charlie, Marie, Mark	Main lounge	Asked Mark to borrow jacket – Mark refused	Happy – looking forward to night out
Thursday evening	Verbal abuse, pushed Charlie against wall	Charlie, Marie, Dev	Kitchen	Wanted ice cream for pudding, none left – it was Charlie's turn to shop	Fed up – a boring day at day centre
Tuesday morning	Verbal abuse, angry, smashed dressing table mirror	Alone	Bedroom	Phone call from ex-girlfriend – does not want to get back together	Grumpy first thing in morning

Use the process of drawing up the table as a time to talk about what led to the incidents, and then try to find any common factors or patterns in the finished table. Patterns can be based on:

- people present
- places
- moods
- triggers
- types of behaviour
- the time of day.

With the table above, you could suggest that Pete look at the triggers. In each case it has been a disappointment – some apparently minor, some quite significant. Each has provoked similar behaviour – verbal aggression and damage to the immediate environment. In one incident there was a threat of physical violence.

In Pete's case it does not look as if it is a particular person who triggers his behaviour, nor does it seem to be a particular mood or a place. Of course, this table only summarises three occasions. In reality, you will probably need to look at quite a few more before you can see patterns emerging.

Evidence indicator

Ideally, this exercise should be done with an individual you work with who is presenting challenging behaviour. However, if this is not possible, you can work with a friend or colleague and use examples of any type of behaviour – it doesn't matter if it is happy, sad, scared or angry.

Produce a table like the one shown on page 161, using at least six incidents. Complete all of the sections and then look for patterns.

Make notes about the patterns and then try to identify the possible causes or triggers. Make notes, with explanations. If you have done this with an individual you are supporting, use what you have learned about human behaviour to make some notes on what you think the underlying reasons for the behaviour may be. Discuss your ideas with your assessor.

Facing up to consequences

One of the difficult tasks you can face when dealing with challenging behaviour is making sure that the person understands there are consequences to what he or she does. For example, if someone is living in a residential setting with other people, and those people are being placed at risk from violent or aggressive behaviour, then ultimately it may be that the person is not able to remain there. Similarly, in a setting such as a supported living environment, someone who is aggressive and disruptive may be asked to leave.

There are inevitably tensions when people share living space – this is true of families, so people without the close bonds of a family are bound to have issues that need to be resolved when they live together. However, there is a difference between everyday tensions and putting people at risk, and if challenging behaviour is placing other vulnerable people at serious risk it cannot be allowed to continue.

Sometimes it is hard to decide between the rights of an individual and your responsibilities to others you support, but the question of risk to others is always the decider.

Depending on the circumstances in which people are living, the consequences of their behaviour may involve the loss of friends, or a partner, parent, or child. It could bring disputes with neighbours or even criminal proceedings.

Challenging behaviour can also have devastating effects on people close to the person involved, and you will need to help them to look at, and face up to, the effects of their behaviour on people they care about. It is not easy to face the fact that your behaviour frightens your children or worries your partner, but we all need to be able to take responsibility for what we do, and make our own choices about how to move forward. The choice may be to change nothing, but if the choice is made with full awareness of the possible consequences, individuals have the right to make it.

● *People need information about the likely consequences of their choices*

Current thinking about the empowerment of individuals, and giving people the right to take risks and make choices, is reflected in the 2005 Green Paper 'Independence, Well-being and Choice' in relation to services for older people, and the White Paper about services across health and social care, 'Our Health, Our Care, Our Say', 2006. This applies as much to choosing to behave in a way that can bring negative consequences as it does to choosing the service provider for personal care.

Your role is to make sure that individuals are aware of what could happen as a result of their behaviour. Sometimes becoming aware of consequences can be a motivator for dealing with behaviour; if people realise that they are at risk of losing their home or people they care about, they may decide to do something about their behaviour.

However, if individuals are living independently, and the only ones at risk from their behaviour are themselves (perhaps because they may be arrested as a result of their behaviour, or they may lose friends or family as a result) the situation is different. You have a responsibility to make sure that they understand what could happen as a result of the way they are behaving, but if they make an informed choice to continue, there is nothing you can do to force them to change.

Facing consequences can also be used positively as part of a strategy to help people address their behaviour. This is called a **restorative** approach, and we will look at it more closely in the next part of this unit.

Other help

Your role is to support individuals. However, some individuals will need more specialist help than you can give in order to understand their behaviour. You will need to discuss with them the possibility of seeking further help, through either their GP or social worker. If a specialist does become involved in providing additional help, it is important that you seek the agreement of the individual to working closely with that specialist and sharing information in the interest of promoting an integrated approach that will bring the maximum possible benefit.

Test yourself

1   Name three different approaches to understanding challenging behaviour.
2   What is the basis for most psychological theories?
3   What is the difference between *reasons for* and *causes of* challenging behaviour?
4   Why is it important for people to understand the consequences of their behaviour?
5   What are the factors that have to be balanced when dealing with the effects and consequences of challenging behaviour?

HSC 337b Work with individuals to agree ways to manage their behaviour

The key to successfully supporting people in managing behaviour is that you work *with* them, supporting people to reach their own decisions, and don't attempt to impose your own solutions. It is not necessary that you agree with the actions people choose to take, as long as they have all the information they need in order to decide what they want to do.

Theories on managing behaviour

In the previous element, you looked at an overview of some of the main areas of psychological theory in relation to the development of challenging behaviour. Each of the schools of thought takes a slightly different approach to managing challenging behaviour.

Behaviourism

The approach of behaviourist psychologists is to offer rewards for acceptable behaviour and sanctions for unacceptable behaviour. This approach is often used in schools, where stars or points are awarded, and there is public recognition of acceptable behaviour.

● *In school, young children are often rewarded for good work and behaviour with a star system*

Approaches based on this theory can work with some adults, although star charts would not be appropriate. A simple example would be someone deciding to stop smoking, and planning to save the money formerly spent on cigarettes in order to buy a treat each week. This offers a reward – positive reinforcement – for not smoking. The sanction for starting to smoke again would be the loss of the weekly treats.

A common approach in social care is that a 'contract' is agreed with an individual which clearly sets out what is acceptable and what is not, and states the 'sanctions' (i.e. the consequences) that will follow any unacceptable behaviour.

Active knowledge

Think of a time when you have used the behaviourist approach in your own life. It may have been something for yourself such as stopping smoking, or losing weight. Perhaps you used it with your children. Make notes about the circumstances, why you used the method and whether it was effective.

Cognitivism

Because this theory focuses on the attitudes and beliefs behind behaviours, the approach to managing challenging behaviour is to provide people with the tools they need to improve the way they respond to 'triggers'. This includes supporting people to develop problem-solving skills, self-control, and improved ways to reduce and cope with stress.

Humanism

This approach works on raising people's self-esteem and their ability to deal with feelings and emotions. It views the ability to form relationships as a matter of key importance in enabling individuals to manage their own behaviour.

Active knowledge

Think about a time when you felt really low and did not like yourself very much. Then someone was supportive and said or did something to make you feel better about yourself. How much did it help the way you were feeling and behaving?

Psychodynamics

The psychodynamic approach supports the use of therapy, counselling and group work to support people to resolve issues rooted in earlier experiences. This approach is often used with people who have experienced abuse in their past. Your role is not to be a therapist or a counsellor, and these types of interventions require specialist training, but you need to be aware that this may be appropriate for some of the people you support, and know how to access this type of specialist help through referral to either a social worker or GP.

Systems theory

Systems theory is based on the view that individuals' responses to the world are based on the 'system' of their living environment. As a result, behaviour can become a vicious circle, because that is the only system in which people are able to function. If someone is part of a system in which the response to what is perceived as aggression from others is to be even more aggressive in return, the vicious circle of aggression leading to more aggression is set up. The approach here is to try to break the circle of behaviour, by replacing the negative responses with more positive alternatives – thus creating a 'virtuous circle'.

For example, an individual could be supported to view the behaviour of another parent complaining about an incident between their respective children as not aggressive but 'strongly protective'. This shift in how behaviour is perceived will lead to a change in response.

Think of an occasion when you have misinterpreted someone's behaviour – perhaps you thought someone was being aggressive or confrontational, but when it was explained to you that he or she was actually very frightened, you felt differently and this changed your response. This applies not only to aggression – think of at least one other type of behaviour you have misinterpreted and how your response changed when you understood it differently.

Interactionist theory

Interactionist approaches work on the basis that there is a genetic pre-disposition towards certain behaviour – a person's 'nature' – but that this is also influenced by the environment and circumstances people are in – or 'nurture'. Managing challenging behaviour using this approach is about recognising and changing the circumstances, or the response to the circumstances, thus reducing the factors that can trigger challenging behaviour, and allowing the positive personality traits to be more in evidence.

Restorative approach

Much of the research currently being carried out in restorative work is in the area of youth (and adult) justice. However, the approach can also be used in many other contexts. The basic principles underpinning restorative approaches are as follows.

1 Positive relationships are at the heart of success.
2 Those who have caused harm should have the opportunity to face those they have harmed.
3 Those who have been harmed should have a chance to be heard and have a say in how the harm should be repaired.
4 Those who have done harm should have the chance to make amends.

The restorative approach manages challenging behaviour by working to restore damaged relationships, viewing the victim's needs as central to the process, looking for ways to make amends and, most importantly, taking account of the needs, views and feelings of all those affected by the behaviour.

If we return to the behaviour chart for Pete on page 161 and look at the ice cream incident, a restorative approach would support Pete in listening to Charlie explaining how he felt when Pete was so angry with him. The harm done needs to be looked at; in this case, the impact on Charlie needs to be explored. Charlie should be able to suggest what Pete needs to do to make amends – perhaps in this case he will feel that an apology is enough, or perhaps Pete will have to take Charlie's next turn at shopping – and face the complaints if he forgets anything!

This approach has the advantage of making Pete look at the consequences of what he did, but also makes it less likely that Charlie will continue to feel aggrieved. Giving Pete the chance to make amends is likely to boost his self-esteem and make him feel more positive about himself.

Deciding to manage challenging behaviour

The key to any work you do to support people is that they have made the decision to try to manage their behaviour. There are some situations where specialists may work with people when behaviour changes are not entirely voluntary, for example working in the prison service or in some areas of mental health, but this is not the case in the work you do.

If an individual has not decided to change the way he or she behaves, you should not begin work on the process. In that situation, you must work on supporting people to make the decision to change.

Planning for change

As with any programme of change, it is important that people set goals and targets and some means of checking when they have reached them. One of your key roles is to support this process by helping people to identify the behaviours they want to change and the way they want to achieve this.

As with other programmes, try to ensure that people do not set themselves unachievable goals. Failing will de-motivate someone, but a small step achieved will make him or her more determined to go on to the next step.

CASE STUDY: Drawing up a plan

Jayne is 47 and has a history of depression, but has been well for the past six years. She lives in a hostel with four other people, all of whom have had mental health problems in the past, but are now well and coping without medication.

Jayne is keen to find a permanent job, but has left every job she has started because as soon as someone tries to explain anything to her, or makes suggestions about what she can do to improve her work, she takes it as criticism. She becomes abusive and storms out, blaming the employer.

She is far less likely to behave in this way in the hostel. She can be quick to take offence, but not in any way that causes serious difficulties.

Following some hard work with Nadeem, the support worker for the hostel, Jayne has been helped to understand that it is her responses that have caused the problems, not anything done by her employers. Jayne has asked Nadeem to help her work out a way to manage her behaviour so that she will be able to find, and keep, a job.

Nadeem begins by supporting Jayne to decide on her overall goal and her targets. They then work on a plan for reaching each of the targets. The final plan is shown on the next page.

Goal: Keep a job

	How	With whom	When	Result
Target 1 Make a plan	Go through everything; write everything down	Nadeem	By end of week	Plan on a spreadsheet
Target 2 Work out the triggers	List all the incidents; do an identification check	Nadeem	By end of June	List of triggers
Target 3 Find boundaries	Look at people at work; talk to mates who are working	Mates in hostel; Nadeem	By end of July	Know what I have to avoid
Target 4 Accept comments from mates	Ask mates in hostel to suggest ways I can improve	Everyone in hostel	By end of August	Don't get angry
Target 5 Accept comments from day-centre staff	Day-centre staff to offer helpful criticisms	Day-centre staff	By end of September	Can follow up suggestions and find them helpful

Boundaries

Boundaries are limits to the behaviour that is acceptable in any situation. For example, it might be acceptable to make an angry comment to the ticket collector at the station because the train has been cancelled yet again, but it is beyond the boundaries to punch him because you are angry. It is acceptable to say that you don't like a particular meal that has been served and to ask for something else, but it is beyond the limits to throw the meal at the wall and shout about 'not eating this muck'.

Some people who present challenging behaviour do so because they have problems knowing, or accepting, boundaries for their behaviour. Most of us learn and conform to boundaries early in life, and each time we move into a new situation, we learn and conform to the boundaries there. Supporting people to recognise and conform to boundaries is a key part of enabling them to manage their own behaviour. You can have a useful role in helping people to find out the

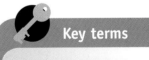

Key terms

Boundary: The limit that defines what is acceptable in a situation.

difference between where they think the boundaries are and where everyone else thinks they are.

This does not have to be a complex task; some straightforward questions about where the individual sees boundaries can start things off. If there are massive differences, or a failure to even recognise boundaries, it can be a useful exercise to provide some visual clues. Clips from films or TV soaps can be helpful in showing people the type of behaviour that is acceptable and that which is beyond the limit. Ultimately, however, the decision to conform to boundaries and limits belongs to the individual – you can support and encourage, but not impose.

● *Most of us learn about boundaries to behaviour early in life, within the family and in the wider world*

Triggers

In the previous element, you looked at ways to identify any factors that seem to trigger challenging behaviour. If obvious triggers have emerged, this is valuable information in the process of managing behaviour because individuals can plan to avoid specific triggers.

Remember

Triggers are the immediate causes of behaviour, and may be something that seems quite insignificant at first sight. **Reasons** are the deeper, psychological influences that affect people.

People can exhibit challenging behaviour as the result of a wide range of causes, and these can be the trigger for an underlying emotional response. Some common causes of distress can be identified and it is helpful for you to be aware of commonly occurring triggers, such as:

- receiving bad or worrying news
- problems with an important relationship
- stress through an overload of work or family pressures
- serious problems such as money issues, problems at work, problems with the family
- the behaviour of others towards them
- something heard, seen or read in the media
- an environment that is perceived as frustrating or restricting
- an environment that is perceived as irritating, such as a noisy or cramped one
- feeling deprived of information and/or fearful
- anxiety about a forthcoming event
- inability to achieve objectives that have been set.

Obviously there are many other triggers that you may come across depending on the individuals you support. Regardless of the type of triggers that emerge from your identification work with an individual, the key task is to look at ways in which they can be avoided or their impact can be reduced.

For example, if someone identifies that contact with a particular person always makes him or her feel angry, look at ways of minimising contacts with that person. Alternatively, use the systems theory approach and replace the 'vicious circle' with a 'virtuous circle' by supporting the individual to regard the annoying behaviour in a different way, thus changing his or her response – perhaps by seeing someone as sad and needing sympathy rather than as being irritating. The key is to either avoid the trigger or change it into something that is no longer a trigger.

Evidence indicator

Identify three potential triggers for challenging behaviour which relate to your own work setting. Make notes on them and how they could be dealt with.

Dealing with challenging behaviour

This unit is about supporting people to manage their own challenging behaviour, but it is important that you have the ability to deal with potentially violent or aggressive behaviour and to defuse a difficult situation.

You need to be able to judge when such a situation is developing and when individuals are starting to show behaviour that may place themselves or others at risk. If you intervene in the early stages, it is often easier to calm a situation.

Physical effects of strong emotions

Definite and measurable physical effects are caused by strong emotional responses. It is useful to be aware of these physical effects of emotion as they can often be an early indicator of a potentially dangerous situation. The physical effects of strong emotion can be:
- pupils dilate, eyes open wider than usual, and the eyes protrude
- the speed and strength of the heart beat is increased
- blood pressure is increased and blood is forced towards the surface of the body – this is clearly noticeable in flushing of the face and neck
- hair can stand up, causing goose pimples
- breathing patterns will change, to be either faster or slower
- lung function alters to allow up to 25 per cent more oxygen to be absorbed
- more sweat is produced – this can often be identified as a 'cold sweat'
- the salivary glands are inhibited – the mouth feels dry

- the digestive system is affected – the gastric fluids are reduced and blood is withdrawn from the digestive organs
- there is an increase in adrenalin, which reinforces all these effects and promotes blood clotting.

These reactions are thought to be a basic human response to a situation perceived as threatening, in which the body physically prepares to fight or run away.

- The body's natural reaction to danger or stress is to prepare to either fight, or run away

There are other noticeable effects in people who are in a highly emotional state. They will often have what appears to be increased energy – they don't speak, they shout; they don't sit or stand still, they run or walk about, slam doors and possibly throw things around.

Recognising the signs

When you have a close working knowledge of an individual's behaviour over a period of time, it becomes easier to identify when he or she is becoming angry or distressed. You will find that you have become attuned to a person's behaviour and can recognise the small signs that indicate a change in mood.

However, you will not always be in a situation of knowing the individual, or you may be dealing with challenging behaviour from a carer or even a work colleague. In these cases there are some general indications that an individual is becoming angry or distressed which you can use in order to take immediate action. You are most likely to notice:

- changes in voice – it may be raised or at a higher pitch than usual
- changes in facial expression – this could be scowling, crying, snarling
- changes in eyes – pupils could be dilated and eyes open wider

- body language demonstrating agitation, or an aggressive stance, leaning forwards with fists clenched
- reddened face and neck
- excessive sweating
- breathing patterns may change and become faster than normal.

Overall, you are likely to notice a significant change in normal behaviour when someone is becoming distressed. Someone who is normally talkative may become quiet, and someone who is normally quiet may start to shout or talk very quickly. It may be that someone who is normally lively sits still and becomes rigid, or someone who is normally relaxed starts to walk around waving his or her arms. You need to be aware of even subtle changes in normal behaviour as they too can indicate escalating emotional responses.

A risk to themselves

Anger is not always directed at others; it can be turned inwards. You may be faced with a situation where distressed, hurt and angry individuals make it clear to you that they intend to harm themselves. You have a responsibility to take immediate action in order to protect the individual in such a case. It is essential that you advise the individual that you will have to take steps in order to protect him or her and prevent any harm.

Although you are required to treat information confidentially, a threat of self-harm is a case where you must break confidentiality in order to obtain immediate assistance for the individual.

It is never acceptable for you to comply with a request to assist an individual in harming himself or herself, or for you to allow people to deliberately harm themselves. If you are faced with such a request you must immediately report it to your manager and arrange for emergency assistance to assess the risk to the individual. An assessment of risk of self-harm needs to be a specialist one in the first instance – you must not make a judgement about the likelihood of someone self-harming. You may be able to contribute valuable information to support the assessment process, but the decision is in the hands of mental health specialists: community psychiatric nurses, approved social workers, psychiatrists or specialist GPs.

Responding to aggressive behaviour

Your organisation will have a policy and procedures about responding to aggressive behaviour. You must act in line with the policies and procedures of your organisation; they will vary in detail, but are likely to include most of the following points.

✔ Keys to good practice: Dealing with aggressive behaviour

✓ Your objective is to calm and de-escalate the situation. First, make sure that any triggers are removed, or that the individual is removed from the trigger.

✓ Provide privacy if possible – if the individual is in a public space, try to move to somewhere private; an audience can often make people feel threatened and more aggressive. If you are alone, simply instruct people to leave. If a colleague is available, ask him or her to move people who do not need to be there.

✓ Do not become aggressive yourself. Try to appear calm (even if you're not!).

✓ Make sure that you are between the individual and the exit; move if necessary.

✓ Speak in a calm voice, clearly and without shouting.

✓ Do not make prolonged eye contact, as this can be perceived as a challenge.

✓ Keep a relaxed posture – sit if possible, or if not, stand in a relaxed way, not directly facing the person.

✓ Make sure that the person has his or her own space.

✓ It is essential that you appear to be in control – remember that the individual needs someone to be in control because he or she is not, and that feels frightening.

✓ Give clear, short instructions, calmly and without raising your voice.

✓ Do not respond to arguments or verbal abuse, but encourage communication – ask individuals to tell you why they are angry, and show that you have understood.

De-escalating requires that you provide a non-challenging situation, so do not threaten or issue an ultimatum – once you have done so, you have created a situation where someone must win and someone must lose, which can only escalate.

Calm, clear communication, a demonstration of understanding and recognition of the causes of the anger or distress are the key to de-escalating the situation.

Physical intervention

Physical intervention should only be used when there is no alternative and all other approaches have been tried. Any physical interventions should be recorded in an incident book (as always, with numbered pages).

You should not attempt to physically intervene in a violent situation unless you have been specially trained. If you feel that such training would be useful for you, raise the issue with your manager.

The 'Valuing People' strategy included guidelines in July 2002 for using physical intervention, jointly issued by the Department of Health and Department for Education and Skills under both the Local Authority Social Services Act 1970 and the Education Act 1966. The guidelines are focused on people with a learning disability or an autistic spectrum disorder, but similar principles are included for all vulnerable adults in 'No Secrets', the strategy for dealing with the abuse of vulnerable adults.

Any policy for physical intervention must be within the framework of the Human Rights Act 1998, which ensures that everyone has the right to:
- respect for his or her private life
- not be subjected to inhuman or degrading treatment
- liberty and security
- not be discriminated against.

All physical interventions must be on the basis of the minimum intervention necessary in order to remove the risk, and must be within local and national policy guidelines.

All organisations should have a plan for physical interventions, so that there is an understood approach for all staff to use, appropriate staff are trained in the techniques that can be used, and risk assessments have been carried out as far as possible.

The impact on you

Do not underestimate how upsetting it can be to deal with someone who is displaying strong emotions. Sometimes people's stories or experiences can be very moving and it is inevitable in such circumstances that we compare their situations with our own. This may make you feel very grateful for your own circumstances, or it could have the effect of making you feel guilty, if you feel that you have a particularly happy situation compared to an individual in very difficult circumstances.

Feeling concerned, upset or even angry after a particularly stressful experience with an individual is perfectly normal. You should not feel that the fact that you continue to have an emotional response after a situation is over is a reflection on the quality of your work or your ability as a care worker.

After dealing with any challenging or emotional situation, most people are likely to continue to think about it for some time afterwards. You should discuss it either with your line manager or another person you find supportive, but always follow the principles of confidentiality if you are talking to anyone other than your manager. If you find after a period of time that you are unable to put a

Did you know?

There are almost half a million (486,000) residential places for older people and people with a physical disability in the UK.

particular incident out of your mind or you feel that it is interfering with your work, with either that individual or others, there are plenty of sources of help available to you, both within your workplace and outside it, and you should talk to your line manager or supervisor to ensure that you have access to any assistance you need.

The distress of others, whether it takes the form of anger, sadness or anxiety, will always be distressing for the person who works with them, but if you are able to develop your skills and knowledge so that you can identify distress, contribute towards reducing it and offer effective help and support to those who are experiencing it, then you are making a useful contribution to the provision of quality care.

Test yourself

1 Why is it important to identify triggers to challenging behaviour?
2 Why do people need to identify boundaries?
3 Why do you need to appear calm when dealing with challenging behaviour?
4 Why is it important to plan the management of challenging behaviour?

HSC 337c Support individuals to evaluate actions to manage behaviour

Recording incidents

Recording any incidents of challenging behaviour is vital. It is especially important if physical intervention has been necessary, but it must be done for any incident.

Your organisation will have procedures and you must follow those in relation to the information you need to record and the format in which you do so. Procedures will vary, but they are likely to include:

- date, time, location
- people present
- full description of incident, including what led up to it
- any interventions, physical or verbal
- how the situation was resolved
- the views of the individual concerned
- the views of any other individuals involved in or witnessing the incident
- implications for management of behaviour
- recommendations for next steps.

Remember that the information you are recording is subject to the Data Protection Act, so if you want to make recommendations for general policy issues or for organisational approaches, you will need to prepare a separate document, which does not identify individuals.

Recording is also very useful for individuals who are working to manage their challenging behaviour. If they and you record any incidents, the records can be used to review progress towards targets and to check whether there are problems, or targets are being missed. Above all, you need to encourage individuals to communicate their thoughts and feelings.

Review and evaluation

As with any other programme undertaken by an individual, it is essential to review and evaluate progress in managing behaviour. If an ongoing process of review is built into the planning, it is easier to pick up approaches that are working, and ones that are not, so that plans can be changed.

There are two different types of review; the first follows a major incident, when it is important that everyone involved has a chance to discuss and evaluate what happened. This is often called a de-brief review, and should involve:

- the individual
- his or her carer or advocate
- the staff involved
- management at the appropriate level.

The review should not be about blaming anyone or deciding who was at fault. It must look at exactly what happened, how it affects those involved, and strategies for preventing it from happening again. The result should provide recommendations for action by the organisation at a policy level and action by the individual in relation to managing his or her own behaviour.

CASE STUDY: Reviewing an incident

K is 61 years old and has very painful arthritis. Her mobility is poor and she has been in residential care in a unit for people with a disability for ten years. Many of the people she lives with are much younger than her, but she was very specific when she had her assessment that she did want to live with 'a load of old people'.

K has been in a lot of pain for some time. Various medications have been tried, but none are very effective, so she is finding things difficult.

One night J, a young man in his twenties, was playing music very loudly in his room. K became very angry at the disturbance, went to J's room, was verbally abusive to him and then hit him with her stick.

1   What factors are important in recording this incident?
2   What needs to be included in a 'de-brief'?
3   How can K be supported?
4   How can J be supported?
5   How could this incident have been avoided?

Individual evaluation

The other type of evaluation is for individuals as part of the process of managing their behaviour. This type of evaluation can be done alone, or with the help of a support worker. The process is straightforward, but it is usually better to work with someone else, rather than do it alone.

The easiest way to review and evaluate progress is to:
- look at the plan
- identify the targets
- judge whether the targets have been met
- if not, try to work out why not and re-schedule, or develop different targets
- if they have been met, move on to the next stage.

● *You can support someone in evaluating his or her progress towards targets*

It is during the process of working out which targets have been met, and which approaches have been successful, that the support of someone else is useful, and you can have an important input at this point. You can encourage individuals to evaluate any changes in their own behaviour. You can also help in drawing up any changes to plans and suggesting alternative ideas.

If matters arise that are outside the scope of your responsibilities or experience, seek specialist help as appropriate.

Evidence indicator

Write up the 'de-brief' report following a serious incident of challenging behaviour. You can use an incident that you were involved in, or are aware of, from your own workplace, or you can take an incident from a TV programme or film, or you can make one up. Make sure you include all the relevant information, along with proposals for action following the incident.

Test yourself

1 Why is recording incidents important?
2 What are the different types of review and evaluation?
3 What is the purpose of each?

HSC 337 UNIT TEST

1 What can be done if individuals decide they do not want to change their challenging behaviour?
2 At what point is physical intervention acceptable?
3 Note down three ways you may notice that someone is becoming angry.
4 What is the key legislation that must be complied with when dealing with challenging behaviour?

Identify the individual at risk from skin breakdown and undertake risk assessment

Treating individuals with skin breakdown costs the NHS millions of pounds every year. As carers you can contribute to reducing this cost, not only in monetary terms but also the cost to the individual in terms of pain, discomfort and poor health. In preventing the breakdown of skin you prevent the potentially life-threatening condition of pressure sores and all the problems associated with them.

This unit looks at preventing skin breakdown by treating individuals holistically – that is, treating each person as a whole. No two people are the same and therefore should not be treated in the same way. You may use the same or a similar approach in the prevention of skin breakdown but you should never expect to obtain the same results or outcomes.

In the first element of this unit you will look at those individuals who are at risk from skin breakdown and identify the factors that create the risks. You will also develop an in-depth understanding of the anatomy and physiology of the skin and how to maintain its health. In the second element you will develop an understanding of what pressure sores are and discover how you should prepare and carry out risk assessments for the prevention of skin breakdown. Finally, in the last element you will look at the reporting, reviewing and updating of risk assessments and identify the reasons for and importance of doing this.

What you need to learn

- Anatomy and physiology of skin
- Individuals at risk from skin breakdown
- External factors to skin breakdown
- Involving the individual
- What are pressure sores?
- Assessment tools used to identify risk of skin breakdown
- Assessment procedures
- Recording, reporting and reviewing risk assessments
- The importance of recording and reporting risk assessments

HSC 358a Identify individuals at risk from skin breakdown

Before you can begin to learn how to identify individuals at risk of skin breakdown, it is important that you develop an understanding of what healthy skin is. Once you develop your knowledge of healthy skin, you should be able to identify more easily those individuals at risk from skin breakdown.

This element will look at what is healthy skin, the individuals at risk from skin breakdown and the external factors that can cause the skin to breakdown. You will also look at how and why you should involve the individual from the beginning in preventing skin breakdown.

Anatomy and physiology of skin

Functions of the skin

The skin provides protection by:
- acting as a barrier to infection
- keeping body tissues moist, preventing them from drying out
- registering sensations such as pain, texture and temperature
- helping to regulate body temperature through sweat glands in the skin
- storing fat as an essential requirement to the body's functioning
- making vitamin D to provide essential nutrients to keep bones strong and healthy
- excreting waste through the skin's pores.

Structure of the skin

There are three main layers to the human skin:
- the epidermis or outer skin
- the dermis or inner skin
- subcutaneous fatty tissue.

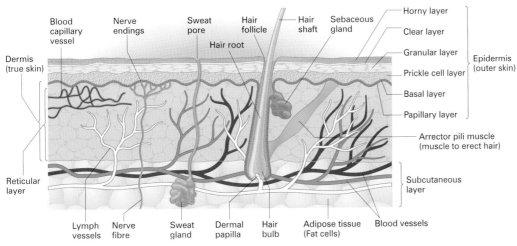

The structure of the skin

The epidermis

The epidermis is the outermost layer of the skin and is constantly dying and shedding itself. In the healthy individual this outer layer of skin replaces itself on a daily basis with the growth of new skin cells. The epidermis is waterproof which keeps the skin dry on the outside while ensuring that the body's internal tissues remain moist. The epidermis does not contain any blood vessels, which is why you do not bleed when you scratch the epidermis.

The dermis

The second layer of skin is known as the dermis. This inner skin is a thick layer of tissue containing:

- sebaceous glands (otherwise known as oil glands)
- sweat glands (also known as sudoriferous glands)
- hair follicles
- blood vessels
- nerve endings.

The nerve endings send information to the brain letting the body know of pain, touch, pressure, temperature and irritation. If you cut yourself you will only bleed if you cut through the epidermis and into the dermis. Within the dermis there are also elastic fibres that help the skin regain its original shape after stretching or moving.

Subcutaneous fatty tissue

The third and innermost layer of the skin is known as subcutaneous fatty tissue. This collection of fatty tissue cells are vital in helping to cushion the body from any excess exertion placed on it. This layer also keeps the body warm and is a source of nutrition. People who are on extreme diets or who are underweight will feel the cold more because of the reduction of this important fatty layer.

What is healthy skin?

Skin which is healthy should be smooth with no breaks or cracks. It should be warm to touch but not hot or red; it should be neither dry nor moist, neither taut nor wrinkled.

Active knowledge

Examine your own skin, especially the skin on your hands and face which is exposed to the atmosphere constantly. Is it:

- smooth or cracked
- warm, hot or red
- taut or wrinkled
- dry or moist?

From your examination would you say you had healthy skin?

For skin to remain healthy it requires nutrition, fluids and oxygen. Look at the skin of a healthy newborn baby: it is soft and smooth, warm to the touch and has a delicate sheen to it. This is because the skin had everything it required in the mother's womb. As a child grows into an adult, the skin can begin to show signs of wear. As the adult ages the signs become more apparent – wrinkles begin to appear on the face especially around the eyes and mouth. Many people prefer to call them 'laughter lines', as wrinkles can be generally seen as a sign of becoming old.

● *As a person ages, the skin begins to show signs of wear and tear*

Maintaining healthy skin

Regardless of the age of an individual, in order to maintain healthy skin you need to ensure three essential ingredients: nutrition, fluids and oxygen.

Nutrition

A well balanced diet will give the body all the nutrition it requires to remain healthy. To ensure a well balanced diet it must contain the following nutrients:
- *Proteins* – for example, lean meat, fish and dairy products.
- *Carbohydrates* – for example, bread and cereals.
- *Vitamins and minerals* – for example, fresh fruit and vegetables.
- *Fats* – for example, nuts and seeds.
- *Fibre* – for example, wholegrain breads, cereals and potato skins.

All of the above forms of foods need to be eaten in moderation and not in excess. Fresh foods contain more nutrition than processed foods and are therefore better for you.

Fluids

The human body requires at least 2 litres (4 pints) of water per day to maintain healthy tissues including the skin. Beverages such as tea and coffee can cause the body to dehydrate (to lose valuable fluids) when taken in large quantities. For this reason it is important for the individual to drink water in addition to tea and coffee. Fluids help the skin maintain its elasticity so it is essential that you drink plenty of fluids to keep the skin supple and moving freely.

● *Fresh foods contain more nutrition than processed foods*

Oxygen

Oxygen is an essential requirement in keeping the body alive. Without oxygen your body's organs will suffocate and die. Blood vessels are responsible for transporting oxygen around the body so you need to ensure these remain healthy.

Blood vessels which become constricted or blocked will not be able to carry oxygen to the body's organs, including the skin. Smoking is one of the major causes of constriction (making blood vessels smaller). Another cause is high cholesterol, which is a build up of fats in the bloodstream. Both of these reduce or prevent the amount of oxygen getting to the skin and other essential organs.

Exercise helps to maintain healthy oxygen levels in the body by keeping the lungs, heart and circulation system in tiptop condition. The good work gained through exercise will, however, be lessened if the individual continues to smoke and eat fatty foods.

Did you know?

Vitamin C promotes wound healing and collagen (protein) formation. The average human needs around 40mg of vitamin C per day to remain healthy. It is found in citrus fruits, berries and currants, tomatoes and vegetables.

Remember

Nutrients + oxygen + fluids = healthy skin

Individuals at risk from skin breakdown

You have examined what makes skin healthy, including nutrition, fluids and oxygen. The breakdown of skin occurs when these factors are compromised.

When considering the risk of skin breakdown, you need to look at the individuals themselves. The individual is a major factor in the risk of skin breakdown in terms of his or her age, ability and general health. This risk is because of the pressure the individual places on particular parts of the body and also the individual's general state of health. Before you look at the groups of individuals at risk you need to understand the areas of the body involved in pressure.

Pressure areas

All individuals have areas on their body which come under pressure from external sources on a regular basis, for example, when sitting down. You may have experienced the sensation of your buttocks becoming numb after sitting in one place for a long time without moving. This is because of the constant pressure placed on your buttocks during the process of sitting. Providing the individual is healthy, this pressure should not result in any skin breakdown.

The most common areas prone to pressure on the body include:
- head – back of head or ear
- shoulder – back of shoulder or side
- rib cage – front of chest
- elbow – back of elbow or side
- spine – along the bones which are prominent
- hip
- buttocks and sacrum (lower spine)
- thigh – inner and outer, front and back
- knees – front and side

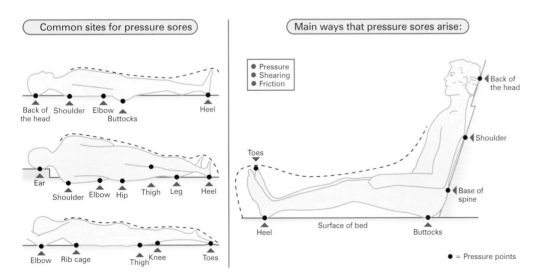

Common sites for pressure sores

Main ways that pressure sores arise:

Pressure
Shearing
Friction

Back of the head · Shoulder · Elbow · Buttocks · Heel

Ear · Shoulder · Elbow · Hip · Thigh · Leg · Heel

Elbow · Rib cage · Thigh · Knee · Toes

Toes · Back of the head · Shoulder · Base of spine · Heel · Surface of bed · Buttocks

● = Pressure points

- Common sites for pressure sores – lying on back, front, side and sitting (Source: Tissue Viability Society)

- calves – back of
- heels
- toes.

This pressure comes from sitting or lying. If it is prolonged in one position and the individual has poor nutrition, oxygen and fluid intake, then he or she is at a greater risk of skin breakdown.

Active knowledge

Take a few minutes to think of your body position while reading this book.
- What areas of your body are under pressure?
- How do you know that they are under pressure?
- Are any areas of your body under more pressure than others?

Active knowledge

Using the knowledge you have gained so far, which groups of individuals do you think would be at risk of skin breakdown? List as many as you can.

Individuals most at risk

If you consider that the risk of skin breakdown is associated with remaining in one position for a long period of time, this will give you a good indicator of those at risk. Combine this with individuals who do not meet the requirements for having healthy skin and you should begin to have a clearer understanding of all the groups of **individuals at risk** of skin breakdown.

Groups of individuals who would be at risk of skin breakdown include:
- those who are immobile
- those with reduced mobility
- those who are acutely ill
- those with an altered mental state
- those who have a sensory impairment to the body.

Immobility

Immobility is a state of not being able to move around the environment. This will affect individuals who are both conscious and unconscious, including people undertaking or recovering from an operation or those under sedation.

The individual who is immobile will be placing constant pressure on one particular area. This is because the person will not be able to change his or her position. This pressure and the inability to relieve it will put the individual at risk from skin breakdown.

Key terms

Individuals at risk:
- those who are unconscious
- very elderly people
- people with reduced mobility or immobility due to surgery, stroke, etc.
- those suffering from malnutrition, dehydration, skin conditions, sensory impairment, acute illness, vascular disease, severe chronic or terminal illness
- those with a previous history of pressure damage or incontinence
- people with diabetes
- those with an altered mental state.

Reduced mobility

Individuals with reduced mobility may have some movement but not sufficient to mobilise freely around their environment or to take regular exercise. People in this group include those who have had recent surgery or have a mobility-reducing condition such as osteoarthritis, Parkinson's disease and the effects of a stroke or other brain injury. Individuals over the age of 70 years may also come under this group when their mobility and skin elasticity begin to decrease.

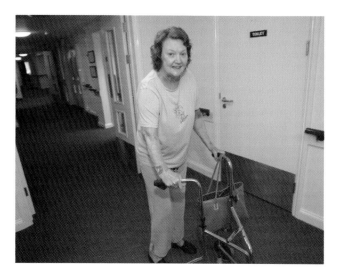

Providing the individual is able to maintain a well balanced diet, take in plenty of fluids and has a good level of oxygen intake, his or her risk of skin breakdown will be reduced but not eliminated. If, however, these factors cannot be maintained, the risk of skin breakdown will be increased.

Acute illnesses

Individuals with an acute illness such as pneumonia can be confined to bed for long periods, and this increases the risk of skin breakdown.

If you have ever had an illness which required you to spend some time in bed, you will know that this can cause you to go off your food. Poor food intake can cause the body's nutritional levels to fall. In addition, a high body temperature or vomiting associated with the illness can result in the individual losing bodily fluids, and this can lead to dehydration. Combining these three factors will put the individual at a higher risk of skin breakdown.

Remember

Illness + poor nutrition/food intake + fluid loss = increased risk of skin breakdown

Other illnesses such as vascular disease can increase the risk of skin breakdown. Vascular disease is a condition affecting the blood vessels and it reduces the flow of oxygen and nutrients to the body's organs, including the skin. It thereby causes the skin tissues to become starved of essential requirements, leaving it at greater risk of breakdown.

Altered mental state

Individuals with depression, who are withdrawn or confused, can be at risk of skin breakdown. The altered **mental state** of an individual can reduce the person's mobility if he or she sees no point in moving about or undertaking

Key terms

Mental state: The mental condition of an individual. It can include the individual being withdrawn, depressed, agitated or confused.

activities. The individual may feel that there is no point to life and may spend many hours in bed or sitting motionless in a chair.

How many times have you been at home alone and thought it was not worth cooking a meal just for you? Eating is generally a sociable activity and if a person lives alone, he or she may not want to eat alone. If a person is depressed, confused or withdrawn, the individual may not be bothered to cook, or may lose interest in eating altogether.

If the individual does not eat properly, he or she will not receive the essential nutrients required to keep the skin healthy. If the individual does not mobilise, he or she runs a greater risk of skin breakdown.

Sensory impairment

For the purpose of this unit, a sensory impairment is one where the individual has no sense of feeling on areas of his or her body. This could be caused by illness, accident, or a condition from birth in which the nerves responsible for transmitting sensations to the brain are damaged.

Sensory impairment means that the individual will not be able to feel pain or discomfort and so will not recognise when the skin becomes sore (if this occurs on an area where no sensation is felt). This could lead to further skin breakdown if the sore area continues to be damaged without the individual realising.

Other predisposing factors

Medication

As you have seen previously (pages 183–184), the skin is maintained by a blood supply feeding it oxygen and nutrients from the body (gained from the air during breathing and by the digestion of food). Some medication can cause nutritional deficiencies in the individual by preventing essential nutrients from being absorbed into the bloodstream or by increasing the body's tendency to eliminate waste. These medications include:

- cytotoxics (used in the treatment of cancer)
- lipid-lowering medicines (those which reduce cholesterol)
- diuretics (those that help the body to eliminate fluids)

Did you know?

In the later stages of dementia, an age-related condition affecting the individual's brain functioning, the individual often loses motivation and does not move for long periods. This lack of movement can lead to pressure sores.

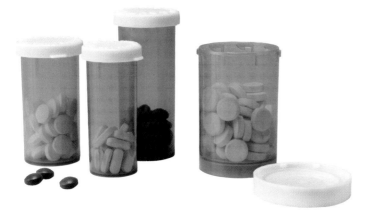

- anti-inflammatory medicines (such as Ibuprofen)
- antacids (these create a lining on the stomach wall)
- laxatives (medicines to aid the elimination of body waste).

Medication that prevents the absorption of nutrients or helps the body to pass fluids or waste can cause essential nutrients to be lost from food. This reduces the skin's healthiness, exposing it to the risk of skin breakdown.

Moisture

The skin requires fluids to be healthy but excess moisture on the skin caused by sweat or incontinence can increase the risk of skin breakdown.

An individual who wears incontinence pads may have excess moisture caused by sweat and urine around the buttocks for longer periods of time. This excess moisture may irritate the skin causing it to breakdown. If the individual has reduced mobility and remains seated, this will only compound the problem, greatly increasing the risk of skin breakdown.

CASE STUDY: Most at risk

You are working on the admissions ward within a busy hospital. During the early part of your shift, two patients are admitted within minutes of each other with differing needs and health problems.

J, a 34-year-old woman, has just been involved in a serious car accident, in which her husband was fatally injured. She has a shattered pelvis, a fractured right head of femur and dislocated ankle. She also has extensive facial injuries. J is fully aware of the fate of her husband but is not displaying any emotions at present. However, she was given a large dose of morphine, by the paramedics, at the site of the accident.

S, 82 years old, appears to have had a stroke, affecting his speech and left side of his body. He is clearly distressed by not being able to communicate his needs and is very confused, asking to go home. His clothes are soaked in urine as he had been alone in his house, on the floor, for several hours before being found by the neighbour.

1   Who is most at risk in the short term? State the reason for your answer.
2   Who is most at risk in the long term? State the reason for your answer.
3   How can you reduce the risk of skin breakdown to both patients in the short term?

Active knowledge

Create a chart to show the factors that put individuals at risk of skin breakdown.

External factors to skin breakdown

External factors are those outside of the body. You have looked quite closely at individuals at risk of skin breakdown and predisposing factors including excess moisture and medication. You now need to consider those external factors which cause skin breakdown and which are preventable.

Pressure on particular areas of the body is the main external factor to skin breakdown. Other factors include:

- shearing
- friction
- poor handling
- poor hygiene
- knocks to the skin.

Shearing

Sitting up in bed or slouching in a chair can cause what is known as shearing forces. Shearing is when the skin slides over muscles and bones and become stretched in one area and wrinkled in another, decreasing the blood supply to the skin. It is the underling tissues of the skin which become damaged and the true damage is not always immediately apparent until it has become extensive.

Most people are guilty of slouching in a chair, especially in front of the television after a hard day. But how many realise the potential damage they are causing, not only to their posture but to their skin as well?

The shearing force is created by the natural gravity of the body pulling in a downward motion. While sitting in a bed or chair your body is naturally pulling itself downwards. If an individual is unable to maintain a seated position, he or she will begin to slip downwards causing shearing. The shearing force places additional risk of damage on the skin and can be reduced by ensuring appropriate seating positions.

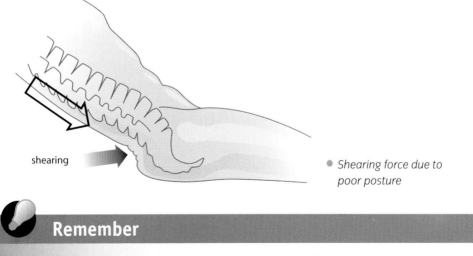

shearing

● Shearing force due to poor posture

Remember

Where shearing forces are present, it only takes half the amount of pressure to create the same amount of damage.

Friction

Friction is the rubbing of the skin on rough or uneven surfaces. You may have experienced damage to the skin caused by friction when wearing new shoes, for example, which can be very painful.

Friction is associated with shearing and can therefore occur when slipping down a bed or chair while sitting in an inappropriate position. The skin rubbing on artificial fibres such as nylon or polyester can also cause friction.

Poor handling

Individuals who require support in moving can be put at risk of skin breakdown by the way the carer handles that individual. Dragging the individual up a bed or chair to reposition him or her can cause shearing and friction. The individual's skin is pulled against the bed sheets or seat covering, which can damage the delicate skin tissue.

The carer's fingernails catching on the individual's skin can also cause it to break down. It is vitally important for carers to keep their fingernails trim and not to wear jewellery, in order to avoid scratching individuals when providing personal care.

Poor hygiene

The human body has a number of areas that require particular attention when cleansing. Any area of the body which has a natural skin fold or where one skin surface lies against another can be susceptible to breakdown if not cleansed and dried thoroughly.

Bacteria grow where there is moisture, warmth and food. Between the natural folds of the skin, warmth and moisture occur naturally; the food supply is the dead skin cells which have been shed by the body. The bacteria will grow and multiply quickly providing they continue to have the moisture, warmth and food they require. It is this build-up of bacteria which causes body odour. If left, the area can become infected, causing the skin to break down. Skin that is also constantly moist from sweat, urine or faeces can become irritated, resulting in damage.

Areas of the body most likely to be affected from poor hygiene include:
- under the breasts
- under the arms
- around the waist (if the individual is overweight and has rolls of flesh)
- in and around the groin area
- between the buttocks
- behind the knees
- behind the ears
- between the fingers and toes.

Remember

Warmth + moisture + food = bacteria

Knocks to the skin

A simple bump to the skin for most people would often go unnoticed and does not generally create any major problems. For some groups of individuals, however, especially those with diabetes or leukaemia, any bump or scrape to the skin can lead to serious conditions of breakdown. The reason is that the skin of those with diabetes or leukaemia takes longer to heal. Because cuts and abrasions on the skin do not heal as quickly, this can lead to them becoming infected. Infected wounds to the skin take even longer to heal and so the problem continues.

It is vitally important for individuals who heal very slowly to be extra careful in preventing injuries to the skin, to avoid any serious skin breakdown.

Keys to good practice: Keeping skin healthy

- ✓ Nutrients, oxygen and fluids are the three main ingredients to healthy skin.
- ✓ Immobility is the leading cause of skin breakdown.
- ✓ Medication can increase the risk of skin breakdown.
- ✓ Poor hygiene, poor handling, friction and shearing are external factors that increase the risk of skin breakdown.

CASE STUDY: The silent risk

F lives in a residential unit along with four other individuals with learning disabilities. She is 48 years old and has a very sociable character, liking to talk with visitors and staff as they pass her in her favourite seat in the conservatory. F enjoys jigsaws, drawing and looking through her photograph album. She enjoys her food, which she eats in her favourite seat, and takes her medication for swollen feet and ankles without any difficulties. She is seen by the staff as a pleasant woman, very quiet and not any bother.

1 Is F at risk of skin breakdown? Give the reasons for your answer.
2 Identify ways of reducing any possible risks of skin breakdown for F. Consider how F can help herself and how staff and others could help her.

Involving the individual

Within each element of this unit you will be looking at ways in which you and other carers can involve individuals in developing their understanding of skin breakdown, so that they can help themselves and monitor their skin for risk of breakdown or damage. In this element you will be looking at how you, as a carer, can support the individual to develop his or her knowledge of the causes of skin breakdown and how to reduce the risks.

Supporting knowledge

Informing and supporting the individual's knowledge of the risk factors involved in the breakdown of skin is essential from the outset and may help to reduce the incidence of skin breakdown.

In 2001 the Department of Health published the document *Essence of Care* in response to concerns about the quality of care individuals were receiving in the National Health Service (NHS). One of the areas of concern was the prevention of pressure sores. The NHS set 'benchmarks' or standards, which all NHS Trusts were to compare with their current practice in order to develop plans for improvement. For pressure sores the benchmark was: 'Patients and/or carers have ongoing access to information and have the opportunity to discuss this and its relevance to their individual needs, with a registered practitioner' (*Essence of Care*, NHS 2001).

A study published in the *Nursing Standard* demonstrates the need for individuals to have further education in this area. The study, funded by South Thames NHSE, consisted of responses to a simple questionnaire on pressure sores. It was posted to a local Patients and Carers Association and some of the results were as follows:

- 53 per cent stated that they had seen a pressure sore.
- 27 per cent thought that pressure sores could be avoidable.
- 95 per cent thought pressure sores were caused by a lack of regular turning.
- 13 per cent related pressure sores to poor nutrition.
- 36 per cent related pressure sores to incontinence.
- 24 per cent believed that not using talcum powder or creams after bathing contributed to pressure sores.
- 45 per cent recognised the relationship between sitting for long periods and the development of pressure sores.
- 10 per cent recognised the relationship between lying on a hospital trolley and the development of pressure sores.
- 4 per cent recognised the relationship between lying on an operating table and the development of pressure sores.

As the results of this study show, individuals need to develop a greater understanding of the risks to skin breakdown. As many as 73 per cent did not think that pressure sores were avoidable; 87 per cent did not relate them to poor nutrition; 64 per cent did not relate them to incontinence; 55 per cent did not recognise the link between sitting for long periods and the development of pressure sores; 90 per cent did not recognise the relationship between lying on a hospital trolley and the development of pressure sores; 96 per cent did not recognise the relationship between lying on an operating table and the development of pressure sores.

As a carer you need to support the knowledge of individuals if they are to play a role in helping to reduce the risk of skin breakdown.

Informing the individual

Individuals should be encouraged to identify their own risk to skin breakdown wherever possible. In order to do this the individual needs to be informed. Informing the individual on the maintenance of healthy skin including nutrition, oxygen and fluids will not only reduce his or her risk of skin breakdown but will support the health of the individual in general.

Educating the individual in all areas of risks to skin breakdown can be achieved through a variety of ways, depending on the person's understanding and communicative abilities. Methods include:

- the use of picture menus to show choices of healthy foods
- the use of books or videos to show different forms of exercise
- individual or group discussions to identify good and bad practices in maintaining a healthy lifestyle
- educational games relating to maintaining a healthy lifestyle
- supported shopping trips to purchase healthy foods.

- *Educating the individual about the risks of skin breakdown can be achieved in a variety of ways*

The information shared with individuals needs to be relevant to them and provided in a format that they will be able to understand and accept. All individuals need to be aware of the requirements of a healthy diet, exercise and fluid intake, but may not necessarily need to be made aware of the problems created by incontinence if they do not have continence difficulties, for example. Not all individuals have the ability to read; for those who cannot, providing the information in written format would be of no use and you may need to use alternatives such as picture symbols. (See Unit HSC 31 for further information.)

In addition to a healthy lifestyle, the individual should be educated and supported in understanding the predisposing and external factors that increase the risk of skin breakdown, including:

- how medication can affect nutritional intake and thus the skin
- the effects of excess moisture (including sweat, urine and faeces) on the skin
- mobility – the risks of sitting or lying in one position for long periods
- friction and shearing forces and the requirement for maintenance of a good seating position; wearing new shoes, callipers or splints
- the importance of good hygiene practices, particularly when cleansing and drying the skin
- the effects of knocks to the skin for some groups (diabetics and those with leukaemia)
- the need to check the skin regularly for any injuries or skin breakdown.

As a carer, you can support the individual's development of this knowledge; dieticians, nutritionists, GPs, health visitors and physiotherapists can also support it. The National Institute for Health and Clinical Excellence (NICE) has produced a document called *Working together to prevent pressure sores – A guide to patients and their carers*. It is an easy-to-read document and avoids the use of technical words. Unfortunately it is not available in any format other than the written word, but it can be easily adapted for use with the individuals you work with, if required.

CASE STUDY: Identifying and reducing the risks

M is a 39-year-old woman with Down's syndrome who lives at home with her elderly parents in the community. M does not attend any daytime activities and spends most of her time watching television while eating chocolate and crisps. She has put on a large amount of weight during the past 12 months, which is affecting her mobility and breathing. You have recently become her care worker, supporting her for four hours per day, three days per week.

1 What risk factors does M have in contributing to skin breakdown?
2 How can you help M to reduce these risks?
3 Who else should you involve to help reduce these risks?
4 What format would you use to inform M on the health information she requires?

Test yourself

1 How can you involve the individual in preventing skin breakdown?
2 Describe the anatomy and physiology of healthy skin and the three main ingredients required to keep it healthy.
3 What does the term 'shearing' mean and how can it be prevented?
4 Identify the sites on the body where pressure can occur.

HSC 358b Prepare for and carry out risk assessment

In this element you will learn about:

- the most common type of skin breakdown – pressure sores
- the different types of assessment tools used to identify the risk of skin breakdown
- how to carry out risk assessments in accordance with health and safety and using a holistic approach.

What are pressure sores?

Pressure sores – otherwise known as pressure ulcers, bedsores or (more technically) decubitus ulcers – are injuries to the skin or underlying tissues caused by increased pressure to the area for a prolonged period.

In the first element you looked at individuals at risk from skin breakdown and established that individuals with little or no mobility were more likely to develop this condition. This is because, for skin to be healthy, it requires oxygen from the blood; individuals who do not relieve the pressure from areas of the skin through moving or turning on a regular basis will cause a disruption of the blood vessels, cutting off the supply of oxygen to the skin.

Did you know?

95 per cent of pressure sores are preventable.

Active knowledge

To develop a good understanding of the disruption of blood to areas of skin caused by pressure, try this simple activity.

Gently place together your thumb and index finger as though you are picking up a tiny object. You will see the change in your skin colour with just a small amount of pressure. Now squeeze your thumb and finger together tightly for no longer than 10 seconds and you will see a greater colour change. This is because your blood supply is being prevented from reaching the tip of your finger. Now imagine the pressure you exert on your buttocks when sitting for hours on end without moving and the damage this is causing due to lack of oxygen.

The development of a pressure sore

There are four stages to the development of a pressure sore.

Stage one pressure sore

- The area of skin affected becomes red or discoloured. Darkly pigmented skin becomes purplish/bluish.
- The area of skin is not broken but may feel warmer than the skin around it.
- The redness or change in colour does not fade within 30 minutes of removing the pressure.

At this stage the pressure sore can be prevented from developing further by removing the pressure from the affected area.

Stage two pressure sore

- Both the epidermis and dermis (outer and inner layers of the skin) are affected.
- The epidermis may blister or may break, creating a shallow pit into the dermis.
- The sore may be weeping or leaking fluid.

At this stage the damage to the skin and underlying tissues is greater than you can see.

Stage three pressure sore

- The break in the skin extends through the dermis into subcutaneous fatty tissue.
- The sore is deeper than stage two.
- Weeping will be evident.
- The sore is likely to be infected.

Stage four pressure sore

- The breakdown extends into the muscle and can extend down to the bone.
- The area of skin blackens from dead and rotting tissue.
- Weeping will be evident.
- Surgery is usually required.

At this stage the sore can create a life-threatening condition such as septicaemia (blood poisoning) or osteomyelitis (infection of the bone).

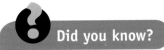

Did you know?

62 per cent of stage four pressure sores never heal and 48 per cent can take more than one year to heal.

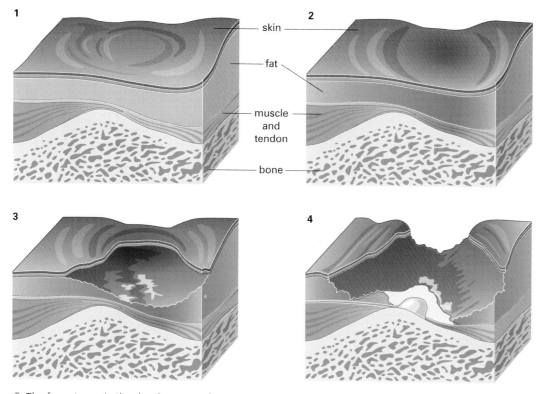

● *The four stages in the development of a pressure sore (Source: Spinal-Injury Network)*

Assessment tools used to identify risk of skin breakdown

Now that you know what to look for in an individual at risk of skin breakdown, you can begin to develop your knowledge of the assessment tools used to identify that risk.

Under the NHS document *Essence of Care* (2001), the benchmark of best practice is 'for all patients identified as "at risk" to progress to further assessment'. This means that once you have identified an individual at risk, through informal assessment, a formal assessment must be carried out.

Assessment for pressure sores requires a holistic approach – one that looks at the individual as a whole rather than at a specific area. In the UK the most widely used risk **assessment tool** for pressure sores is the Waterlow Scale. There are also other forms of assessment tools, including the Gosnell Scale, Norton Scale and the Braden Scale. You will be examining all of these assessment tools in this element.

Gosnell Scale

Devised by D.J. Gosnell, the Gosnell Scale looks at the risk to the individual of pressure sores developing using five particular areas:

- *Mental status* – an assessment of the level of response to the environment.
- *Continence* – the amount of bodily control of urination and defecation.

Key terms

Assessment tool:
In relation to skin breakdown, a process of assessment using a variety of risk factors, including continence, weight and nutritional status, against which a score is identified clarifying the degree of risk that an individual's skin will break down. Assessment tools have various names according to their authors or developers.

- *Mobility* – the amount and control of movement of the body.
- *Activity* – the ability to ambulate (walk).
- *Nutrition* – the process of food intake.

In addition, evaluation includes recording of:
- the vital signs of temperature, pulse, respirations and blood pressure
- skin appearance
- diet
- medication
- 24-hour fluid intake and output.

Each area is scored with points from 1 up to 5. The minimum score an individual can attain is 5 and the maximum score is 20. These are worked out as shown in the table on page 200.

Each of the expected findings per area come with a clear description of the definition of what the carer should be looking for. This can aid the carer in his or her understanding and ensures that everyone assesses individuals following the same criteria. Individuals scoring 5 are said to be at a very low risk of developing pressure sores; those scoring 20 are said to be at a very high risk of developing pressure sores.

Norton Scale

Devised by Doreen Norton, the Norton Scale looks at the risk of the individual to pressure sores using five particular areas. These include:
- physical condition
- mental condition
- activity
- mobility
- incontinence.

Each area is scored on a points system from 1 to 4. Unlike the Gosnell scale, the higher point is awarded for the positive findings, as shown in the table on page 201. Individuals are seen to be at risk of developing pressure sores if their overall score is below 14. The lower the individual's score, the more he or she is at risk.

Area	Finding	Description	Points
Mental status	Alert	Responsive to all stimuli; understands explanations	1
	Apathetic	Forgetful, drowsy; able to obey simple commands	2
	Confused	Disorientation to time, person and place	3
	Stuporous	Does not respond to name or simple commands	4
	Unconscious	No response to painful stimuli	5
Continence	Fully controlled	Total control of urine and faeces	1
	Usually controlled	Incontinence of urine or faeces no more than once every two days	2
	Minimally controlled	Incontinence of urine or faeces at least once every 24 hours	3
	Absence of control	Consistently incontinent of both urine and faeces	4
Mobility	Full	Able to move at will	1
	Slightly limited	Movement is restricted slightly and requires assistance, but will initiate movement	2
	Very limited	Unable to initiate movement but can assist a person who helps the individual to move	3
	Immobile	Unable to move without assistance	4
Activity	Ambulatory	Can walk unassisted	1
	Walks with help	Walks with help from another person, braces or crutches	2
	Chairfast	Walks only to chair or is confined to wheelchair	3
	Bedfast	Confined to a bed 24 hours a day	4
Nutrition	Regular intake of food	Eats some food from each basic food category each day	1
	Occasionally misses food	Occasionally refuses a meal or frequently leaves more than half of meal	2
	Seldom intakes food	Seldom eats a complete meal and only a few bites of food	3

● *The Gosnell Scale*

Area	Finding	Points
Physical condition	Good	4
	Fair	3
	Poor	2
	Very bad	1
Mental condition	Alert	4
	Apathetic	3
	Confused	2
	Stupor	1
Activity	Ambulant	4
	Walks with help	3
	Chairbound	2
	Bedbound	1
Mobility	Full mobility	4
	Slightly limited	3
	Very limited	2
	Immobile	1
Incontinence	None	4
	Occasional	3
	Usually urine	2
	Urine and faeces	1

● *The Norton Scale*

Braden Scale

Devised by Barbara Braden and used widely in the United States, the Braden Scale looks at the risk of the individual to pressure sores using six particular areas (one more than the Norton Scale and the Gosnell Scale). These six areas are:

● *Sensory perception* – the ability to respond meaningfully to pressure-related discomfort.
● *Moisture* – the degree to which skin is exposed to moisture.
● *Activity* – the degree of physical activity.

- *Mobility* – the ability to change and control body position.
- *Nutrition* – the usual food intake pattern.
- *Shear and friction* (see pages 190–191).

As with the previous scales, each area is broken down into findings, with points awarded. Like the Norton Scale, the higher point is given to the most positive finding.

Area	Finding	Points
Sensory perception	No impairment	4
	Slightly impaired	3
	Very limited	2
	Completely limited	1
Moisture	Rarely moist	4
	Occasionally moist	3
	Very moist	2
	Constantly moist	1
Activity	Walks frequently	4
	Walks occasionally	3
	Chairfast	2
	Bedfast	1
Mobility	No limitations	4
	Slightly limited	3
	Very limited	2
	Completely immobile	1
Nutrition	Excellent	4
	Adequate	3
	Probably inadequate	2
	Very poor	1
Friction and shear	No apparent problem	3
	Potential problem	2
	Problem	1

- *The Braden Scale*

Individuals with a total score of 16 or less are considered to be at risk of developing pressure sores:

- a score of 15 or 16 is considered mild risk
- a score of 13 or 14 is considered moderate risk
- a score of 12 or less is considered high risk.

Braden Scale research studies

Several studies have been made on the Braden Scale, including Bergstorm et al (1998) and Nixon & McGough (2001). Both of these studies looked at the validity of the Braden Scale in predicting individuals at risk from pressure sores.

Bergstorm et al (1998) randomly sampled 843 inpatients from three different care settings; some of the inpatients were free from pressure sores on admission although it has been acknowledged that pressure damage to tissues can take three days to become visible. Research nurses were used to collect the information from the three care settings and were regularly monitored to ensure correct use of the assessment tool. From the studies made, Bergstorm et al (1998) identified that the mean (average) age of those who developed pressure sores was higher than those who did not. From this it could be concluded that age is a risk factor which needs to be considered within the assessment tool. It was also suggested that an individual scoring 18 on the Braden Scale indicates the risk of pressure sores (the original 'mild risk' score is 16). It was explained that, by raising the score to 18 to identify those at risk, more individuals would be identified, but equally, more individuals would be falsely identified. This would be beneficial to the individual but could create an increase in expenditure to the care organisation.

Waterlow Scale

The Waterlow Scale, devised by Judy Waterlow in 1985 and revised in 2005 to incorporate research undertaken by Queensland Health, is a comprehensive assessment tool widely used within the UK. You may already be familiar with this scale if it is used within your organisation. However, many organisations have adapted the format to suit the area in which it is used, while retaining many of the original scoring areas.

The Waterlow Scale looks at a total of ten areas potentially contributing to risk of pressure sores, more than the Braden, Gosnell and Norton scales. These areas include:

- build/weight for height ratio
- continence
- skin type visual risk areas
- mobility
- sex and age
- malnutrition screening tool
- tissue malfunction
- neurological deficit

- major surgery or trauma
- medication.

A version of the table is shown below.

WATERLOW PRESSURE ULCER PREVENTION/TREATMENT POLICY
RING SCORES IN TABLE, ADD TOTAL. MORE THAN 1 SCORE/CATEGORY CAN BE USED

Build/weight for height ◆		Skin type visual risk areas ◆		Sex / Age ◆		Malnutrition screening tool (MST) (Nutrition vol. 15, No.6 1999 – Australia) ◆	
Average BMI = 20–24.9	0	Healthy	0	MALE	1	A – Has patient lost weight recently?	B – Weight loss score
Above average BMI = 25–29.9	1	Tissue paper	1	FEMALE	2	YES - Go to B	0.5–5 kg = 1
Obese BMI > 30	2	Dry	1	14–49	1	NO - Go to C	5–10 kg = 2
Below average BMI < 20	3	Oedematous	1	50–64	2	UNSURE - Go to C and score 2	10–15 kg = 3
BMI = Wt(kg)/Ht(m²)		Clammy, pyrexia	1	65–74	3		>15 kg = 4
		Discoloured grade 1	2	75–80	4	C – Patient eating poorly or lack of appetite	Unsure = 2
		Broken/spots grade 2–4	3	81+	5	NO = 0 YES = 1	NUTRITION SCORE If > 2 refer for nutrition assessment/intervention

Continence ◆		Mobility ◆	
Complete/catheterised	0	Fully	0
Urine incontinent	1	Restless/fidgety	1
Faecal incontinent	2	Apathetic	2
Urinary & faecal incontinence	3	Restricted	3
		Bedbound, e.g. traction	4
		Chairbound, e.g. wheelchair	5

Special risks

Tissue malfunction ◆		Neurological deficit ◆	
Terminal cachexia	8	Diabetes, MS, CVA	4–6
Multiple organ failure	8	Motor/sensory	4–6
Single organ failure (respiratory, renal, cardiac)	5	Paraplegia (max of 6)	4–6
Peripheral vascular disease	5		
Anaemia (Hb < 8)	2		
Smoking	1		

Major surgery or trauma	
Orthopaedic/spinal	5
On table > 2 hr#	5
On table > 6 hr#	8
	Max of 4

MEDICATION – cytotoxics; long-term/high dose steroids; anti-inflammatory

#Scores can be discounted after 48 hours provided patient is recovering normally

© J Waterlow 1985 Revised 2005*
Obtainable from The Nook, Stoke Road, Henlade TAUNTON TA3 5LX
* The 2005 revision incorporates the research undertaken by Queensland Health.   www.judy-waterlow.co.uk

SCORE
10+ AT RISK
15+ HIGH RISK
20+ VERY HIGH RISK

- The Waterlow Scale

The Waterlow Scale, designed to be used with its accompanying prevention and treatment policy, also has a manual to inform the user on how to interpret and use the assessment tool correctly. This manual was also updated in 2005 to incorporate clarification on the areas assessed.

To ensure your understanding of the Waterlow Scale, some of the definitions include:

- *BMI* – Body Mass Index (the amount of fat within the body), calculated using the formula: Weight (kg) ÷ Height (m^2).
- *Oedematous* – collection of watery fluid in the body's tissues.
- *Pyrexia* – raised body temperature above 37°C.
- *Apathetic* – lack of interest.
- *Terminal cachexia* – life-threatening muscle wastage.
- *Peripheral vascular disease* – build up of plaque (atherosclerosis) in the arteries outside the heart, reducing blood flow.
- *MS* – Multiple Sclerosis.
- *CVA* – Cerebral Vascular Accident.
- *Cytotoxics* – medication used in the treatment of cancer.
- > – more than.
- < – less than.

Active knowledge

Using the correct formula, calculate your own BMI.

Waterlow research studies

Studies conducted by Dealy (1989), Edwards (1995), Watkinson (1996) and Cook et al (1999) all assessed real patients using the Waterlow Scale. The outcomes of these studies have shown that the tool lacks inter-rater reliability. Inter-rater reliability is when two assessors, assessing independently, rate the same score for the areas assessed. It is difficult to determine if the outcomes of the studies made were as a result of the different perceptions of the patients by the assessor or because of the different interpretations of the Waterlow Scale itself.

To try and identify Waterlow's inter-rater reliability more accurately, another study was conducted of 110 qualified nurses all experienced in using the Waterlow Scale. Each nurse was given the same case study to assess using the scale. The case study was fairly detailed, sufficient to determine if there was a risk to pressure sores and the level of that risk. Having read the case study and completed the Waterlow Scale:

- 65 per cent of the nurses overrated the risk
- 23 per cent underrated the risk
- only 12 per cent correctly rated the level of risk.

One difficulty the nurses faced was accurately working out the case study's BMI. Without a calculator this can be fairly difficult to do – without knowing the formula it would be impossible. Waterlow addressed this difficulty in her revision of the scale in 2005 by giving the formula for calculating BMI and the ranges for each score. The use of a BMI conversion table, like the one below, should also help.

Waterlow has also addressed other difficulties encountered by the nurses in her revision of the scale, including clarification on skin types, malnutrition screening tool and major surgery or trauma scoring.

The conclusion of this study showed that, as an assessment tool, the Waterlow Scale was successful at identifying the individual at risk, if not entirely accurately in terms of the level of risk. Not using the tool in the way it was intended, however, created part of this problem. With sufficient training this could be excluded but additional studies will need to be put in place to show any improvement on the Waterlow's inter-rater reliability.

Body Mass Index (BMI) Table																	
BMI	19	20	21	22	23	24	25	26	27	28	29	30	31	32	33	34	35
Height Weight (in pounds)																	
4'10" (58")	91	96	100	105	110	115	119	124	129	134	138	143	148	153	158	162	167
4'11" (59")	94	99	104	109	114	119	124	128	133	138	143	148	153	158	163	168	173
5' (60")	97	102	107	112	118	123	128	133	138	143	148	153	158	163	168	174	179
5'1" (61")	100	106	111	116	122	127	132	137	143	148	153	158	164	169	174	180	185
5'2" (62")	104	109	115	120	126	131	136	142	147	153	158	164	169	175	180	186	191
5'3" (63")	107	113	118	124	130	135	141	146	152	158	163	169	175	180	186	191	197
5'4" (64")	110	116	122	128	134	140	145	151	157	163	169	175	180	186	192	197	204
5'5" (65")	114	120	126	132	138	144	150	156	162	168	174	180	186	192	198	204	210
5'6" (66")	118	124	130	136	142	148	155	161	167	173	179	186	192	198	204	210	216
5'7" (67")	121	127	134	140	146	153	159	166	172	178	185	191	198	204	211	217	223
5'8" (68")	125	131	138	144	151	158	164	171	177	184	190	197	203	210	216	223	230
5'9" (69")	128	135	142	149	153	160	167	174	181	188	195	202	209	216	223	230	236
5'10" (70")	132	139	146	153	160	167	174	181	188	195	202	209	216	222	229	236	243
5'11" (71")	136	143	150	157	165	172	179	186	193	200	208	215	222	229	236	243	250
6' (72")	140	147	154	162	169	177	184	191	199	206	208	215	222	229	236	243	250
6'1" (73")	144	151	159	166	174	182	189	197	204	212	219	227	235	242	250	257	265
6'2" (74")	148	155	163	171	179	186	194	202	210	218	225	233	241	249	256	264	272
6'3" (75")	152	160	168	176	184	192	200	208	216	224	232	240	248	256	264	272	279

● BMI conversion table

E was born on 12 June 1928. He is 5 feet 8 inches tall and currently weighs 12 stone 4 pounds; he did weigh 14 stone 3 pounds five weeks ago. E is in the later stages of dementia and is very confused and withdrawn, often spending one or two days in bed not wanting to get out. He is incontinent of urine and faeces and has dry skin. Blood tests show his haemoglobin levels are 7.2 and he has traces of protein in his urine. Using the Waterlow Scale:

1   What score would you give E under the heading sex/age?
2   What is E's BMI?
3   What total score would you give E under mobility, malnutrition and special risk?
4   How would you score E overall in terms of risk?

Keys to good practice: Knowing about skin

✓ Develop a good knowledge of the factors contributing to healthy skin.

✓ Know what healthy skin should look like for individuals of different skin pigmentation.

✓ Know what signs to look for indicating skin breakdown.

✓ Know what the four stages of pressure sores look like.

✓ Have an in-depth knowledge of your organisation's pressure area risk assessment tool and practise how to use it correctly.

Assessment procedures

As with any assessment you undertake as a carer, there are certain criteria you must follow to ensure an accurate outcome. For risk assessments on skin breakdown these include:

- standard precautions
- timescales
- safe handling techniques
- working within your own sphere
- involving the individual.

Pressure area risk assessment tools are not designed to replace the clinical judgement of the professional. They are there to support the care given to the individual in conjunction with the expertise of the multidisciplinary team.

Standard precautions

Using the appropriate assessment scale is essential – it should also be one that has been approved by your organisation for use when assessing individuals at risk of pressure sores. The assessment scale should be valid, reliable and culturally sensitive:

- It is valid if it accurately assesses what it claims to assess.
- It is reliable if, when used by different people, it gives the same outcome.
- It is culturally sensitive if it does not unfairly discriminate against any individual because of the person's ethnicity or preferred language.

The Department of Health, in its *Guidance On The Single Assessment Process* (2004), suggests the Waterlow Scale as an assessment tool to use in assessing risk of skin breakdown. However, it is important to add that it does not endorse this or any of the suggested assessment scales used within the Health Service.

To prevent infection and cross-infection you must ensure you follow **standard precautions** with hand washing before undertaking the assessment, during and after the assessment. You should also wear the appropriate **protective clothing** such as disposable gloves and aprons, ensuring they are removed after interaction with one individual and replaced with clean protection before interaction with another individual. Failure to follow these actions could result in individuals becoming exposed to infection transmitted from one individual to another. Some of these infections could increase the risk to the individual of skin breakdown, especially if the infection affects the person's health, for example, vomiting and diarrhoea.

For individuals who already have open sores, the risk of infection is even greater. Infection can be transferred from one individual to another by the carer who has

- *To prevent infection and cross-infection you should wear the appropriate protective clothing*

Key terms

Standard precautions and health and safety measures: A series of interventions which minimise or prevent infection and cross-infection, including: hand washing; cleansing before, during and after the activity; the use of personal protective clothing and additional protective equipment, when appropriate.

Key terms

Personal protective clothing: Items such as plastic aprons, gloves (both clean and sterile), footwear, dresses, trousers and shirts, and all-in-one trouser suits. These may be single-use disposable clothing or reusable clothing.

Key terms

Additional protective equipment: Types of personal protective equipment such as visors, protective eyewear and radiation protective equipment.

not followed health and safety guidelines appropriately. This infection can enter the individual's blood stream through the open sore and cause serious illness, if not death.

Remember

Protect yourself to protect the individual.

Timescales

As an old saying goes, 'a stitch in time saves nine'. As with many things, the sooner something is carried out the better. Individuals can be protected from the long-term suffering of pressure sores if they are assessed and appropriate treatment put in place sooner rather than too late.

Following NICE guidelines (2005) all individuals should be assessed for the risk of pressure sores on admittance to the care environment. This could be undertaken immediately on an informal basis and, if the individual is felt to be at risk, a more formal assessment should be carried out within six hours of admittance. For individuals living in the community the risk assessment should be carried out during the first home visit.

Remember

Failure to assess an individual in time can potentially put the person's life at risk.

Safe handling techniques

To avoid creating additional risk factors, such as friction and shearing, you must ensure during your risk assessment and at any other time that you handle the individual using safe techniques. Under the Health and Safety at Work Act 1974, as stated by the Manual Handling Regulations 1992, all employees carrying out manual handling tasks must be suitably trained in this area and be given regular update training as required.

Friction and shearing are contributory factors to skin breakdown. You as the carer can cause both of these if you use inappropriate methods of moving and handling. When supporting or moving an individual, you must always ensure that his or her body is lifted clear of the bed or chair. This is to prevent the skin being dragged against the mattress or seat, creating friction and shearing. You must follow the manual handling guidelines in the individual's care plan and use any equipment provided, such as a hoist, to assist in the move appropriately and as trained.

Working within your own sphere

To ensure the individual receives the best care or treatment, it should be given by those who have the ability through appropriate training and experience. It is highly unlikely that you would ask or even trust your local vet to remove your painful tooth, even though your vet may be very experienced in removing animals' teeth.

As a carer you have a responsibility to work at the level of your own competency without exceeding that level. To do so could place yourself and the individual at harm through misjudgement. The NICE guidelines state that all staff undertaking risk assessment in pressure area care should be suitably trained in the use of the assessment tool and have a good knowledge of appropriate preventative measures.

If you have any difficulties assessing individuals at risk it is important that you seek support from someone more senior. Asking for help or support is not a sign of weakness; in fact it is the opposite. It is a positive strength to admit you need help. Seeking the help and support you need will develop you as a person and in turn help the individual you are caring for. Failure to seek support could put the health of the individual at severe risk. Other health and social care staff you could turn to would include:

- *Tissue Viability Nurse* – a qualified nurse who has been specially trained in the role of assessing skin and the risks of breakdown. The Tissue Viability Nurse is usually employed by the health service to work in hospitals, clinics and in the community, alongside community nurses and health visitors.
- *Team leader* – responsible for staff within his or her team. This person leads through advice and example. If you need support your team leader should be the first person to turn to. If he or she cannot offer the expertise a situation requires, then he or she will be able to refer any difficulties to other professionals.
- *Social worker* – the individual may have a social worker who works closely with him or her. Although not medically trained the social worker may have built up a relationship with the individual and may be able to support you in the initial introductory stages to the individual. In many cases in the community it is the social worker who refers the individual to other specialities to obtain the support the person requires.
- *GP (General Practitioner)* – the GP will have the individual's medical history, including any current medications, health conditions or disabilities, which could contribute to the individual's risk of skin breakdown.

Involving the individual

The NICE (2001) guidelines state that 'individuals who are willing and able should be encouraged, following education, to inspect their own skin.

Individuals who are wheelchair users should use a mirror to inspect areas that they cannot see easily or ask others to inspect them'.

These guidelines go back to the importance of supporting and educating individuals in recognising what is healthy skin. In addition to this, the individual and his or her carers should also be informed on what to look out for as indicators to skin breakdown. This can be done through the use of pictures or a checklist of initial indicating factors, such as reddening skin, skin that is warm to the touch, swelling or skin loss. An example of a checklist is given below.

What to look for	What to do
1: An area of the skin becomes pale or lighter in colour.	Keep moving your body position so that you do not stay in one position for too long.
2: Skin becoming red, warm or swollen.	Stay off areas of redness until skin returns to normal colour. Do not rub the area or put anything on it.
3: A blister appears over the red area of skin.	Stay off the area. Call your doctor or nurse.
4: The centre of the blister turns brown or black and is leaking fluid.	Stay off the area. Cover area with a sterile dressing. Call your doctor.

● *Pressure area care checklist for individuals and their carers*

If you are assessing an individual, it is important that you inform the person what actions you need to take and obtain his or her prior permission before undertaking those actions. Pouncing on an individual and starting to prod and poke him or her will not help you in obtaining the information you need. Apart from startling the unsuspecting individual and appearing very rude, you will also be breaching the person's rights and many of your organisation's policies, procedures and codes of conduct.

Individuals must be given appropriate information in the most suitable format to their needs, to enable them to make informed decisions. Approaching the individual and explaining to him or her what you need to do and why will help the person to be involved in his or her care. Obtaining consent from the individual to assess the risk of skin breakdown will supply you with the accurate information you need. The consenting individual will be more willing to answer your questions, and will have a better understanding of what information you are requesting if he or she knows why you need the information.

● *Observation plays a crucial role within care*

✔ Keys to good practice: Risk assessments

When undertaking a risk assessment ensure that you:

✓ follow standard precautions

✓ carry it out in required timescales

✓ use safe handling techniques

✓ work within your own sphere

✓ always include and involve the individual.

Evidence indicator

Describe in detail how you have followed your organisation's pressure area risk assessment procedure and included the following requirements:

● standard precautions

● timescales

● safe handling techniques

● working within your own sphere

● including the individual.

HSC 358c Report on, review and update risk assessment

In this element you will learn:

- how to record and report your findings from the risk assessment and the importance of doing so accurately
- the frequency of reviewing and reporting of pressure area risk assessments
- the types of change in the individual's condition which need to be reported and recorded.

Recording, reporting and reviewing risk assessments

A risk assessment, however well carried out, will only be as good as the information recorded and reported from it. You could assess an individual following all the required criteria of the assessment but fail to record it appropriately. The recording and reporting of risk assessments and how this is done is vitally important, as is the regular reviewing of the condition of skin.

Frequency of reviewing risk assessments

Risk assessments should not be carried out once and then forgotten about. To ensure the individual receives the appropriate ongoing care, risk assessments should be reviewed or repeated at intervals agreed by the team and your organisation.

If an individual is identified as being at risk to pressure sores, a formal reassessment should be carried out as follows:

Waterlow Score	Frequency of reassessment
< 10	Weekly
10–15	Every 72 hours
16–20	Every 72 hours
> 20	Every 48 hours

The individual should also be reassessed:

- following any surgical or medical procedure
- after receiving an epidural (injection into the spinal cord to produce a loss of sensation below the waist)
- following signs of deterioration or improvement in his or her condition
- upon transfer to a new ward or care environment.

Did you know?

Approximately 65 per cent of individuals hospitalised with hip fractures develop pressure sores.

Active knowledge

Identify your organisation's policy on pressure area risk assessment. What timescales does it state for reviewing and reassessing individuals at risk?

As a carer you should assess the individual's skin condition informally on a regular basis during general care procedure interactions, such as changing dressings or incontinence aids. You should also examine the individual's skin each time you change his or her position. This information should be recorded on a chart such as the example given on page 215.

Some individuals may be identified as not being at risk of skin breakdown. However, this could change if the individual's condition changes, and each person should be reassessed accordingly.

CASE STUDY: Frequency of assessment

G has been transferred to your rehabilitation unit following a stroke. She arrived on your unit at 10.20am by hospital transport. From the case notes accompanying her, G had a Waterlow Score of 21 when she was first admitted to hospital, where they diagnosed her stroke; this has since been reduced to 17 following her last assessment two days ago. G is no longer incontinent of faeces but regularly has 'accidents' because she does not want to bother staff when she needs to urinate and leaves it until the last minute.

1 When should you undertake an informal assessment of G's risk of skin breakdown?
2 By what time should a formal assessment be carried out?
3 If G's risk assessment outcome remains the same as it was before her transfer to your unit, how often should you review it?
4 By how much would G's score have been reduced when it was assessed that she was no longer faecal incontinent?
5 How can you help G to reduce further her risk of skin breakdown?

PATIENT TURNING CHART

Frequency of patient turning should be agreed by the team and recorded in the patient care plan

Name: *Phillip Young*   **Hospital number:** *JL56002316*

Date: 21.08.06

Time	Position	Skin Grading	Signature	Status
01.00				
02.00				
03.00				
04.00				
05.00				
06.00				
07.00				
08.00				
09.00				
10.00	B	2 – on admission	L Harding	SW
11.00				
12.00	R	2	L Harding	SW
13.00				
14.00	P	2	L Harding	SW
15.00				
16.00	L	2	N Green	Staff Nurse
17.00				
18.00	B	2	N Green	Staff Nurse
19.00				
20.00	R	2	N Green	Staff Nurse
21.00				
22.00	P	2	Andrew Pitts	B Grade
23.00				
24.00	L	2	Andrew Pitts	B Grade

Patient position key:

SM – Self mobilising
L – Left side
R – Right side
P – Prone
B – Back
AC – Arm Chair
T – Therapy
I – Investigation

Plan of positions:

1. Change position every *2(two)* hour/s.
2. Patient can sit in arm chair for *1(one)* hour/s only.

● *Patient turning chart*

Information to be reported and recorded

All formal and informal risk assessments relating to skin breakdown should be reported, recorded and made available to all members of the care team. This is to ensure that all staff involved in the individual's care are kept up to date with any changes in the individual's condition.

Individuals with stage 1 pressure sores and above should have in-depth recordings made of the following information:

- *Grade of pressure sore* (e.g. Waterlow Grade 2) – when monitoring and recording on pressure sores which are healing it is important to record the grade of the sore as it originally was and to state on the record that it is healing. Pressure sores can deteriorate from a grade 3 to a grade 4 but should not be graded back up when healing.
- *Cause of the pressure sore* (e.g. rubbing on splint).
- *Area affected* (e.g. upper left calf, elbow).
- *Size of the pressure sore* (e.g. 2cm x 1cm).
- *Any signs of infection* (e.g. skin red 1cm out from edge of sore).
- *Odour emitting from sore* (e.g. no odour detected).
- *Pain* (e.g. individual complaining of moderate pain).
- *A photograph of the pressure sore* should be taken to help identify healing or further breakdown.

An example review is shown on page 217.

Any change within an individual's condition should be reported and recorded immediately. The change may require that the individual's care plan is reviewed and altered accordingly. Changes that need to be reported and recorded include:

- *Changes to the skin* – e.g. colour, spots, dryness.
- *Rise in temperature* – the individual can become sweaty, increasing the risk.
- *Change of continence ability* – e.g. the insertion or removal of a catheter.
- *Development of health condition* – e.g. cancer, anaemia, diabetes, MS.
- *Changes to mobility* – becoming ambulant or losing mobility.
- *Changes to appetite* – an increase or decrease in appetite.
- *Weight loss or weight gain.*
- *Prescription of risk-increasing medicines* – e.g. steroids, cytotoxics.

Some organisations, especially larger ones such as the NHS, may have a collective report form that needs to be completed. This form enables the organisation to collect information relating to the incidence or number of individuals developing pressure sores while in the care of the organisation. This information would be collated by the Tissue Viability Service on a weekly basis and aids them to identify any increase or decrease in individuals developing pressure sores.

Did you know?

The fibres of the fabric linen absorb the body's perspiration. These fibres then swell and release moisture into the air creating a self-cooling effect. As a result, linen is a popular choice for bedding, especially in hotter climates.

Patient Pressure Area Review Record

Name: Marion Spierrs   **Hospital No:** JJ4235633

Ward: Ward 17 Rehabilitation

<table>
<tr><td colspan="2">TO BE COMPLETED FOLLOWING REASSESSMENT USING THE FOLLOWING TIMESCALES</td><td rowspan="6">AFFIX PHOTOGRAPH HERE</td></tr>
<tr><td>Waterlow score:</td><td>Frequency of review:</td></tr>
<tr><td>< 10</td><td>Weekly</td></tr>
<tr><td>10 – 15</td><td>Every 72 hours</td></tr>
<tr><td>16 – 20</td><td>Every 72 hours</td></tr>
<tr><td>> 20</td><td>Every 48 hours</td></tr>
</table>

Grade of pressure sore	1 ≥	2	3	4
Area affected	Left heel			
Cause of the pressure sore	Rubbing on splint			
Size of the pressure sore	2cm by 2cm			
Any signs of infection	No signs indicated at present			
Odour emitting from sore	No odour detected			
Pain	Marion states she only has pain when pressure is put onto the heel			

Completed by: Lucy Harding   **Status:** Support Worker

Date of last review: Not applicable

Date of this review: 19.8.06

● *Patient pressure area review record*

NHS Trust
Weekly Pressure Report Form

Unit/Ward: Ward 17 - Rehabilitation

Week Ending: 20 August 2006

Total number of patients on ward: 18

Total number of patients with pressure sores: 3

Patient's Name OR Hospital Sticker	Hospital Number	Date of Admission	Waterlow Score	Grade of Pressure Sore
Joseph Wilson	HR2758921	02.08.06	21	2
Marion Spierrs	JJ4235633	19.08.06	14	1
Joy Masters	MJ4530076	19.08.06	18	1

Name: Lucy Harding   **Signature:**   Lucy Harding

Status: Support Worker   **Date:**   20.08.06

● *A weekly report form*

Active knowledge

Find out what your organisation's policy is for recording and reporting on pressure area risk assessments for the individual and collectively.

Did you know?

Up to 80 per cent of individuals with a spinal cord injury will develop a pressure sore, and 30 per cent will develop more than one.

An increase in the incidence of pressure sores does not necessarily indicate that staff are not doing their job – this may be due to the susceptibility of the individuals receiving treatment at that time. However, regular increases may need to be looked into to ensure that staff are suitably trained and are following the guidelines correctly.

Remember

A risk assessment will only be as good as the information recorded and reported from it.

The importance of recording and reporting risk assessments

The passing on of information within a care environment is important to enable the continuity of care for that individual. If information relating to an individual was not reported or passed on appropriately, then staff, professionals and the individual would not know what care had been given or indeed needed to be given. The environment would be chaotic – nobody would know what to do and the individual would not receive the care that he or she required.

Records relating to an individual's care are just as important as the care that is given. Records can be used:
- to collate information for the individual's treatment
- to monitor areas of change within the individual
- to inform other staff or professionals on the individual's progress
- for legal purposes – for example, a coroner's inquest.

Following the Data Protection Act 1998 all records completed by you must be accurate, legible and complete. Risk assessments on pressure areas must be recorded accurately and legibly to ensure the correct level of care is given to the individual following the assessment. If you record the assessment inaccurately or incorrectly, this wrong information will be passed on to others and the individual would receive the wrong type of care.

To ensure your recording is legible you must write clearly to prevent any misinterpretation of the record. If you make any mistake while writing the report you should simply cross out your mistake with a single line and rewrite the word. Trying to correct your mistake by going over the word or changing the letters within the word could lead to difficulties in reading it correctly. To ensure your report is complete you should include the date and your initials or signature to confirm when the report was completed and by whom. Initialling your report will allow other staff to identify you as the person completing it, should they need to clarify any areas of the report.

It is just as important to report pressure area assessment outcomes to the appropriate staff, including the person in charge and the individual concerned, to ensure immediate care can be given as appropriate. Informing the individual of the risk assessment outcome is not only the person's right, it is also important to obtain the individual's understanding and co-operation with his or her treatment.

Remember

Records within a care environment are a legal requirement.

Following risk assessment the information you identify and record will need to be incorporated into the individual's care plan. This plan would detail what care the individual requires and how it should be given. If you fail to record the outcome of the risk assessment accurately this will lead to the care plan being developed using inaccurate information and therefore the individual will be provided with the wrong treatment.

Evidence indicator

Undertake a risk assessment on an individual in your care using your organisation's assessment tool. Report and record your findings and incorporate the outcome into the individual's care plan.

You should now see how important it is to record information accurately, legibly and completely. As a carer you play a very important role in the care of individuals alongside other staff. If you do not follow your role completely, this will have an adverse effect on others – especially the individual.

Keys to good practice: Recording assessments

✓ The outcome of the risk assessment must be incorporated into the individual's care plan.

✓ You must ensure you record accurately, legibly and completely.

✓ Changes in the individual, whether positive or negative, must be reported and recorded.

✓ Assessment must be reviewed on a regular basis.

Test yourself

1 Why is it important to report and record your findings of risk assessment?
2 What do the terms 'accurate', 'legible' and 'complete' mean? How can you ensure this?
3 How often should you reassess an individual?
4 **a)** What changes within an individual should be reported and recorded?
   b) When should these changes be reported and recorded?
   c) Why is it important to report and record these changes?

1. What responsibilities do you have under national legislation, guidelines and policies in relation to pressure area care?

2. Describe in detail why it is important for you to work in your own sphere of competence.

3. Describe in detail how you can involve the individual during the whole process of identifying those at risk and pressure area risk assessment.

4. What other health care staff can support you in pressure area risk assessment?

5. When should the following be carried out and why?
   a) Initial assessment
   b) Reassessment
   c) Reviews

6. Describe in detail the layers of the skin and the purpose of each layer.

7. Describe the predisposing factors to pressure sore development.

8. Describe the external factors to pressure sore development.

9. Describe three assessment tools used in assessing pressure area risk.

10. What is the importance of recording and reporting pressure area care?

Prepare for and undertake physiological measurements

This unit will give you the required knowledge for taking physiological measurements of basic body systems. To ensure the body is working correctly and to identify underlying health problems it is important to take appropriate physiological measurements as required. These measurements include blood pressure, pulse, temperature, respirations and body mass index.

You will gain an understanding of how to prepare the environment for each of the measurements to be taken; this includes the individual and his or her comfort and rights, as well as a range of care environments. You will learn about and identify the different types of equipment used for each of the measurements and how to follow correct procedures for their use. This will include developing an awareness of your limitations and of health and safety issues.

What you need to learn

- The importance of informed consent
- Legislation and organisational policies and procedures
- Policies for safe use of equipment and techniques
- Job roles and responsibilities
- The importance of taking accurate body measurements
- Blood pressure
- Pulse
- Temperature
- Respirations
- Measuring height and weight
- What physiological measurements can indicate
- Records and documentation

In this section we will be looking at how to prepare the environment and resources for taking physiological measurements. It is important to remember the individual in this preparation period – he or she is just as important to prepare, if not more so.

The importance of informed consent

When preparing the environment for clinical procedures, the rights and choices of the individual must be taken into consideration. Full information about the procedure needs to be given to the individual, as this will help him or her to feel more at ease when you take the measurements. Each person has the right to information about his or her care or treatment, to ensure that any decision he or she makes is an informed one. Knowing what is happening, when and how, also empowers the individual to make choices around his or her beliefs, preferences, choice, needs and expectations. By ensuring the individual is fully informed, more accurate readings can be taken, as he or she will be less stressed and more co-operative.

What is consent?

Consent can be defined as an individual's agreement to prescribed therapy or treatment. Consent can be either written, spoken or implied. If an individual rolls up her sleeve when informed of the need to take a sample of blood, this can be taken as the individual consenting. If the person is not able to physically assist in his treatment but does not resist, this can also be taken as consent.

CASE STUDY: Obtaining consent

H is 21 years old. He lives at home with his parents and sister. He has cerebral palsy, no speech and requires assistance with his daily activities. You are one of the team of care workers who assist him and his family. You provide respite once a week for the family by sitting with him while his family go out. It is a very hot day and H has indicated he would like to go out into the garden. You are aware that his skin burns very easily in the sun and needs to be protected by sun cream.

1   How can you obtain consent from H before applying the sun cream?
2   If H were not co-operative with you applying sun cream to his skin, pulling his arm away and screaming, what actions would you take?

Regardless of the individual's physical or mental ability you need to ensure that he or she is given the full correct information on the treatment. This is known as informed consent. If an individual has no verbal or physical means of showing consent, treatment can be given if it is necessary to the individual's health.

Legislation and organisational policies and procedures

Current European and national legislation

A range of legislation covers the rights of the individual; these are laws that must be adhered to. They are set by the national government and also the European Union. It is important to understand your own responsibilities related to the legislation to ensure good practice.

The table on page 225 lists some of the European and national laws that affect both the rights of the individual and your responsibilities as a care worker.

Active knowledge

Read the table on page 225 then identify further pieces of legislation that relate to health and social care settings, for example, the Disability Discrimination Act 1995 or Care Standards Act 2000. How do these laws affect the rights of the individual and your accountability as a care worker?

How the law influences practice

When a law is passed it then becomes necessary to ensure that the law is enforced in practice. This means that steps must be taken to ensure that those people to whom the law applies are informed of their new responsibilities under that law and act accordingly. For example, the Data Protection Act 1998 changed the law on how information is held about people; thus all people who store confidential information, such as contact details and medical records, need to be fully informed about how the law requires them to hold information on people (Freedom of Information Act 2000).

It is the responsibility of all staff to ensure that their working practices are in accordance with their workplace's guidelines and procedures.

Legislation	Rights of the individual	Responsibility of the care worker	Responsibility of the employer
The Human Rights Act 1998	The rights and freedoms of individuals are guaranteed by this Act. These include the right to privacy and the right to equal treatment.	To ensure that all care provided to the individual meets with his or her rights, beliefs and choice.	To ensure all staff are following the requirements by ensuring they are suitably trained and have the necessary resources to meet individuals' needs.
Equal Opportunities Act 2004	Individuals have a right to be given equal access to facilities, treatments, investigations and all other aspects of care.	To ensure individuals are given equal access to required facilities and that individual differences are respected.	To ensure all staff have full understanding of the policy, and that facilities, including access, meet with the varied needs of individuals.
Health and Safety at Work Act 1974	Individuals have a right to be kept safe and all practices should ensure that health, welfare and safety are maintained.	To ensure that all working procedures are adhered to and carried out safely, and that your acts or omissions do not put others at risk.	To ensure all staff have full training on health and safety practices, such as manual handling. To ensure equipment is regularly checked and maintained. To ensure the environment is fit for employees and individuals.
The Data Protection Act 1998	Information relating to the individual shall be processed fairly and lawfully. It will be kept safely and securely and used only for the purpose intended.	To ensure that all information is accurately recorded and stored in the appropriate place to prevent misuse or access by those who do not have permission. To ensure confidentiality of the individual's details by sharing information with others on a 'need to know' basis only.	To provide suitable storage for records; to ensure staff are maintaining records appropriately; to ensure records are used only for the purpose intended and are kept no longer than required.
Control of Substances Hazardous to Health (COSHH) Regulations 2002	Individuals have a right to be protected from exposure to substances hazardous to their health.	To ensure that all chemical substances are stored, handled and disposed of appropriately, and used as per manufacturers' instructions.	To ensure a suitable, lockable storage area is provided and clearly marked and maintained.
Reporing of Injuries, Diseases and Dangerous Occurrences Regulations (RIDDOR) 1995	The individual has the right to expect any injury, disease or dangerous occurrence within the scope of this legislation to be reported.	To ensure that all injuries, diseases or dangerous occurrences are recorded and reported within the scope of this legislation as per procedures and job role.	To ensure all requirements under this legislation are met by those responsible.

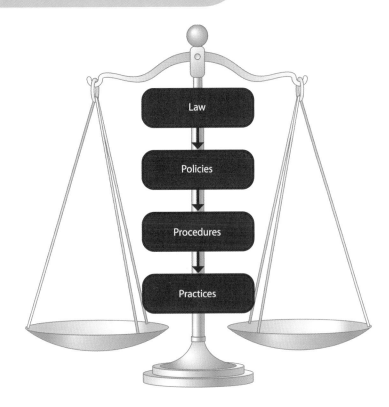

How the law influences practice

Remember

Laws in themselves do not ensure good practice – the media reports every day on situations in which laws have been broken. Being fully aware of your workplace policies and procedures and ensuring you follow them will enable you to meet standards of good practice.

The role of the inspectorate

All social care services are now inspected to ensure that workplace policies and procedures are in place and are being adhered to. The Commission for Social Care Inspection (CSCI) is responsible for ensuring social care providers meet the National Minimum Standards. The CSCI has a duty to inspect care settings regularly to ensure that the care received by individuals meets the current legislation; this includes checking clinical skills and the recording of physiological measurements. To find out more visit the commission's website at www.csci.org.uk.

Did you know?

CSCI requirements are not relevant to those working in healthcare settings at present. However, this will change with the merger of the CSCI and the Healthcare Commission in 2007.

Organisational policies and procedures

As well as current legislation, your workplace will have policies and procedures for you to follow when taking the physiological measurements of individuals. It is important to remember that these have been produced to ensure that your practices are safe and that the results you obtain are accurate.

It is your responsibility as a care worker to ensure that you are familiar with all your organisation's policies and procedures. Each care environment will have its policies and procedures clearly recorded for all staff to access.

Evidence indicator

Identify the policy and procedure file where you work. Look at the policies and procedures for taking physical measurements and write a brief account of your responsibilities relating to these procedures.

Principles of good practice

Policies defined in the care services are set around principles of good practice. There are three main principles of good practice, as described below.

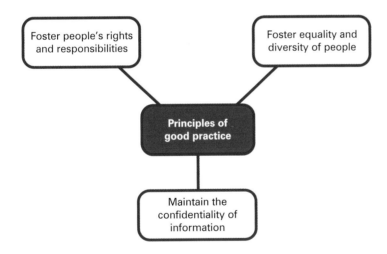

- *Foster people's rights and responsibilities*
  When working in a care setting, tensions may arise between your values (what you see as being right) and those of other people. We all have different values and there may be times when an individual wants to do something which you do not agree with. This could be as simple as wanting to remain in the communal area of the residential home while his or her blood pressure is taken. You need to separate your values from those of other people. You may not think it is appropriate for the individual to stay where everyone else can see him or her having a blood pressure check. However, you need to recognise individuals' rights and

responsibilities, and providing a request does not cause harm to the individual or to others, you must respect the individual's right to choose.

- *Foster equality and diversity of people*

  Each individual has his or her own personality, likes and dislikes. This is what makes people different from each other. Within the principles of good practice you need to ensure individuals are treated equally but differently. Everyone should be given the same opportunity but offered different means of meeting that opportunity according to their values, beliefs, preferences and choice. It is important as a care worker that you recognise an individual's diversity (difference). This could be in culture, religion, age, sex or ability. By meeting an individual's diverse needs you are promoting anti-discriminatory practices. When preparing equipment or environments for individuals you need to be mindful of their needs, ensuring that you take account of each individual's rights to equality and diversity.

- *Maintain the confidentiality of information*

  You must have a clear knowledge and understanding of workplace policies, procedures and guidelines for storing and transmitting information. This includes the recording systems and security arrangements for all information. When preparing records prior to taking physiological measurements, you must be aware of the possible consequences of leaving records unattended and prevent this from occurring.

Key terms

Needs of the individual: Needs relating to individual characteristics that influence the choice and setting up of equipment and other resources, e.g. mobility needs.

CASE STUDY: Principles of good practice

F is a young woman who is visiting the outpatients' clinic of her local hospital for the first time. F has lived in the UK most of her life and is a devout Muslim. On arriving in the department she is informed by the male doctor that he needs to take her blood pressure. F lowers her head and leaves the room immediately. The doctor follows her out into the corridor, asking what is wrong rather loudly.

1 What are F's rights in this situation?
2 Were F's rights to equality and diversity respected in preparation for taking physiological measurements?
3 What should F do now?
4 What should the doctor do now?

Active knowledge

The principles of good social care practice have been defined within the National Minimum Standards.

1 If you work in social care, connect to the website www.csci.org.uk and research the standards for your area of work. Healthcare staff should obtain a copy of their organisation's Code of Practice.
2 With reference to your job description, identify how these standards or Codes of Practice are transferred into your working practice.

Policies for safe use of equipment and techniques

Health and safety

Following health and safety policies and procedures keeps individuals, your colleagues, yourself and all visitors to the workplace safe. This is a particularly important part of your duties when preparing environments and resources for use.

When selecting and preparing environments and resources you must ensure they are correct for the task to be undertaken. The resource or equipment must be in full working order and clean. This is to reduce the risk to the individual or yourself from harm, injury or infection. It will also ensure accurate measurements are taken.

Environmental considerations should include the following:

- The room temperature: if the room is too hot or cold, this could provide inaccurate readings. For example, a person's body temperature may be recorded as very high if the environment is too hot.
- The room layout: is it suitable to ensure privacy and dignity; are there curtains at the windows; can the door be closed securely?
- Poor ventilation or strong fragrances may possibly affect the individual's breathing, and this could give inaccurate readings when taking measurements relating to the individual's breathing.

Infection control

Infection control is important when taking any physiological measurement as it prevents cross-infection and ensures the accuracy of results.

- This poster formed part of the NHS 'Clean your hands' campaign launched by the National Patient Safety Agency (NPSA)

Infection control should be a standard precaution in health and safety measures. This means preventing infection and cross-infection by washing hands before, during and after preparation of environments and resources, as well as wearing protective clothing such as gloves, aprons and masks where required.

How to wash your hands

Handwashing is the most effective way of reducing cross-infection and contamination. See the step-by-step instructions below.

Using a sterile field

In some circumstances you may be required to undertake physiological measurements in a sterile field. A sterile field is an area that has been cleaned with chemicals to ensure that it contains no pathogens (bacteria or viruses). When commencing a procedure that requires a sterile field, sterile gloves must be used, hands must be washed correctly, and equipment must also be sterilised to reduce the risk of cross-infection.

Key terms

Standard precautions and health and safety measures: A series of interventions which will minimise or prevent infection and cross-infection, including handwashing/cleansing before, during and after the activity, and the use of personal protective clothing and additional protective equipment where appropriate.

1 *Wet your hands thoroughly under warm running water and squirt liquid soap onto the palm of one hand.*

2 *Rub your hands together to make a lather.*

3 *Rub the palm of one hand along the back of the other and along the fingers. Then repeat with the other hand.*

4 *Rub in between each of your fingers on both hands and round your thumbs.*

5 *Rinse off the soap with clean water.*

6 *Dry hands thoroughly on a disposable towel.*

Wearing protective clothing

Employers now have a legal duty to provide protective clothing to employees. Protective clothing reduces the risks of cross-contamination to both individuals and staff. It ensures that good hygiene is adhered to and protects personal clothing from damage. Some staff wear their work clothes outside of the working environment. This can increase the risk of cross-contamination by transferring bacteria and viruses to other environments.

Wearing disposable aprons and gloves when working with body fluids and/or chemicals, and ensuring that they are changed after each task, ensures that you are meeting your health and safety responsibilities and keeps individuals safe.

Key terms

Contaminated: Items can become contaminated with body fluids, chemicals or radionucleatides. Any pack/item opened and not used should be treated as contaminated.

How to use disposable gloves

1 *Check gloves before putting them on. Never use gloves with holes or tears. Check that they are not cracked or faded.*

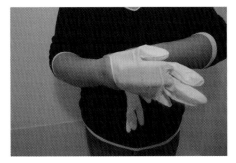

2 Pull gloves on, making sure that they fit properly. If you are wearing a gown, pull the gloves over the cuffs of the gown.

3 *Take the gloves off by pulling from the cuff – this turns the glove inside out.*

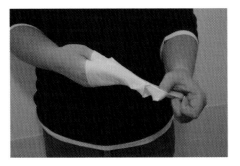

4 *Pull off the second glove while still holding the first, so that the two gloves are folded together inside out.*

5 *Dispose of the gloves in the correct waste disposal container and wash your hands.*

CASE STUDY: For whose protection?

A and S work as health care assistants in a residential home for older people. They have had a very hectic day because a number of the individuals have stomach bugs. They decide to go to the local shopping centre for a coffee before going home. Both are still wearing their uniforms.

1 Do you feel this is acceptable practice?
2 Discuss this with your colleagues to identify their views.

Active knowledge

What is your organisation's policy on wearing work clothes outside of the working environment?

Storage and handling of equipment

These policies cover procedures for the appropriate storage and handling of equipment used for taking physiological measurements, such as portable blood pressure monitors.

Storing equipment

Storing equipment inappropriately increases the risks to both individuals and colleagues. For example:

- leaving a portable blood pressure monitor in the middle of the room could lead to an individual or colleague tripping over it and sustaining a serious injury
- leaving cleaning fluid on the work surface in the kitchen could lead to someone drinking it, resulting in poisoning. It could also contaminate food if spilt, again poisoning individuals.

If an individual or colleague were to sustain injury from equipment being stored incorrectly or not being stored at all, he or she could take legal action against whoever failed to follow the correct procedures.

Using equipment

Equipment can be a potential hazard: when using any equipment you must always check that it is in full working order. The use of faulty equipment is unprofessional, shows poor practices and a lack of judgement. Its use could result in injury to yourself or the individual.

Key terms

Personal protective clothing: Items such as plastic aprons, gloves (both clean and sterile), footwear, dresses, trousers and shirts, and all-in-one trouser suits. These may be single-use disposable clothing or reusable clothing.

Electrical equipment should be checked to ensure there are no loose or exposed wires and that any electrical cable is not frayed or split. You must also check that the electrical item has had a recent electrical test by a qualified electrician.

When you check equipment and find it is faulty, it is your legal responsibility to label it to ensure that no one else uses it and to report the fault to the person in charge.

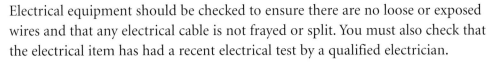

Key terms

Additional protective equipment: Types of personal protective equipment such as visors, protective eyewear and radiation protective equipment.

Evidence indicator

Discuss with your assessor:

1 How you should check that equipment is fit for use.
2 Why you should report faulty equipment to the person in charge.

Active knowledge

1 **a)** Identify the policies and procedures file in your workplace and a policy relevant to taking physiological measurements.
   b) Read the policy thoroughly, noting all relevant information.
   c) Discuss the policy with a colleague, sharing the information that you have found. Identify three principles of good practice that form the basis of the policy.

Job roles and responsibilities

Each job has its own role and responsibilities which are set out in the job description. Following these roles and responsibilities ensures a safe and effective working environment. Knowing and understanding your role and responsibilities promotes good practice.

A safe practitioner is one who is aware of the limitations of his or her experience and job role, and as a result never tries to do something outside of those limitations. If you are unsure of how to prepare the equipment or environment, it is safer for you and the individual to ask for help. This will not show you as being weak – quite the opposite. Asking for help is a strength: you will be demonstrating that you know what you are capable of and what you need support with.

Remember

Both you and your employer are accountable for your acts and omissions under the Health and Safety at Work Act 1974 (see page 225).

Accountability when taking physiological measurements

Accountability can be defined as working responsibly within the limitations of your job role. This includes your responsibilities to the individual and to your colleagues. You are responsible for everything that you do and do not do in your work.

There is a line of accountability from the managers through to you. Your job description will state to whom you are accountable within your area of work; this is usually your line manager. You are also accountable to the individual in respect of ensuring that he or she receives the treatment to which he or she is entitled, in the way in which he or she is entitled to receive it.

Accountability covers a range of issues when taking the physiological measurements of an individual. These include:

- awareness of your job role and your limitations within that role
- ensuring that you attend all training that is provided
- ensuring that the equipment is used safely; this includes ensuring that the equipment is in working order after use, storing it appropriately for others to use and reporting any equipment that is faulty
- awareness of the environment in which the equipment will be used
- awareness of the needs of the individual on whom the equipment is to be used.

Awareness of your job role and your limitations within that role

To ensure that employees are aware of their job role and responsibilities, every employer provides a job description. This describes all tasks that employees are responsible for and details the role that they will play. It sets out the line of accountability by explaining who you are responsible to and what you are responsible for.

Active knowledge

1 Read through your job description.
   a) Identify the daily tasks that you do in relation to your job role.
   b) Are there any things that you have been asked to do at work that have been outside of your job role? If the answer is yes, what did you do?
   c) Is there anything you would do differently now that you have re-read your job description?
   d) How does knowing your job description help you to achieve good practice?
2 With your colleagues, discuss what you have learned from this activity. You do not have to give full details of actual examples; this activity is more concerned with your own reflections and learning.

Test yourself

1 What is meant by consent?
2 What legislation relates to the rights of individuals?
3 What is meant by 'the principles of good practice'?
4 Describe the correct hand washing procedure.
5 Why is it important to store and use equipment appropriately?
6 What pieces of equipment would you not be willing to use because of the limitations of your role?
7 Why is it important to receive appropriate training before using any equipment?
8 How would you know if a piece of equipment has been maintained properly? Examples of equipment that you may like to find out about are:
   - blood pressure monitor
   - digital thermometer
   - spirometer.
9 If a piece of equipment is faulty, what should you do?
10 To whom are you accountable in your job role?

HSC 361b Undertake physiological measurements

Physiological body measurements are the signs of life in a person. They indicate the health and well-being of the individual, and monitoring them enables assessment of the level at which an individual functions physically. This section will look in turn at each of the following physiological measurements:

- blood pressure
- pulse
- temperature
- respirations
- body mass index (BMI).

Did you know?

Stress affects the body in many ways:
- blood pressure rises and the pulse rate becomes faster
- breathing becomes shallow and quick
- the skin becomes clammy and sweaty.

It can also affect the physiological measurements you take, which can lead to false readings.

For each physiological measurement described in this section you will learn about:

- the body system it is measuring
- what the measurement can tell you about an individual's health
- the equipment that is used
- how to use the equipment
- any health and safety considerations.

All of the physiological measurements can be observed, measured and monitored. Baseline measurements are an essential part of planning appropriate care of the individual. A baseline measurement is one taken before any treatment or further measurements are taken. It is this first measurement to which all further measurements are compared; therefore baseline measurements are essential in keeping track of any improvements. Gaining an understanding of the individual's 'normal' readings and the general physiological norms will ensure that appropriate care can be given.

For each of the body measurements there is specific equipment and set procedures. Ensuring that the equipment is in full working order is a health and safety requirement and should always be the first stage of the procedure. Ensuring that all equipment is gathered and to hand when commencing the monitoring is also an important part of the preparation.

When taking physiological measurements it is essential that the individual receives the type of care which meets his or her full range of needs. Correct preparation of the environment demonstrates your competence and shows good working practice, which in turn can instil confidence and give reassurance to the individual. Discussing the tests with the individual also gives you the opportunity to assist him or her with repositioning of clothing in order to access the required parts of the body, if necessary.

The importance of taking accurate body measurements

Accurate readings which are monitored, recorded and reported can ensure early interventions and treatment. In this way, accurate readings will help individuals to make informed life choices regarding their health and lifestyle.

It is important to know how to take accurate body measurements as well as why they are being taken. This is a form of preventative healthcare designed to help and encourage us to live a healthier lifestyle, and is part of the government's white paper 'Choosing Health'.

Blood pressure

What is blood pressure?

Blood pressure is the pressure exerted by the blood on the walls of the blood vessels as it travels along. Every time the heart beats, its natural pumping action pushes a volume of blood away from the heart into the arteries and around the body. This puts the blood under pressure and this is what is monitored when taking a blood pressure reading.

Understanding what blood pressure is will ensure that appropriate action is taken once the task has been completed. Communicating all of your findings ensures that an appropriate diagnosis can be made and that appropriate treatment can be given to the individual.

To fully understand what blood pressure (and pulse) is, you need to have a good understanding of the cardiovascular system.

The cardiovascular system

The cardiovascular system consists of the heart, lungs, blood vessels and blood. This system is also known as the circulatory system because it circulates blood around the body within vessels, mainly veins and arteries, with the aid of a pump – the heart.

Arteries are the largest of the blood vessels. They connect to smaller arterioles, which connect to the tiniest of all the vessels – capillaries. Capillaries then connect to venules, which are smaller versions of veins. Arteries, arterioles, venules and veins all have the ability to dilate and constrict (open and close) which helps move blood along.

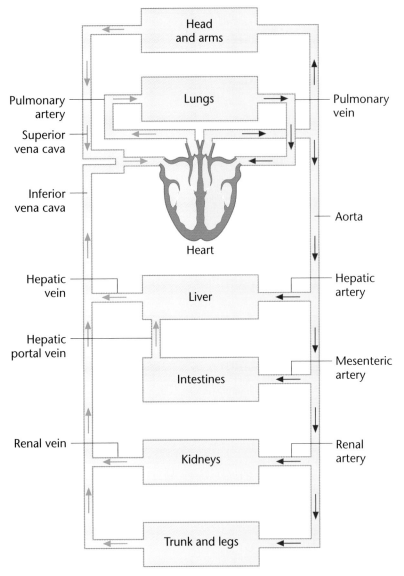

● *Some of the main blood vessels in the blood circulatory system*

The main role of the cardiovascular system is to circulate blood around the body while carrying:

- vital substances that the body needs in keeping its cells and tissues healthy – these include oxygen, food, water, hormones and enzymes
- waste products from the cells and tissues to the lungs and kidneys to be excreted – these include carbon dioxide and toxins
- heat around the body.

Did you know?

The adult human body has on average 5.6 litres or nearly 10 pints of blood. This amount circulates through the body three times every minute.

How the cardiovascular system links to the respiratory system

The body needs a constant supply of oxygen to function properly. Oxygen is inhaled into the body via the lungs during breathing (inspiration), where it is absorbed into the blood supply. The oxygen-rich blood, known as oxygenated blood, then circulates from the lungs through the body, giving oxygen to the body's tissues, organs and cells. As oxygen is passed to the cells it is exchanged for the waste product carbon dioxide. The blood containing carbon dioxide (deoxygenated blood) now returns to the lungs, where the carbon dioxide passes out and is exhaled from the body during breathing (expiration). With this, the process of passing oxygen to the blood and carbon dioxide from the blood starts again – this process is known as gaseous exchange. (For more on the respiratory system, see pages 261–62.)

The heart

The heart is a large muscular organ which is divided into four chambers. The upper two chambers are called atriums and the lower chambers are called ventricles; thus the heart's four chambers are:

- the left atrium
- the right atrium
- the left ventricle
- the right ventricle.

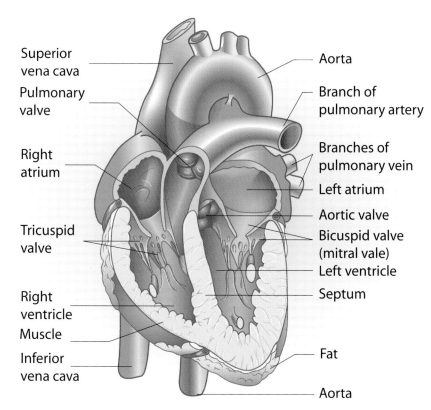

The structure of the heart

Blood is pumped from the atrium to the ventricle through a one-way valve. The right side of the heart receives deoxygenated blood from the body through the veins. This blood is then pumped to the lungs where gaseous exchange occurs, i.e. carbon dioxide passes from the blood to the lungs and is exhaled during breathing, and oxygen which has been inhaled during breathing is taken up by the blood. The oxygenated blood then returns to the left side of the heart where it is pumped out to the rest of the body. This process is then repeated.

Blood pressure readings

Blood pressure is measured when it is at its highest and lowest, giving two figures:

- The highest pressure is the pressure in the artery when the heart contracts and the blood is pumped out. This is known as systolic pressure.
- The lower pressure is the pressure in the arteries when the heart is being filled up with blood as the heart relaxes. This is known as diastolic pressure.

These two numbers are usually written with the systolic measurement over the diastolic measurement. On average, a healthy blood pressure reading in adults is 120/70 mmHg.

Did you know?

Blood pressure is measured in millimetres of mercury (mmHg).

The range of blood pressure	Measurement
Low	99/60 or less
Healthy	100–130/61–80
Moderate	131–140/81–90
Severe	141–160/91–100
Crisis	161/101 or higher

The above table should act as a guide only. An individual's blood pressure reading can mean a variety of things depending on that individual. Low blood pressure could indicate either good physical fitness or internal bleeding or a heart attack. You must ensure you record and report any recordings which:

- you are unsure of
- give you cause for concern
- are different from the individual's baseline measurement (see page 236).

High blood pressure

High blood pressure is also known as hypertension. It usually has recognisable symptoms, as shown in the diagram below. However, some individuals do not present any indications of having high blood pressure, which is why there is a need for regular monitoring.

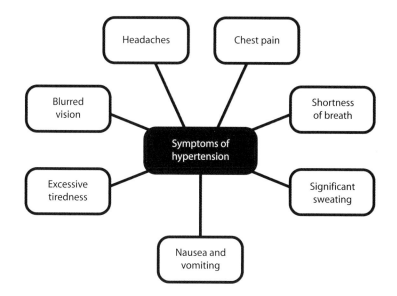

Types of hypertension

There are two types of hypertension:

- *Primary hypertension,* also known as essential hypertension. There is no clear cause for this type of hypertension; however, there are indications to suggest that it is hereditary. This means that you are more likely to get it if a close member of your family has it. Primary hypertension can also be linked to high salt and fat intake in food and excessive amounts of stress. Regular monitoring is essential for individuals who fit into either of these categories.

- *Secondary hypertension.* The signs and symptoms of secondary hypertension are not always exhibited and it is only during routine examination that it is picked up. This type of hypertension has a link to a recognised cause, which may be a symptom of another disease or illness. These include:
  – kidney disease
  – narrowing of the aorta
  – pre-eclampsia in pregnancy
  – adrenal gland disease.
  Some forms of medication can also cause secondary hypertension, including steroids and some types of contraceptive pill.

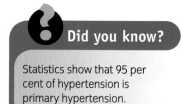

Diseases associated with hypertension

People with hypertension have a risk of major illnesses, which include those shown in the diagram below.

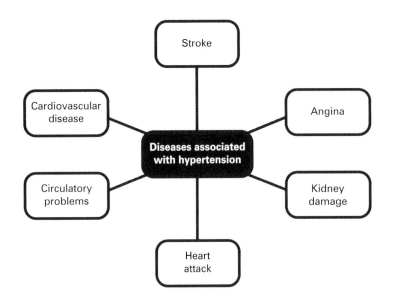

Treating hypertension

Hypertension treatment may include a range of medication; however, there are lifestyle changes that can help to reduce high blood pressure. These include:

- losing weight if overweight
- stopping smoking
- reducing alcohol intake
- reducing salt intake
- reducing fat intake
- eating at least five portions of fruit and vegetables a day
- taking regular exercise.

It is good practice to encourage individuals who have high blood pressure to consider the above lifestyle changes and include all of them, if applicable, in their daily regime. Studies have shown that losing weight combined with a low salt and low fat diet significantly reduces hypertension, therefore avoiding the need for medication.

Low blood pressure

Low blood pressure is also known as hypotension. This occurs when the pressure of the blood circulating around the body is lower than normal. Blood pressure that is too low results in an inadequate amount of blood circulating around the body to vital organs.

Low blood pressure is only a problem if it has adverse effects on the body. It is important to remember that different people have different blood pressures;

some individuals will have a naturally low pressure in comparison to others but are healthy.

When taking an individual's blood pressure reading it is important to ask questions about the person's medical history if his or her blood pressure is low. These questions may help other professionals to find a possible cause and will ascertain whether a low blood pressure reading is normal for the individual or not. It is important that you record the individual's responses to these questions in his or her notes and report any concerns immediately to the shift leader or supervisor.

✔ Keys to good practice: Taking an individual's blood pressure

You should ask the following questions when taking blood pressure.

- What is your normal blood pressure?
- Have you been eating and drinking normally?
- Are you taking any medication? What medication are you taking?
- Have you recently had an illness?
- Have you recently been involved in an accident?
- Do you feel dizzy or light-headed when standing up from either sitting or lying down?

Symptoms of hypotension

Sudden blood loss will reduce the blood pressure leading to shock and, in the most serious of cases, unconsciousness. Others symptoms of hypotension that can build up over time include:

- fainting
- weakness
- dizziness
- tiredness
- light-headedness when standing from either sitting or lying – this is known as postural hypotension.

Causes of hypotension

There are many causes for low blood pressure as shown in the diagram on the next page. To accurately diagnose this condition, professional medical attention should be sought. If the individual's blood pressure is below 99/60 (see page 240) and he or she is experiencing the above symptoms, this would generally suggest hypotension and the individual should immediately be referred for further investigation.

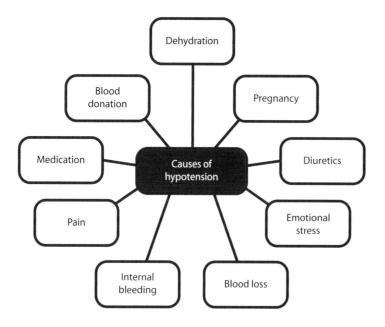

How to take a blood pressure reading

Blood pressure readings can be taken using:

- a manual sphygmomanometer
- a digital sphygmomanometer.

When using a manual sphygmomanometer, a stethoscope is also used. Manual sphygmomanometers used to be made with mercury, but these are now being replaced with aneroid sphygmomanometers. This is because mercury creates health, safety and environmental risks.

Digital sphygmomanometers are modern and easy to operate. A stethoscope is not required, making them practical to use in a noisy environment, and they have become the preferred method within many health care settings. However, digital monitors can be affected by heat and moisture, and can be less effective if the individual's heartbeat is irregular. Some health care workers therefore find a manual sphygmomanometer and stethoscope give a more accurate blood pressure reading (if used correctly).

Using a manual sphygmomanometer

A manual sphygmomanometer consists of an inflatable cuff which wraps around the upper arm. It is important to use the correct cuff size for the individual, to ensure an accurate reading can be taken. Cuffs are available in small, medium, large and extra large, and the sizes are shown on the label of the cuff.

The individual should be encouraged to sit down and rest his or her arm on a table; alternatively, if lying down then the arm can be rested at the side on the bed. The appropriate cuff should be wrapped around the individual's upper arm just above the elbow.

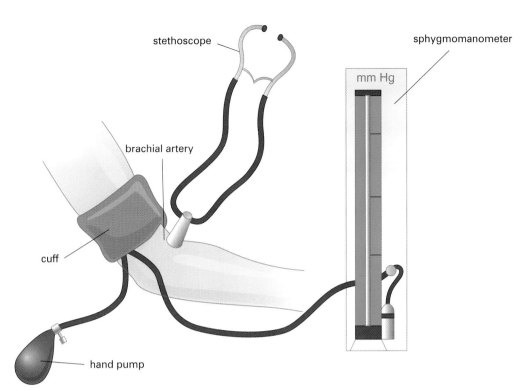

stethoscope

sphygmomanometer

mm Hg

brachial artery

cuff

hand pump

● *Taking a blood pressure reading with a manual sphygmomanometer and a stethoscope*

The valve on the inflator bulb should be checked and confirmed as closed. By placing the head of the stethoscope over the brachial artery, on the inside of the elbow joint, you should be able to hear the 'thumping' of the pulse through the stethoscope. The cuff should be inflated by squeezing the inflator bulb until the pulse can no longer be heard or felt. Inflating the cuff too much can cause the individual a great deal of discomfort.

Once the pulse sound has disappeared, the valve on the inflator bulb should be released slowly while you listen for the return of the pulse through the stethoscope. The first recording is taken at the point on the gauge when the pulsing can first be heard while deflating the cuff – this is the systolic pressure, the top number when recording. You must ensure you continue to deflate the cuff slowly until the pulsing sound disappears again. The bottom number – the diastolic pressure – is the recording taken at the point on the gauge when the pulsing can no longer be heard.

Remember

You only need to inflate the cuff on a manual sphygmomanometer until you can no longer hear or feel the brachial pulse. Inflating the cuff excessively can cause the individual a great deal of discomfort.

Keys to good practice: Taking blood pressure using a manual sphygmomanometer

1 Select the appropriate equipment and the correct cuff size.

2 Explain the procedure to the individual and encourage him or her to sit with the arm extended on a table and to the front.

3 Wrap the cuff snugly around the upper arm.

4 Locate the brachial artery, placing the stethoscope over it so you can hear the pulse.

5 Close the valve on the inflator bulb and ask the individual to be as quiet as possible.

6 Pump up the cuff until you can no longer hear the brachial pulse.

7 Deflate the cuff slowly and steadily.

8 Listen for the pulsing of the systolic pressure to return and note the point on the gauge where this occurred.

9 Continue deflating the cuff and listen carefully until you can no longer hear the pulsing (this is the diastolic pressure). Note the point on the gauge where this occurred.

10 Deflate the cuff rapidly and completely.

11 Remove the cuff from the individual.

12 Record the blood pressure on the appropriate forms.

13 Put the manual sphygmomanometer away in its appropriate storage place.

14 Report any concerns or deviations from the baseline measurement to the shift leader or supervisor.

Using a digital sphygmomanometer

A digital sphygmomanometer has an inflatable cuff which automatically inflates when the monitor is switched on. The cuff is fitted on to the individual's upper arm as with a manual sphygmomanometer. However, it is important that the tubing leading from the cuff to the monitor is positioned on the inner middle of the individual's arm. Once the machine has inflated the cuff sufficiently it will begin deflating, taking digital recordings as it is doing so. Once the machine has detected both the systolic and diastolic readings, it will give an audible sound indicating it has finished. The cuff will then automatically completely deflate. The readings of the individual's blood pressure measurements will be displayed on the digital screen.

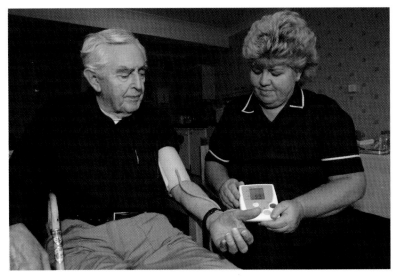

Taking a blood pressure reading using a digital sphygmomanometer

Remember

Always check the equipment is clean and in full working order before using.

Keys to good practice: Taking blood pressure using a digital sphygmomanometer

1 Select the appropriate equipment and the correct cuff size.

2 Explain the procedure to the individual and encourage him or her to sit with the arm extended on a table and to the front.

3 Wrap the cuff snugly around the upper arm, ensuring the tubing is running along the inner arm.

4 Switch the machine on, following manufacturer's instructions.

5 Allow the machine to fully inflate the cuff and finish taking all of its reading.

6 On hearing the audible signal indicating the measurements have been completed, remove the cuff from the individual's arm.

7 Record the blood pressure on the appropriate charts.

8 Put away the equipment in its appropriate storage place.

9 Report any concerns or deviations from the baseline measurement to the shift leader or supervisor.

The manual or digital sphygmomanometer will not produce a clear result if the cuff is put over clothing. You should therefore remember to ask the individual to roll up his or her sleeve, or assist him or her to slip the arm out of a sleeve if it is too restrictive.

Evidence indicator

Show your assessor how you set up and use a manual or digital sphygmomanometer, according to your organisation's availability of equipment.

Test yourself

1 What is blood pressure?
2 What is the difference between systolic and diastolic pressure?
3 What is the normal range for blood pressure?
4 What equipment is used for taking blood pressure?
5 List three things that can affect the blood pressure.

Pulse

The pulse is the wave of pressure from the heart. It is the force felt when blood is pushed from the left ventricle of the heart around the body (see page 239). An individual's heart rate may be very fast but his or her pulse may be slower if the individual suffers heart failure or severe blood loss. This is because, although the heart is pumping quickly, the pressure and volume of blood within the arteries and veins is reduced.

Pulse points

The pulse can be felt at various points in the body, which are known as pulse points. At each pulse point a steady beat can be felt. This beat is the expansion and constriction of the artery as the blood passes through it. Each pulse point is named after the artery from which the pulse is measured.

The main points in the body for taking a pulse are as follows:
- *Neck* – the pulse point at the neck is called the carotid pulse. It can be felt by putting the forefinger and middle finger on the side of the neck, running them alongside the outer edge of the trachea.
- *Wrist* – the pulse point felt at the wrist is called the radial pulse. This is felt by pressing the forefinger and the middle finger on the radial artery at the base of the wrist (see diagram on next page). This pulse point is possibly the one that is most familiar to you.
- *Groin* – the pulse point felt in the groin area is called the femoral pulse. This is felt by pressing your forefinger and middle finger into the groin area. It can be found by imagining a line running from the hip to the groin, with the pulse being located approximately two-thirds of the way in from the hip.

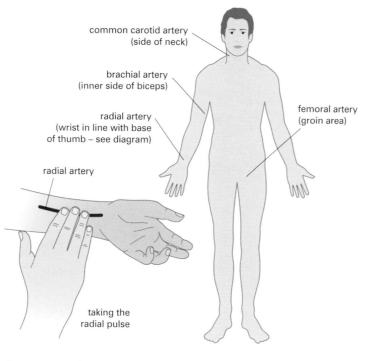

common carotid artery
(side of neck)

brachial artery
(inner side of biceps)

radial artery
(wrist in line with base
of thumb – see diagram)

femoral artery
(groin area)

radial artery

taking the
radial pulse

Common pulse points

You should always use the radial pulse when taking this body measurement as a general routine check-up. Pulses at the neck and groin are generally used in medical emergencies.

The average pulse is 72 beats per minute, and the normal range of a resting adult pulse is between 60 and 90 beats per minute. A normal heart beat is steady and rhythmical – it is so regular that the next beat can be predicted.

How to take a pulse reading

You can take a pulse reading using one of two methods:
- manually with the aid of an accurate watch or clock with a second hand or stopwatch facility
- electronically with the aid of a pulse oximeter, which is a digital machine connected to a two-sided probe that is clipped to the finger tip or ear (see page 250).

Procedure for taking a pulse using a watch or clock

Human error can affect the pulse reading.
- Moving about while taking a pulse will give an inaccurate reading.
- The thumb has a pulse of its own; therefore you should not use your thumb to take a pulse.
- Not using enough pressure on the site when taking a pulse can also give inaccurate readings, as beats may be missed or mistaken for being weak.

Taking a pulse from the wrist

Keys to good practice: Taking a pulse reading manually with the aid of a watch or clock

1 Ensure your watch or clock has a second hand or stopwatch facility and is working correctly.

2 Explain the procedure to the individual.

3 Place your forefinger and middle finger gently on the radial artery at the base of the wrist.

4 Locate the radial pulse, palm side up, just below the wrist.

5 Count the beats for 1 minute.

6 Take a note of the strength of the beats and how regular the beats are.

7 Record the number of beats on the appropriate recording form.

8 Record the strength and regularity of beats on the recording form.

9 Report results to shift leader or supervisor if you have any concerns or if there is a deviation from the baseline measurements.

Procedure for taking a pulse using a pulse oximeter

Pulse oximetry is a non-invasive process that measures the pulse and the amount of oxygen that is being taken up by the blood via the lungs (see also pages 238–40 and 263). Although a pulse oximeter measures the pulse it is rarely used just for this (taking the radial pulse, as described above, is still the favoured method for taking a pulse reading on its own).

When using a pulse oximeter, it is placed over the individual's index finger (see illustration opposite) or ear. A two-sided probe transmits infrared light through the body tissue, the majority of which is absorbed by the tissue. The probe on the other side of the finger tip detects the small amount of light that is not absorbed and this measures the amount of haemoglobin saturation. The sensors in the pulse oximeter also recognise the pulse of the individual and these are displayed either in wave form or numerically. (For more on pulse oximetry, see pages 263–64.)

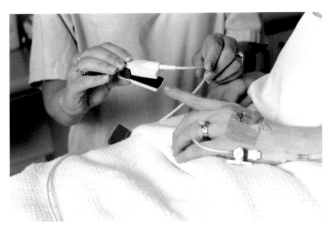

● *Taking a pulse reading from the finger using a pulse oximeter*

When a pulse oximeter is switched on it will start by going through a series of checks to ensure that it is in full working order. Some oximeters are powered by rechargeable batteries and the machine must be plugged in after each use to ensure that it is properly charged.

1 Gather the equipment needed and ensure it is in full working order.

2 Check the machine's battery power is sufficient or plug into an electrical socket if required.

3 Turn the pulse oximeter on and wait for the machine to complete its checks.

4 Select the correct size probe for the finger or ear that you are going to put it on.

5 Put the probe on the finger or ear.

6 Allow several seconds to pass to ensure pulse and oxygen saturation are detected.

7 Check on the display for a waveform.

8 Note the recordings on the display and record them appropriately.

9 Report any concerns or deviations from the baseline measurement to the shift leader or supervisor.

Remember

Always remember to check the charge before using a pulse oximeter – you may charge it up but never assume that the person who used it before you has done so.

Factors that can interfere with the use of a pulse oximeter

- Extremely bright lights can mislead the device, giving an inaccurate result; this is because the machine determines oxygen levels by reading light strengths.
- Very dark nail polish, such as blue, green or black, can affect the reading as the infrared light is unable to penetrate the dark colour. This will give an inaccurate result.
- The environment or individual being very cold may give an inaccurate result.
- The individual shivering can affect the reading.
- An inaccurate result may be given if the probe is placed on a finger where there is a reduced blood supply caused by serious injury, for example, a fractured wrist.

Understanding reasons for different pulse rates

Variations in an individual's pulse which could be a sign of illness include:

- irregular pulse
- weak pulse
- rapid pulse
- slow pulse.

These are explained in more detail below.

Irregular pulse

An irregular pulse is one that is unsteady and not evenly spaced, with missing or skipped beats. An irregular pulse can indicate a range of illnesses including congestive heart failure, shock, internal bleeding, heart attack, stroke or cardiac arrest.

Weak pulse

A weak pulse is a pulse that is not strong or is difficult to feel. It can be indicative of internal bleeding, shock or heart failure.

Rapid pulse

A rapid pulse is one that exceeds the average normal pulse rate of 60–90 beats per minute. Stimulants such as caffeine or cigarettes, and medication such as amphetamines and some decongestants can increase the pulse rate. Stress, cardiac problems, infection and exercise all increase the pulse as the body needs more oxygen at these times. The blood is pumped around the body more quickly in the need to deliver oxygen where it is required.

Slow pulse

A slower pulse reading, one generally below 60 beats per minute, might be attributed to medication prescribed for hypertension, such as Beta blockers or digoxin, which is intended to reduce the pulse rate. However, if the individual is extremely physically fit then his or her pulse rate could be expected to be below 60 beats per minute.

Evidence indicator

Show your assessor how you prepare and undertake an individual's pulse measurement using the manual method and, if available, using an oximeter.

Test yourself

1   List the different sites for taking a pulse.
2   How long should you count a pulse for?

Temperature

What is body temperature?

An individual's body temperature is an indicator of the body's ability to generate and get rid of heat. The body is usually effective at keeping its temperature within a very tight range, unless there is a problem with the individual's health. We will look at this in more detail later in this section.

Normal body temperature, when taken orally, is 37°C. Maintaining the body's temperature close to 37°C is essential for the effective functioning of cells.

How body temperature is maintained

Cooling the body down

When a person is too hot, the blood vessels in the skin dilate so that more blood circulates to the outer areas of the body. This allows more heat from the body to escape through the skin into the air. This is why the skin goes red when you are hot, for example, after running. The body also perspires or sweats when it is hot. This perspiration evaporates on the skin's surface, which cools the body down.

Warming the body up

When a person is cold, the blood vessels constrict taking the blood supply into the body, away from the skin and extremities to supply heat to the vital organs, such as the heart, lungs and kidneys. This conserves the heat in keeping the body warm. This explains why the fingers and toes are the first body parts to feel cold. Shivering also helps to warm the body up, as the extra muscle movement involved in the shivering process generates more heat within the body.

The role of the nervous system in temperature regulation

The nervous system provides a network of communication between different areas of the body so that all the systems remain in contact with each other and the body maintains co-ordination. The nervous system also acts as a receiver for information from the external environment so that the body knows what is happening in its surroundings and can respond in the appropriate way. These external stimuli are transmitted by sense organs in the form of sensations.

Did you know?

Temperature is no longer measured in degrees Fahrenheit (°F). The preferred measurement is degrees Celsius (°C).

Did you know?

Body temperature varies depending on where you measure it. Normal body temperature when measured orally (under the tongue) is 37°C; when measured in the ear (tympanic) is 38°C; and a normal axillary (under the arm) temperature is 36.5°C.

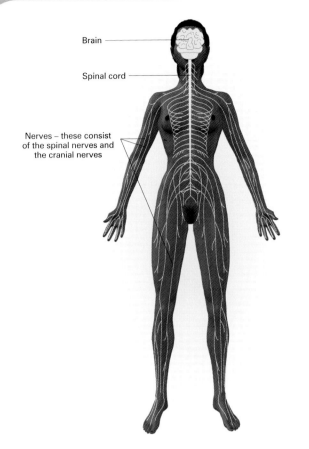

Brain

Spinal cord

Nerves – these consist of the spinal nerves and the cranial nerves

● *The nervous system*

The nervous system consists of two main parts. The central part consists of the brain and spinal cord and is called the central nervous system (CNS). The part around the rest of the body is called the peripheral nervous system (PNS) and is made up of nerves and receptors.

Body temperature is controlled by the central nervous system. The brain is the message centre of the body and all messages that go to and from the brain travel via the spinal cord. Receptors in the body register temperature and send messages to the brain, which then sends messages back, causing the blood vessels to either constrict or dilate in response.

Understanding conditions where body temperature may be high or low

Hyperthermia

Hyperthermia is when body temperature goes above the 'normal' measurement due to environmental factors; for example, a person may suffer sunstroke and heatstroke. The body can have difficulty in cooling down and so overheats, causing hyperthermia.

Pyrexia

Body temperatures above 37°C, when measured orally, are generally known as pyrexia. This is usually a result of an internal imbalance, such as an infection or illness. In adults, a body temperature of over 38°C measured orally is considered high and requires medical assistance to investigate the cause.

Causes of high temperature include:
- infection – for example, infected wounds on the body, meningitis
- illness – for example, influenza, shingles, chicken pox
- hormones – a woman's body temperature can rise slightly during the menstrual cycle and during menopause
- dehydration.

A very high temperature (hyperpyrexia) can cause confusion, delirium, unconsciousness or even death. In these extreme cases the body is unable to cool itself down because it stops sweating and is unable to lose heat.

Hypothermia

Hypothermia is when the body temperature falls below the 'normal' measurement. A temperature below 36.1°C is classed as low. Older people and children are more susceptible to hypothermia as they have difficulty controlling body temperature. During cold weather they will therefore require closer monitoring owing to the increased risks.

Causes of hypothermia include:
- exposure to the cold
- diabetes
- hypothyroidism
- alcohol or drug use
- shock.

The most common signs and symptoms of hypothermia include:
- Shivering – this is the body's natural way of trying to warm up.
- The 'umbles':
    - grumbles (the individual complains)
    - fumbles (the individual is unable to grasp small objects)
    - stumbles (the individual falls over frequently)
    - mumbles (the individual's spoken language is not very clear).
    These reflect the stages that someone with hypothermia goes through as his or her co-ordination and levels of consciousness change.

How to measure body temperature

Body temperature can be measured using a thermometer. There are several different types available:

- disposable thermometers
- digital thermometers
- tympanic (ear) thermometers.

Glass thermometers which contain mercury are no longer recommended for use because of the risks associated with mercury poisoning. If you find a mercury thermometer in the workplace, inform your manager. If a glass thermometer breaks, contact your local poison control centre immediately.

Active knowledge

Find out the telephone number and address of your local poison control centre.

Using a disposable thermometer

A disposable thermometer is a thin, flat piece of plastic which has coloured dots and temperature markings on it. When placed in the mouth, under the armpit or on the skin the dots change colour, which records the temperature. These are intended for single use only and are then disposed of.

- A disposable thermometer

A disposable thermometer reduces the risk of cross-infection as it is used on one occasion only and then thrown away.

Using a digital thermometer

A digital thermometer is made of plastic. It is flat with a probe at one end (see illustration at top of next page). The flat side of the thermometer has a display screen on it to record the temperature. This type of thermometer can be used for taking oral and axillary temperatures.

It is important to check that the equipment is in full working order. Some of the thermometers are battery operated, so these must be checked regularly to ensure the accuracy of results.

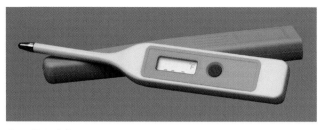

A digital thermometer

Using a tympanic thermometer

Tympanic thermometers are also known as ear or infrared thermometers. There is a small cone-shaped probe at one end of the thermometer which is inserted gently into the ear. The eardrum and surrounding tissues in the ear give off heat; it is this which the tympanic thermometer measures. The results are then displayed on the screen on the thermometer.

To keep the probe clean and to prevent cross-infection, a disposable probe cover should be used. Attach the disposable cover to the probe each time it is used.

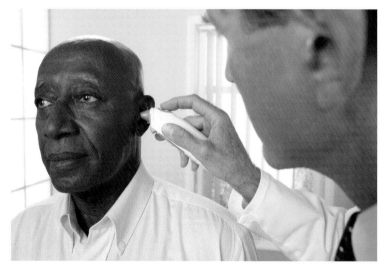

Using an ear thermometer

Active knowledge

You have been asked to take the temperature of one of the individuals in your workplace. You can only find a mercury thermometer. What would you do?

General procedure when taking a body temperature

When taking a body temperature you will need to:

- Check that the individual has not consumed hot or cold food or drinks within the past hour, as this can affect body temparature.
- Ensure that you have explained the full procedure to the individual.
- Ensure you have the appropriate equipment and that you have checked to ensure that it is in working order.
- Ensure the individual is comfortable and that he or she is not sitting in a draught or too near a heater as this may affect the reading.
- Ensure that the thermometer is left in place for the correct amount of time as per manufacturer's instructions. The amount of time required to take an accurate reading will vary depending on the method and equipment used.
- Ensure all readings are recorded.
- Ensure all equipment is cleaned appropriately and put away in its correct storage place.
- Report any concerns or deviations from the baseline measurement to the shift leader or supervisor.

Step-by-step procedures for measuring temperature

Taking an oral temperature

1   When using a digital thermometer, ensure it is covered with a disposable cover to prevent cross-infection.

2   Place the digital or disposable thermometer under the tongue, just to one side of the centre, and ask the individual to close his or her lips tightly around it.

3   Leave the thermometer in place for the stated time as per manufacturer's instructions. Time yourself if necessary, with a clock or watch. Some digital thermometers give a series of short beeps when the reading is done.

4   Remove the thermometer and read it. On average, a normal oral temperature reading will be approximately 37°C.

5   Remove and dispose of the protective cover from the digital thermometer, or dispose of the disposable thermometer as it is intended for single use only.

6   Record the measurement.

Taking an axillary (armpit) temperature

1   When using a digital thermometer, ensure it is covered with a disposable cover to prevent cross-infection.

2 Place the thermometer under the individual's arm with the bulb in the centre of the armpit.

3 Ensure the arm is held against the body and leave the thermometer in place for the stated time as per manufacturer's instructions. Time yourself if necessary, with a watch or clock.

4 Remove the thermometer and read it. On average, a normal axillary temperature reading will be approximately 36.5°C.

5 Remove the disposable cover before storing correctly.

6 Record the measurement.

Taking a tympanic temperature

1 Check that the probe is clean and in working order. Ensure that the probe is covered with a disposable cover to prevent cross-infection.

2 Turn the thermometer on.

3 Centre the probe tip in the ear and push gently inward toward the eardrum.

4 Press the 'ON' button to display the temperature reading. On average, a normal tympanic temperature reading will be approximately 38°C.

5 Remove the thermometer and dispose of the used probe cover.

6 Record the measurement.

Reasons for inaccurate readings

Possible causes of inaccurate body temperature readings include:
- Temperature being taken within an hour of consuming hot or cold foods or drinks – the hot or cold food or drinks affect the oral temperature.
- Temperature being taken within an hour of exercise – exercise warms up the muscles and in turn the body's temperature can rise slightly.
- Temperature being taken within an hour of having a hot bath – as with exercise, the water can cause the body's temperature to rise slightly.
- Not leaving the thermometer in for the correct length of time – the thermometer is not able to register the correct body temperature.
- The individual not keeping his or her mouth closed when taking an oral temperature – the inside of the mouth is cooler when the mouth is open.
- Not following correct procedures will give an inaccurate reading.
- Faulty equipment may give inaccurate results.

CASE STUDY: Recording body temperature

J is a health care assistant working on a medical ward. She has been asked to complete the hourly observations for four individuals in one of the bays. However, she is running late so decides to save time by leaving the thermometer in for half the required time. She hurriedly completes the observations with no discussions or explanations with the individuals.

1 What implications will this have for the results?
2 What possible implications could this have for the care of the individual?
3 Why is it important to always follow set procedures?
4 Is this an example of good practice? Explain your answer.
5 Discuss with a colleague how you could improve on J's practices.

Evidence indicator

Show your assessor how you prepare the individual and environment for taking body temperatures. Using one of the above methods, show your assessor how you accurately take an individual's body temperature.

Test yourself

1 What is considered 'normal' body temperature?
2 What is another term for a high temperature?
3 What is hypothermia?
4 Describe the different types of thermometers available to take body temperatures.
5 Give an alternative word for the different places a temperature can be taken:
   a) armpit
   b) under the tongue
   c) in the ear.
6 List five factors that might increase the body's temperature.
7 List three factors that might lower the body's temperature.

Respirations

In order to understand respirations, it is first necessary to look at the respiratory system.

The respiratory system

The respiratory system comprises the lungs, trachea, bronchioles, bronchi and alveoli.

- There are two lungs, which flank the heart in the thoracic cavity (the chest).
- The diaphragm is a sheet of muscle which separates the chest from the abdominal cavity. When it moves up and down the lungs inflate and deflate, and this movement is known as breathing.

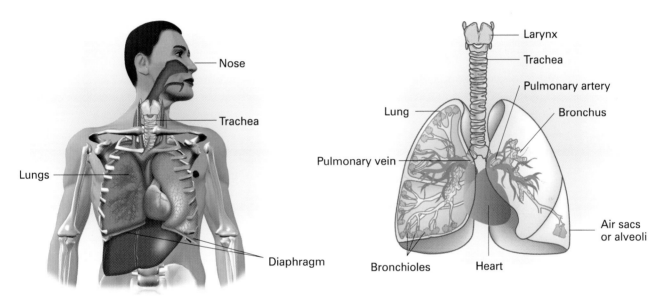

The respiratory system

During inspiration (breathing in), oxygen enters the lungs via the air. The oxygenated air is taken in to the bronchi, bronchioles and alveoli. Alveoli are sacs inside the lungs and here the oxygen is transferred into the blood through gaseous exchange (see also pages 238–39). There, it oxygenates the blood by binding itself to haemoglobin in red blood cells, forming oxyhaemoglobin.

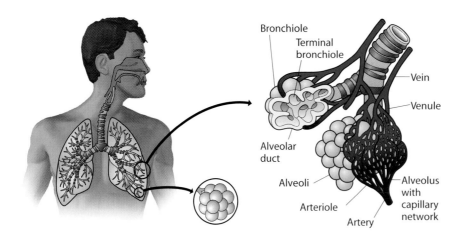

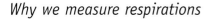 Gaseous exchange takes place in the alveoli

During expiration (breathing out), carbon dioxide, a waste product from the body's cells, is released from the haemoglobin and diffuses out of the blood through the walls of the alveoli to be breathed out. Thus, the purpose of breathing in and out is to keep the oxygen concentration high and the carbon dioxide concentration low in the alveoli.

Measuring respirations

Respirations are counted by the number of times the chest rises in one minute and are recorded as breaths per minute. You will need a watch or clock with a second hand or stopwatch facility to be able to time a full minute. The number of times that you breathe in and out in one minute is known as the respiratory rate.

The average respirations of an adult are 12–20 per minute; however, this will change throughout the day for a variety of reasons. You will breathe faster when you are doing physical exercise or when you are excited or scared. Breathing is slower when a person is calm and relaxed; it also slows down during sleep.

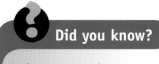

Did you know?

Tachypnea is rapid respirations (over 20 per minute) in an adult.

Why we measure respirations

The way a person breathes can be an indicator of possible lung conditions such as:
- bronchitis
- lung cancer
- tuberculosis
- emphysema.

Active knowledge

Research the above lung conditions to identify how each of these can affect the way an individual breathes.

1 Gather together the equipment needed and ensure that it is in full working order.

2 Avoid explaining the procedure to the individual as this can affect the manner and speed of his or her breathing.

3 Ensure the individual is lying or sitting down.

4 Count the times the chest rises in one full minute using a clock or watch with a second hand or stopwatch facility.

5 Listen to the individual's breathing, noting if it is steady, shallow (fast), deep (slow) or wheezy. Always write down any abnormal noises that you notice concerning the individual's breathing. These noises could indicate a chest infection, fluid on the lungs or an obstruction.

6 Record all of your observations on the appropriate chart.

7 Report any observations that cause concern to the shift leader or supervisor. Reasons to inform the shift leader include:
   - respiratory rate is higher or lower than the individual's 'normal' rate
   - you are concerned about any abnormal noises when monitoring respiration.

Measuring the oxygen saturation of haemoglobin using a pulse oximeter

It is important to measure the oxygen saturation of haemoglobin (how much oxygen the blood contains) in order to monitor the individual's health and promote recovery. As you read earlier (page 238), the body requires oxygen to ensure effective maintenance and repair of its cells and organs.

The usual range of the total amount of haemoglobin (blood) that is filled with oxygen is 96–100 per cent. Generally, a reading of 90–95 per cent would require the individual to be given oxygen. However, if the individual has heart failure or chronic lung disease, a reading of 90–95 per cent may be seen as 'doing well' without oxygen. Below 90 per cent could indicate a life-threatening condition and the individual will need oxygen to be administered. Oxygen is classed as a drug and therefore has to be prescribed by a doctor or suitably qualified nurse.

The full procedure for using a pulse oximeter is described on pages 250–51.

Did you know?

Pulse oximetry readings can vary suddenly, going from the normal range to apparently life-threatening very quickly. This can be due to the sudden movement of the individual or the probe being fitted incorrectly.

Remember

There are many factors that can affect the accuracy of the results when using a pulse oximeter. False low readings can be caused by anything that absorbs light, such as dried blood and dark nail polish, so it is essential to remove them and clean the skin thoroughly before putting the probe on.

Measuring lung capacity using a spirometer

Lung capacity is a medical term used to describe the amount of air an individual can hold within his or her lungs. A spirometer is used to measure lung capacity and lung function, and to monitor lung disease. The spirometer has a tube to blow into attached to a machine. This tube should be fitted with a disposable mouthpiece each time it is used, to prevent cross-infection. A spirometer measures how much air is expelled from the lungs when the individual blows out and how quickly the air is expelled. This measurement is based on how much air can be expelled within the first second of expiration (known as Forced Expired Volume, or FEV1) and the maximum volume of air that can be forcibly expelled in total (Forced Vital Capacity, or FVC).

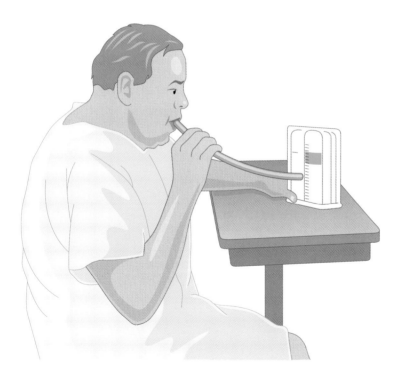

* *Using a spirometer*

1 Gather the appropriate equipment together and ensure a disposable mouthpiece is fitted.

2 Explain the procedure to the individual.

3 Ensure the individual is sitting down.

4 Encourage the individual to take a deep breath.

5 Encourage the individual to close his or her mouth over the mouthpiece of the spirometer and blow out as forcibly as possible.

6 Read the recordings on the display.

7 Repeat the procedure two more times.

8 Record the highest reading from the three measurements on the appropriate forms.

9 Remove the disposable mouthpiece, clean and put the equipment away in its appropriate storage place.

10 Report any concerns or deviation from the baseline measurement to the shift leader or supervisor.

Remember

Ensuring that the equipment is in full working order is essential for the accuracy of results.

Cleaning the equipment after each use reduces the risk of cross-infection; in addition, disposable inserts should be used in the end of the tube.

Did you know?

You should never clean plastic casing of equipment with alcohol-based cleaning fluid as it causes the plastic to become brittle and crack.

Measuring lung capacity using a peak flow meter

A peak flow meter is a portable tube with a reading gauge on the side. A disposable mouthpiece covers the end of the tube, which is blown into very quickly (see illustraton on next page). Peak flow readings indicate how open the airways are and this helps to determine any airway or lung changes. A peak flow meter measures how quickly and forcibly air is expelled from the lungs, and is another tool to help measure lung capacity. It gives a good picture of what is going on inside an individual's lungs.

● *Using a peak flow meter*

✔ Keys to good practice: Using a peak flow meter

1 Gather the appropriate equipment together and ensure a disposable mouthpiece is fitted.

2 Discuss the procedure with the individual.

3 Ensure the gauge is returned to the zero point.

4 Ensure the individual is standing up.

5 Ask the individual to take as deep a breath as possible.

6 Ask the individual to place the meter in his or her mouth, closing the lips around the mouthpiece.

7 The individual should blow as hard and as fast as possible.

8 Write down the value on the gauge.

9 Repeat the process two more times and record the highest of the three recordings.

10 Put all the equipment away in its appropriate storage place.

11 Report any concerns or deviations from the baseline measurement to the shift leader or supervisor.

Remember

- Always reset the gauge before using to ensure accuracy of results.
- Ensure that you use a disposable mouthpiece.
- Clean properly after each use to reduce the risk of cross-infection.

Asthma

Asthma is a condition where the airways become irritated and inflamed. They become narrower and produce excessive mucus, which makes it more difficult for air to flow in and out of the lungs. In extreme cases, asthma can prove fatal.

There are three types of symptoms associated with asthma, and each varies depending on environmental conditions, physical health and time of day. The symptoms include:
- wheezing and coughing
- feelings of tightness in the chest
- shortness of breath.

What causes asthma?

The exact cause of asthma is not fully known as it can sometimes flare up for no apparent reason. There are, however, some common triggers that appear to set off an asthma attack or make the symptoms worse. Allergies can narrow the airways triggering an attack, as can some chemicals found in the workplace. Chest infections, colds and flu are possible causes of increased symptoms, and the weather can also affect asthma sufferers.

There are other factors that can indicate a predisposition towards asthma. It tends to run in families so it has a hereditary link. Research indicates that boys are more likely to be asthmatic as children; however, this trend changes in adulthood with women becoming those more likely to develop asthma.

How can peak flow meter readings help in the management of asthma?

Peak flow meter readings can be used to assess the severity of asthma and check responses to asthma treatments and monitor their effectiveness. Peak flow readings will drop before other signs and symptoms of asthma getting worse are detected. This is a very good preventative method, giving early warnings so that medication and other treatments can be altered whenever necessary. When monitoring peak flow it is therefore important to constantly review the findings to ensure that the best values are maintained. This will also assist with ensuring effectiveness of treatment.

The traffic light system

The traffic light system is a recognised system to monitor peak flow and offers guidelines to help manage asthma (see table on page 268).

Did you know?

The developed world is no longer exposed to the range of infections that it used to be, so natural immunity is reduced. In some cases the immune system overreacts to what used to be harmless substances, for example, house dust mites, medicine and animals, causing asthma. This idea is known as the hygiene hypothesis.

Green zone	Peak expiratory flow rate (PEFR) is anywhere between 80 and 100 per cent of the individual's personal best. (The individual's personal best is based on what he or she, as an individual, is capable of achieving.) This indicates relatively symptom-free asthma and the effectiveness of treatment.
Yellow zone	PEFR is anywhere between 50 and 80 per cent of personal best. This is the zone indicating the need for caution. A temporary increase in treatment may be required, so it is essential that the individual visit the asthma clinic or his or her GP.
Red zone	PEFR is below 50 per cent of personal best and is in the danger zone. Treatment is ineffective and urgent consultation is needed with the asthma clinic or GP to control the symptoms and treat any underlying cause such as a chest infection.

The traffic light system of asthma management

Test yourself

1 Why should you avoid informing the individual that you are measuring his or her rate of breathing?
2 When counting respirations, what would you be checking?
3 What is the normal rate for respirations?
4 List three things that can increase respirations.
5 List three things that can decrease respirations.
6 What does a pulse oximeter measure?
7 What does a spirometer measure?

Evidence indicator

Prepare the environment and individual for taking respiration measurements. Show your assessor how you undertake these measurements correctly using one or more of the methods described above.

Measuring height and weight

A person's weight in relation to height can indicate the extent to which his or her health is being put at risk by being excessively underweight or overweight. There are ideal weights for height which have been calculated to present the least risk to health. These can be identified by:

- a height/weight chart
- body mass index (BMI).

Using a height/weight chart

One way of checking height and weight is to plot them on a chart which will give an indication of whether you are overweight, underweight, clinically obese or within the normal range. An example of a height/weight chart is shown below.

Active knowledge

Research the term 'clinically obese' and identify what this means.

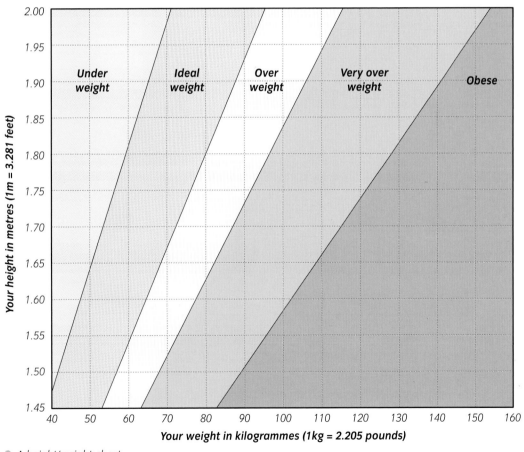

A height/weight chart

Measuring weight

Wherever possible when measuring weight, individuals should stand on a set of scales; any heavy items of clothing should be taken off. The individual should stand still until the scales record the weight. Weight should be recorded in kilograms (kg) in the individual's notes.

● *Using scales*

Measuring height

Height should be measured using a fixed ruler which is attached to the wall. In order to achieve an accurate recording, the individual should stand with his or her back to the wall in bare feet, with the heels touching the wall and the back as straight as possible. The measuring bar is then moved down the ruler until it sits gently on the individual's head. The height is then read from the ruler and recorded in the individual's notes. Height should always be measured in metres (m) and centimetres (cm).

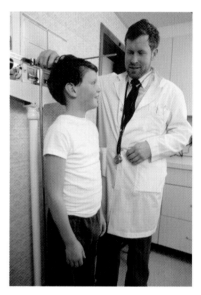

● *Using a height stick*

❶ Active knowledge

Using the height and weight chart on the previous page, plot your height and weight. What do the results indicate about your health?

Measuring BMI

Body mass index (BMI) is a comparative measurement of a combination of the individual's height and weight. It is used to identify an individual's ideal weight and to check whether he or she is over- or underweight and by how much (see the chart on the next page).

An individual's BMI is identified by dividing weight in kilograms by height in metres squared.

$$\text{Body mass index} = \frac{\text{weight (kg)}}{\text{height (m)}^2}$$

BMI < 20	Underweight
BMI 20–24.9	Normal
BMI 25–30	Overweight
BMI > 30	Obese
BMI > 40	Severely obese

Did you know?

Obesity is rising in the UK. The current statistics are:
- 43 per cent of men and 33 per cent of women are classed as overweight (a BMI of 25–30).
- 22 per cent of men and 23 per cent of women are classed as obese (a BMI of over 30).
- Childhood obesity is also rising, with 20 per cent of boys and 25 per cent of girls aged 2–15 years being classed as obese (a BMI of over 30).

CASE STUDY: Measuring BMI

R weighs 12 stone and is 5 feet 4 inches tall.

1 Find a conversion chart and identify:
   a) R's height in metres.
   b) R's weight in kilograms.
2 Using the above BMI calculation, work out what R's BMI is.
3 Using the BMI scale above, what does R's BMI reveal?

Active knowledge

Using your own height and weight, calculate your BMI.

BMI readings and health

Body mass index can be used to monitor and encourage the individual to reach a healthy weight, which in turn reduces the risks to health. It is a useful guide when assessing health and can be used in conjunction with exercise and healthy eating.

Using the example given in the case study above, you should have identified that R is overweight verging on obese. To assist R with her health needs and to reduce the risks associated with obesity, you can encourage lifestyle changes such as those examined on page 242. These changes can be monitored with regular weight checks and BMI calculations to see if they are working effectively. Plotting the results on a graph will give R a visual representation of her achievements and will show her clearly when she reaches the ideal BMI range (a BMI of 20–24.9).

It would be unrealistic and a medical risk for R to aim to go from a BMI of 30 to a BMI of 20 in the space of one week – small targets over a longer period are healthier and more achievable.

Health risks associated with being overweight or obese

There are many health risks associated with being overweight and obese. These include:

- gall stones
- diabetes
- coronary heart disease
- mobility difficulties.

Active knowledge

Choose one of the above health risks and identify how being overweight can cause the problem.

There are also some illnesses and treatments which can affect the weight of an individual and these include:

- the use of steroids
- hyper- or hypothyroidism
- pituitary gland conditions
- hormone imbalances
- heart failure
- liver failure.

Active knowledge

Choose two of the above illnesses or treatments and identify how these can affect an individual's weight.

Test yourself

1 How is body mass index calculated?
2 What is the 'normal' range for body mass index?
3 What does a BMI of 34 indicate?
4 What action would you take if an individual's BMI were outside the normal range?
5 Which professionals could be involved with an individual with a high BMI and why?

What physiological measurements can indicate

Signs of a heart attack

A heart attack is damage to the muscle of the heart caused by insufficient blood supply. This occurs when a coronary artery becomes blocked, preventing blood reaching a part of the heart muscle. Signs of a heart attack include:

- chest pains – the individual will feel as though the chest is being tightly squeezed; the pains originate in the centre of the chest and last for more than a few minutes
- discomfort in other areas of the upper body, including pain in the arms, stomach, jaw or back
- shortness of breath, light-headedness, nausea and a cold sweat.

CASE STUDY: Contributory factors

E is 45 years old and works for a large company in the city. He has been working very long hours, not eating regularly, smoking and drinking alcohol frequently. He is on his way out of the office when he feels a pain in his chest. He finds it hard to breathe and his skin becomes clammy. A colleague notices his discomfort and takes him to hospital where he is diagnosed as having had a heart attack.

1   What factors may have contributed to E's heart attack?
2   What advice would you give E about making lifestyle changes?

Signs of cardiac arrest

Cardiac arrest is different from a heart attack because the heart stops. It strikes without warning and the signs are:

- no signs of circulation (no pulse, purple lips)
- abnormal breathing (or none)
- sudden loss of responsiveness or unconsciousness.

Signs of a stroke

A stroke is the temporary or permanent loss of blood supply to part of the brain. This prevents oxygen reaching part of the brain, causing it to become damaged. Sign of a stroke include:

- sudden severe headache
- sudden dizziness or loss of balance or co-ordination
- sudden difficulty with mobility
- sudden confusion
- sudden trouble speaking or understanding
- sudden numbness in the face, arms or legs; this would usually be in one side of the body.

The common word here which will aid in the diagnosis of a stroke is 'sudden'.

1 **a)** Why is it important to ensure that you have all the necessary equipment for taking the desired physiological measurement?

   b) Why is it important to ensure that all equipment is in full working order?

   c) How might both of these affect the results?

2 **a)** List at least five different pieces of equipment used for taking physiological measurements.

   b) Explain what each piece of equipment is used for.

3 Why is it important to take a set of baseline observations on an individual?

4 Give definitions for each of these words:

   a) hypertension

   b) blood pressure

   c) pulse

   d) respiration

   e) hypotension.

Records and documentation

The recording and reporting of the different body measurements is an important part of the overall process. There would be little point in taking the measurements if they were not recorded, since there wouldn't be anything to compare them with to see whether the individual's health was improving or had deteriorated. Diagnosis would be affected, as would the accuracy of treatment, and the needs of the individual would be less likely to be met.

If you have concerns about an individual's physiological measurement, you should report these to your shift leader or supervisor, or a registered practitioner. Failure to verbally report any irregular physiological measurement could have serious health implications for the individual. However, it would not be appropriate to report all of your findings all of the time; you should only do so if you have cause for concern, are unsure about the reading, or if this is your organisation's policy.

How records are kept

Records are required to keep together all information relating to the individual. Records are now kept in two ways:

- handwritten notes
- computerised records.

Access to records must be restricted to ensure confidentiality and to protect the individual's rights. All records need to be accurate, legible and complete as they are legal documents; therefore the method of recording is essential as they can be used in a court of law.

- Accurate means 'containing the correct information of fact not opinion'.
- Legible means 'Everyone is able to read it and obtain the same meaning without difficulty or misinterpretation.' Any mistakes should be crossed out with a single line and your initials inserted above. Correction fluid should not be used.
- Complete means 'the inclusion of date of entry and your signature, name and status'.

Active knowledge

1 Identify your organisation's policy on reporting physiological measurements to a registered practitioner.

2 The Medical Records Act 1990 is a relevant piece of legislation for the recording of physiological measurements. Research it and explain how it affects your working practices.

Recording physiological measurements

All measurements should be recorded on the appropriate forms and charts using the correct unit of measurement. These are shown in the chart below.

Measurement	Correct unit of measurement (with abbreviation)
Height	Centimetres (cm) and metres (m)
Weight	Kilograms (kg)
Blood pressure	Millimetres of mercury (mmHg)
Pulse	Beats per minute (bpm)
Respirations	Respirations per minute (rpm)
Temperature	Degrees Celsius (°C).

Other members of the care team will refer to the recording forms; therefore you need to ensure they are accurate, legible and complete for continuity of care to be given. Accurate and clear records ensure that correct information about the individual is collected. This is also a requirement of the Data Protection Act 1998.

The Data Protection Act covers all records and individuals have the right for this information to be kept confidential. All records must be accurate and fair, so it is important to ensure that correct training is received in how to complete paperwork.

✔ **Keys to good practice:** Record keeping and confidentiality of information

✓ Only pass on information to the people who have a right and a need to know.

✓ Keep records safe so that they cannot be seen or accessed by people who do not have a right to see or access them.

✓ Always write in black ink so that records are clear and are easy to photocopy.

✓ Always write what you see and hear, not what you assume. This keeps records accurate.

✓ Handwritten records must be legible.

✓ Records must only contain relevant information.

Active knowledge

Each working environment will have specific charts and forms for each of the measurements. Collect one for each measurement then practise filling them in. You could do this by practising some of the procedures on colleagues and then recording the measurements accurately.

Evidence indicator

Show your assessor any recording documents you have completed when taking physiological measurements. Ensure they conform with the Data Protection Act 1998 in that they are accurate, legible and complete. Explain to your assessor why you have completed them the way you have.

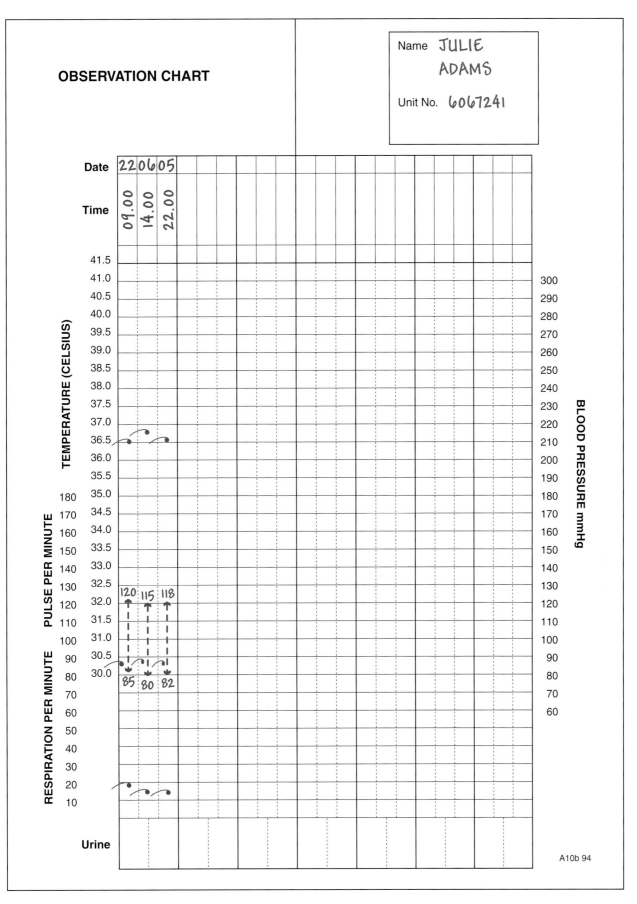

Example of a chart for taking body measurements

CASE STUDY: Making notes

M works in a small care setting with adults who have learning disabilities. V, one of the individuals, has not been well. He appears confused, looks sweaty and hot, and complains of headaches. He is also sleeping a lot and this has caused concerns regarding his health.

M has accompanied V to the doctor's, where V has had his temperature, blood pressure, pulse and respirations measured. All are raised above normal levels, and on listening to his chest the doctor diagnosed that V has a chest infection, prescribing him antibiotics.

On returning to the care home M writes the following entry in V's case notes:

25/9 – Took V to the GP and was told he has a ~~infarction~~. infection. MP

1   How do you think M's entry into V's case notes will benefit V's health?
2   What essential information do you think M should have included in the case notes?
3   If you were working at the same setting as M, how do you think M's actions would affect your own practice?
4   To whom should M have reported the information given by the doctor?

Keeping good records is important in any care setting as it not only ensures continuity of care but it also informs other care workers as to what has been done and what needs to be done.

When taking physiological measurements, clear records are a good indicator of whether treatment is working and they help with accurate diagnosis.

Test yourself

1   Name three pieces of legislation relating to accurate record keeping.
2   Give two reasons why it is important to accurately record measurements.
3   What measurement is used for temperature?
4   Where should confidential records be kept?
5   To whom should you report your observations on body measurements?
6   Computerised records need to be protected – by what?
7   Who is responsible for recording the body measurements once you have taken them and why?
8   What do you measure respirations in?
9   What is recorded by one number over another?
10 Records are kept in two ways; name them both.

1   Read through the table below, which shows potential problems when taking physiological measurements and how to resolve them.
2   Suggestions have been given for how to resolve the first two problems. For the remaining four problems identified in the table below, suggest how these could be resolved.
3   Finally, identify a further two problems and suggest how these problems could be resolved.

Problem when taking physiological measurement	How to resolve the problem
Cannot locate pulse (individual is conscious).	• Try again with a little more pressure • Find a different site • Report to senior staff
Manual sphygmomanometer cuff will not inflate.	• Ensure that you have closed the valve. • Check the equipment is in working order. • Use an alternative piece of equipment. • Report to senior staff.
Individual keeps on moving while you are trying to take his or her pulse.	
The individual becomes distressed while you are trying to take a tympanic temperature.	
The individual refuses to roll up his or her sleeve for the blood pressure measurement to be taken.	
The pulse oximeter is in working order but results appear erroneous.	

Glossary of key terms

Abuse   Causing physical, emotional, sexual and/or financial harm to an individual and/or failing or neglecting to protect him or her from harm.

Abusive and aggressive behaviour   Behaviour that causes harm; it may be verbal or non-verbal and can be social, physical, sexual or emotional in nature.

Active support   Support that encourages individuals to do as much for themselves as possible to maintain their independence and physical ability and encourages people with disabilities to maximise their own potential and independence.

Assessment tool   A process of assessment using a variety of risk factors, for example assessing the risk of skin breakdown using factors such as continence, weight and nutritional status. Assessment tools have various names according to their authors or developers.

Boundary   The limit that defines what is acceptable in a situation.

Care plan   A plan including all aspects of the individual's care needs that must be adhered to within any setting in which the individual is placed. It addresses the holistic needs of the individual.

Danger   The possibility that harm may occur.

Discrimination   In care work, discrimination means treating some categories of people less well than others. People are often discriminated against because of their race, beliefs, gender, religion, sexuality or age.

Empowerment   Making sure that people have choice, that their self-esteem and confidence are promoted, and that they are encouraged to take action for themselves where possible.

Evaluation   The judgement made following a review process.

Harm   The effects of an individual being physically, emotionally or sexually injured or abused.

Hazard   Something with the potential to cause harm.

Mental state   The mental condition of an individual, including being withdrawn, depressed, agitated or confused.

Personal protective clothing   Items worn for protection such as plastic aprons, gloves and footwear, which may be disposable or reusable.

Protective equipment   Equipment that provides extra protection, including visors, protective eyewear or radiation-protection equipment.

Quantitative   Relating to quantity (such as size, number or amount) and its measurement.

Qualitative   Relating to quality (such as conditions, opinions or feelings) and its measurement.

Risk assessment   A document that identifies actual and potential risks and specifies actions related to specific activities and functions.

Risk   The likelihood of a hazard being realised. Risks can be to individuals in the form of danger, harm and abuse, and/or to the environment in danger of damage and destruction.

Review   The process of discussion and examination of information gained from monitoring a service.

Self-concept   How we see ourselves.

Self-image   How we value ourselves.

Standard precautions and health and safety measures   A series of measures that minimise or prevent infection and cross-infection, including handwashing and the use of personal protective clothing and equipment.

Knowledge specification

In the unit specifications, the required knowledge points are detailed under the headings 'Values', 'Legislation and organisational policy and procedures' and 'Theory and practice'.

The following grid shows how to pinpoint material relating to these knowledge points in the text. The points are addressed on and following the page numbers shown. (Values point 1 is common to most units, except the practical caring units, and is not included in the grid, since its content is fundamental to the information given in the whole unit.)

HSC 331 Values	
2	10, 21, 24
3	10, 17, 24
4	10, 17, 21, 24
Legislation and organisational policy and procedures	
5	10, 20, 24, 26
6	10, 24, 26
7	10, 24, 26
8	26
Theory and practice	
9	10, 20, 26
10	4, 9
11	4, 9, 12
12	2, 3, 12, 14, 17
13	17, 21, 24
14	2, 3, 6, 12, 17
15	10, 12, 17, 20
16	10, 14, 17, 21, 24
17	10, 12, 14, 17, 21, 24

HSC 332 Values	
2	37, 38
3	42
4	43
Legislation and organisational policy and procedures	
5	35
6	35, 54
7	35, 38
8	42, 55
9	55
Theory and practice	
10	42
11	35, 52
12	29, 31, 48
13	33, 39, 40
14	42, 44
15	38
16	41
17	37, 38, 42, 44
18	30, 31, 39, 48

HSC 335 Values	
2	75, 79, 81
3	70, 75, 80, 81
4	68, 75, 86

Legislation and organisational policy and procedures	
5	59, 61, 75, 78
6	63, 83, 95
7	59, 74, 91
8	59, 93, 95
9	94, 98

Theory and practice	
10	59, 93
11	59, 61, 76, 78, 90
12	70, 72, 75
13	61, 62
14	59, 61, 69, 70, 72, 84
15	61, 70, 81
16	61, 62, 70
17	74, 76, 78, 81, 91, 93
18	84, 91
19	59, 61, 74, 75, 86, 91
20	59, 70
21	61, 72
22	62, 74, 84, 86, 91
23	61, 62, 70, 75
24	78, 81, 91, 93
25	93, 95
26	93, 95

HSC 351 Values	
2	102, 108, 116, 122
3	108, 116, 120
4	116

Legislation and organisational policy and procedures	
5	103, 109, 119, 121
6	121, 125
7	109, 119, 121

Theory and practice	
8	102, 103
9	102, 110
10	102, 111
11	102, 103
12	108, 109, 116, 120
13	105
14	102, 106, 108, 109, 110
15	108, 109, 116, 120
16	103, 125

HSC 329 Values	
2	128, 132, 142
3	131, 142
4	131, 139, 146, 148, 150
5	128, 131, 135, 142, 146

Legislation and organisational policy and procedures	
6	128, 131
7	128, 131, 139, 142
8	128, 131
9	131, 135, 142

Theory and practice

10	131, 135
11	128
12	132, 139, 143
13	132
14	130
15	129, 132, 139, 143
16	132, 139, 142, 146
17	146
18	128, 135
19	133, 135
20	146
21	131, 135, 140, 142, 145
22	140, 142, 145, 149

HSC 337
Values

2	160, 162, 164
3	154, 155, 162, 173
4	155

Legislation and organisational policy and procedures

5	156, 163, 175
6	163, 175, 176
7	163
8	156, 176
9	175

Theory and practice

10	156, 164
11	163, 164, 175
12	156
13	162, 168, 171

14	161, 162, 164, 168, 176
15	155, 163, 164
16	171
17	153, 156
18	156, 160, 170
19	164
20	168, 171
21	164, 168
22	173

HSC 358
Legislation and organisational policy and procedures

1	193, 198, 208
2	193, 198, 208, 209

Theory and practice

3	210
4	208
5	198, 209
6	193, 210
7	198
8	210
9	181, 186, 190, 196
10	209
11	213
12	186, 190, 193
13	181
14	196
15	190
16	188
17	185
18	198

Index

A

abuse
  see also abusers; abusive
    situations
  of carers 80
  of children 76
  discriminatory 68
  financial/material 66–7, 70–1
  institutional 71
  long-term 71
  neglect 69–70
  physical 62–4, 71
  psychological 65, 66
  reporting 98–9
    confidentiality 91–3
    line managers 93
    preserving evidence 95
    recording 94–6
    referrals 96
  risk factors 72–3
  serial 70–1
  sexual 64–5, 70–1
  situational 71
abusers 62, 72–3, 78
abusive situations 61–2
  dealing with 97
access, barriers in relationships 15
activities
  care worker's role 116–17
  consent for 119–20
  development 110–11
  equipment preparation 117–18
  evaluations 124
    qualitative 122–3
    quantitative 122–3
  feedback, importance of 120–1
  health and safety, risk assessments 21
  information 120
  planning
    for the individual 112–13
    process 113–15
  reports 125

    confidentiality 125
    types of 111–12
addressing service users 42
adversity, and resilience 159
advocates, roles of 24–5
aggressive behaviour
  see also challenging behaviour
  effect on care workers 175–6
  guidelines 173–4
  physical interventions 174–5
aging, skin 183
Anti-Social Behaviour Act 2003 10
assessments
  agreeing areas of concern 106
  consent 109
  formal 104–5
  individual's involvement in 108–9
  informal 105
  needs 102
  observations 106–7
  pre-activity 109–10
  single assessment process 131–2, 136–9
  standardised tests 104
asthma 267–8

B

balanced diet 183–4
baseline measurements 236
bedsores *see* skin breakdown
behaviourism 31
  and challenging behaviour 157, 165
behaviour management
  evaluations 178
  reviews 177
  theories 164–8
blood
  oxygenation 261–2
  oxygen saturation, pulse oximeter 263
  and skin 184
blood pressure 237
  cardiovascular system 237–8
    heart 239–40

monitoring 143–4
predictable 51
reactions to 52–3
support at times of 52–4
unpredictable 51–2
children
abuse of 76
family relationships 9–10
friendships 7–8
human needs 29–30
restrictions on contact with 10
clothing
personal 232
protective 208, 231
CNS (central nervous system), and body temperature 253–4
cognitivism 31
and challenging behaviour 158, 166
Commission for Social Care Inspection (CSCI)
35, 85, 86, 226
communication
as barrier in relationships 15
skills, and relationships 21
Community Care Act 1990 69
Community Care Assessment Directions 2004 131
confidentiality
assessments 125
breaking, abuse cases 91–2
records 11, 228
consent 81, 223–4
for activities 119–20
assessments 109
informed 223–4
and mental capacity 82–3
refusal of 81–2
skin breakdown, assessment procedures 211
contacts 2
see also social contacts
contamination 231
Control of Substances Hazardous to Health (COSHH)
Regulations 2002 225
court proceedings 75
Courts of Protection/Public Trust Office 67
Criminal Justice Act 1998 63
criminal record checks, care workers 90
cross-infections 229–30

CSCI (Commission for Social Care Inspection)
35, 85, 86, 226
cultural values, service users' 42–3
culture, and self-esteem 41–2

D

danger 59
Data Protection Act 1998 92–3, 224, 225
decision-making, records 26–7
decubitis ulcers see skin breakdown
dermis 181–2
development
activities 110–12
and needs 102
Directors of Social Services 128
direct payments 133–4, 143
Disability Discrimination Act 1995 68
discrimination 68
discriminatory abuse 68
disposable gloves 231
divorce, orders under 10–11

E

electrical equipment 233
emotions, physical effects of 171–2
empowerment 75, 132–3
vulnerable adults 75–7
environmental barriers, in relationships 15
environmental considerations, health and safety 229
epidermis 181–2
Equal Opportunities Act 2004 225
equipment
electrical 233
preparation, activities 117–18
safe storage 232
safe usage 232

F

families
children's relationships 9–10
long-term abuse in 71
networks within 5
relationships within 6, 7
structures 8–9
working patterns within 9

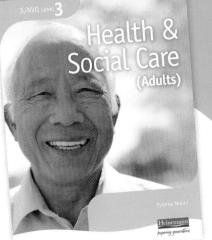